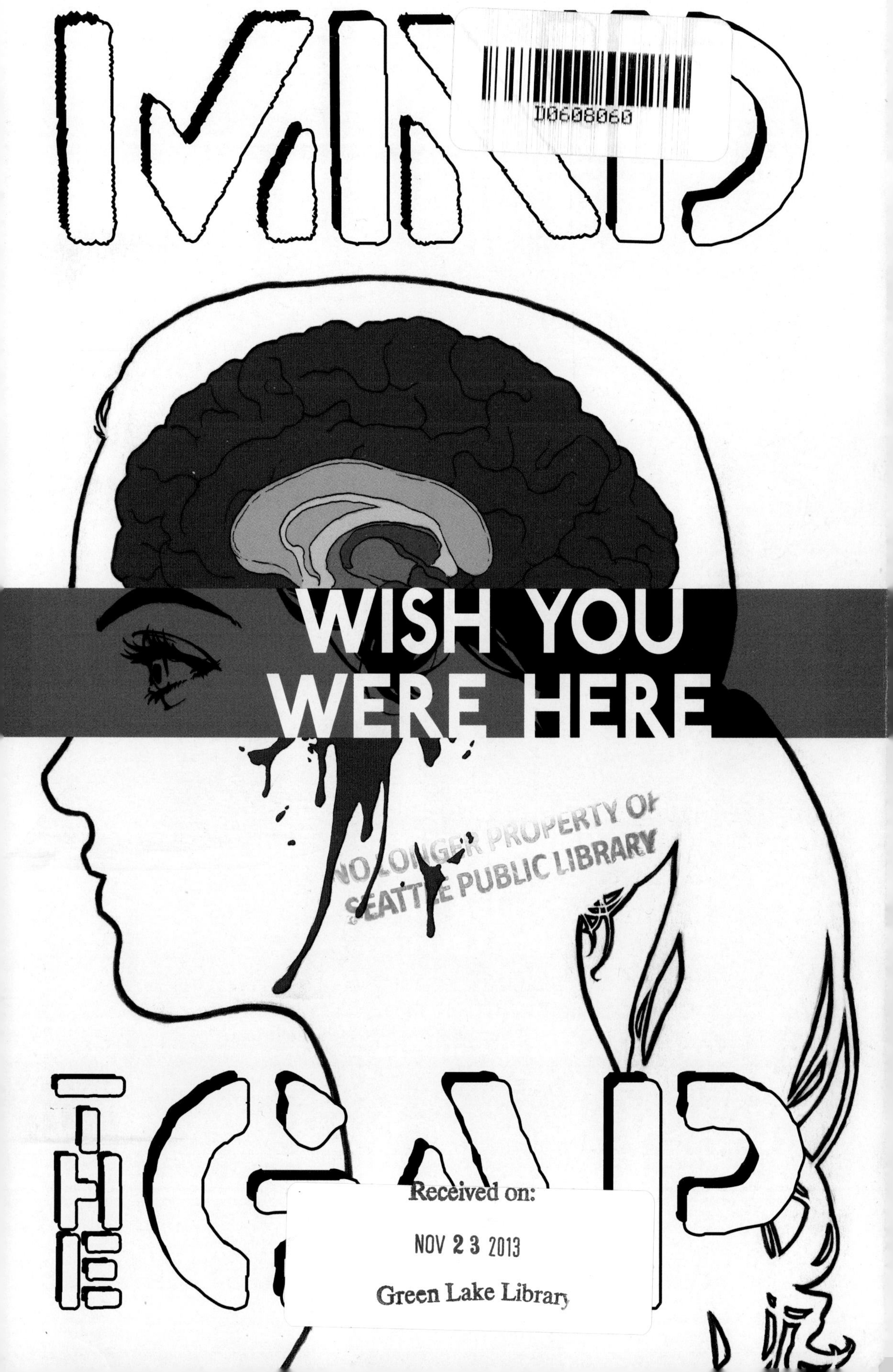
WISH YOU
WERE HERE
THE

Written by Jim McCann

MIND

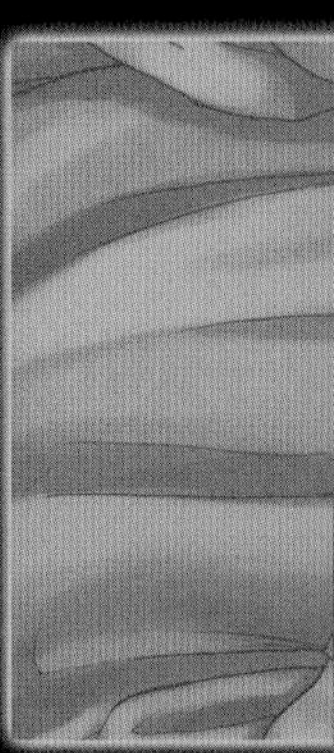

Production and Graphic Design by Damien Lucchese

Edited by Rob Levin

Cover by Rodin Esquejo

MIND THE GAP, VOL. 2: WISH YOU WERE HERE
ISBN: 978-1-60706-733-7
First Printing

Published by Image Comics, Inc. Office of publication: 2001 Center Street, 6th Floor, Berkeley, CA 94704. Copyright © 2013 Jim McCann. Originally published in single magazine form as MIND THE GAP #6-10. All rights reserved. Logo and all character likenesses are trademarks of Jim McCann, unless otherwise noted. Image Comics and its logos are ® and © 2013 Image Comics, Inc. All rights reserved. No part of this publication may be reproduced or transmitted, in any form or by any means, (except for short excerpts for review purposes) without the express written permission of Image Comics, Inc. All names, characters, events and locales in this publication are entirely fictional. Any resemblance to actual persons (living or dead), events or places, without satiric intent, is coincidental. For information regarding the CPSIA on this printed material call: 203-5953636 and provide reference # RICH - 495859 PRINTED IN THE UNITED STATES For international rights, contact: foreignlicensing@imagecomics.com

IMAGE COMICS, INC.

Robert Kirkman - chief operating officer
Erik Larsen - chief financial officer
Todd McFarlane - president
Marc Silvestri - chief executive officer
Jim Valentino - vice-president
www.imagecomics.com

Eric Stephenson - publisher
Ron Richards - director of business development
Jennifer de Guzman - pr & marketing director
Branwyn Bigglestone - accounts manager
Emily Miller - accounting assistant
Jamie Parreno - marketing assistant
Jenna Savage - administrative assistant

Kevin Yuen - digital rights coordinator
Jonathan Chan - production manager
Drew Gill - art director
Tyler Shainline - print manager
Monica Garcia - production artist
Vincent Kukua - production artist
Jana Cook - production artist

Art by
Rodin Esquejo

with Special Guest Artist
Dan McDaid
on "Speechless"

Colors by
Arif Prianto of STELLAR LABS,
with Beny Maulana, Jessica Kholinne,
& Fahriza Kamaputra of STELLAR LABS

Letters by
Dave Lanphear

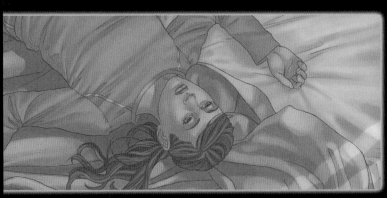

**MIND THE GAP
created by
Jim McCann**

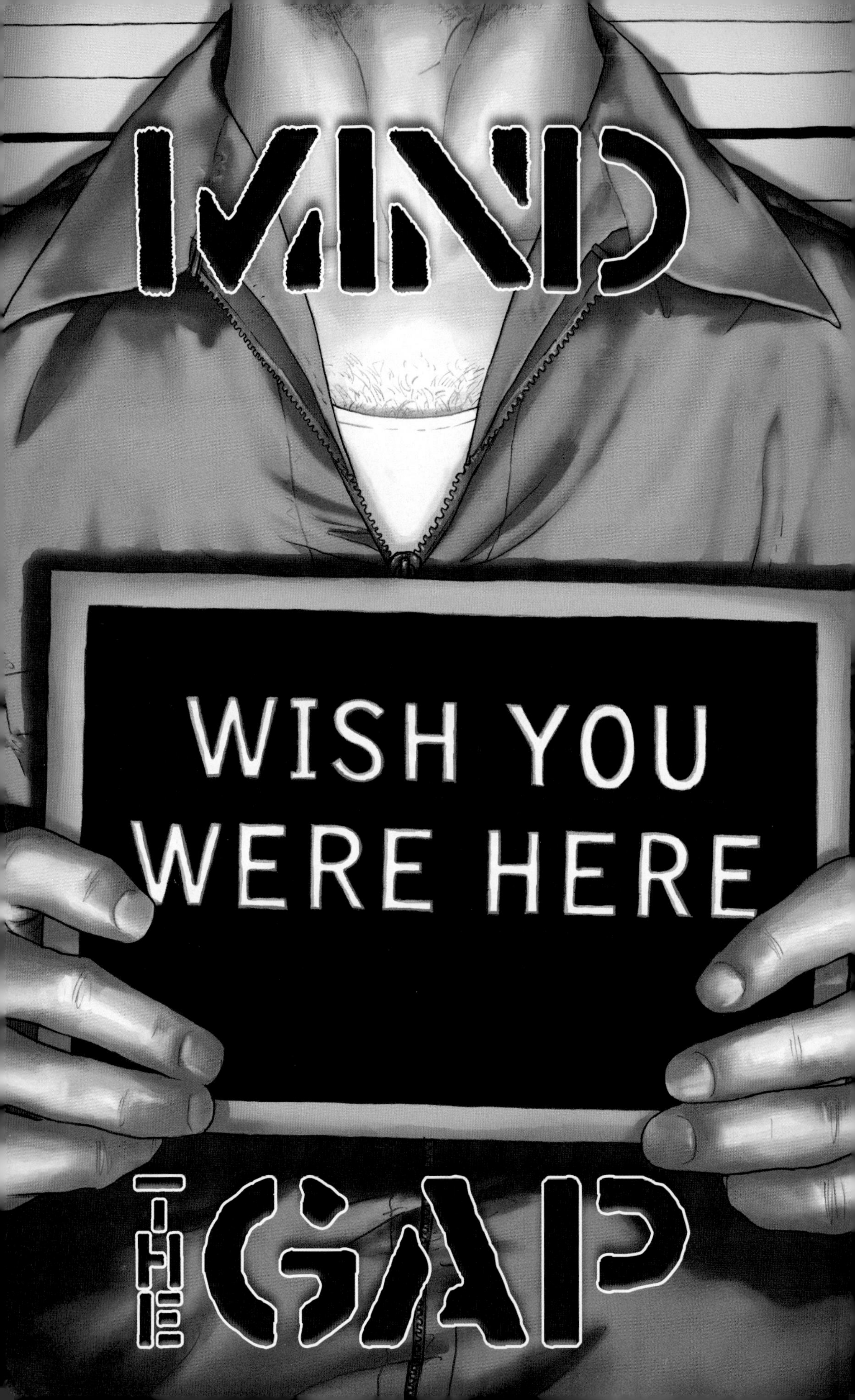
MIND
WISH YOU
WERE HERE
THE GAP

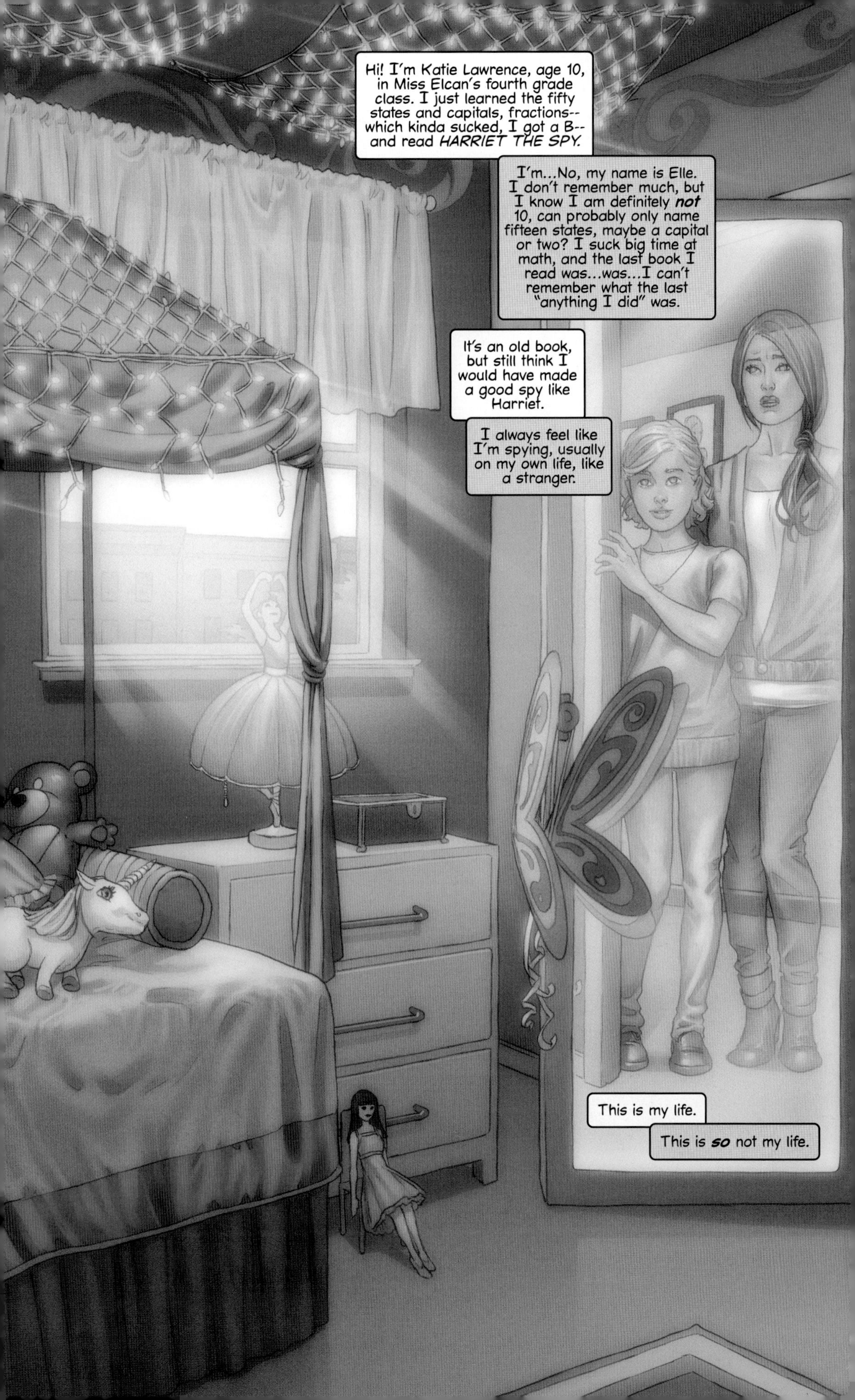
Hi! I'm Katie Lawrence, age 10, in Miss Elcan's fourth grade class. I just learned the fifty states and capitals, fractions--which kinda sucked, I got a B--and read HARRIET THE SPY.
I'm...No, my name is Elle. I don't remember much, but I know I am definitely **not** 10, can probably only name fifteen states, maybe a capital or two? I suck big time at math, and the last book I read was...was...I can't remember what the last "anything I did" was.
It's an old book, but still think I would have made a good spy like Harriet.
I always feel like I'm spying, usually on my own life, like a stranger.
This is my life.
This is **so** not my life.

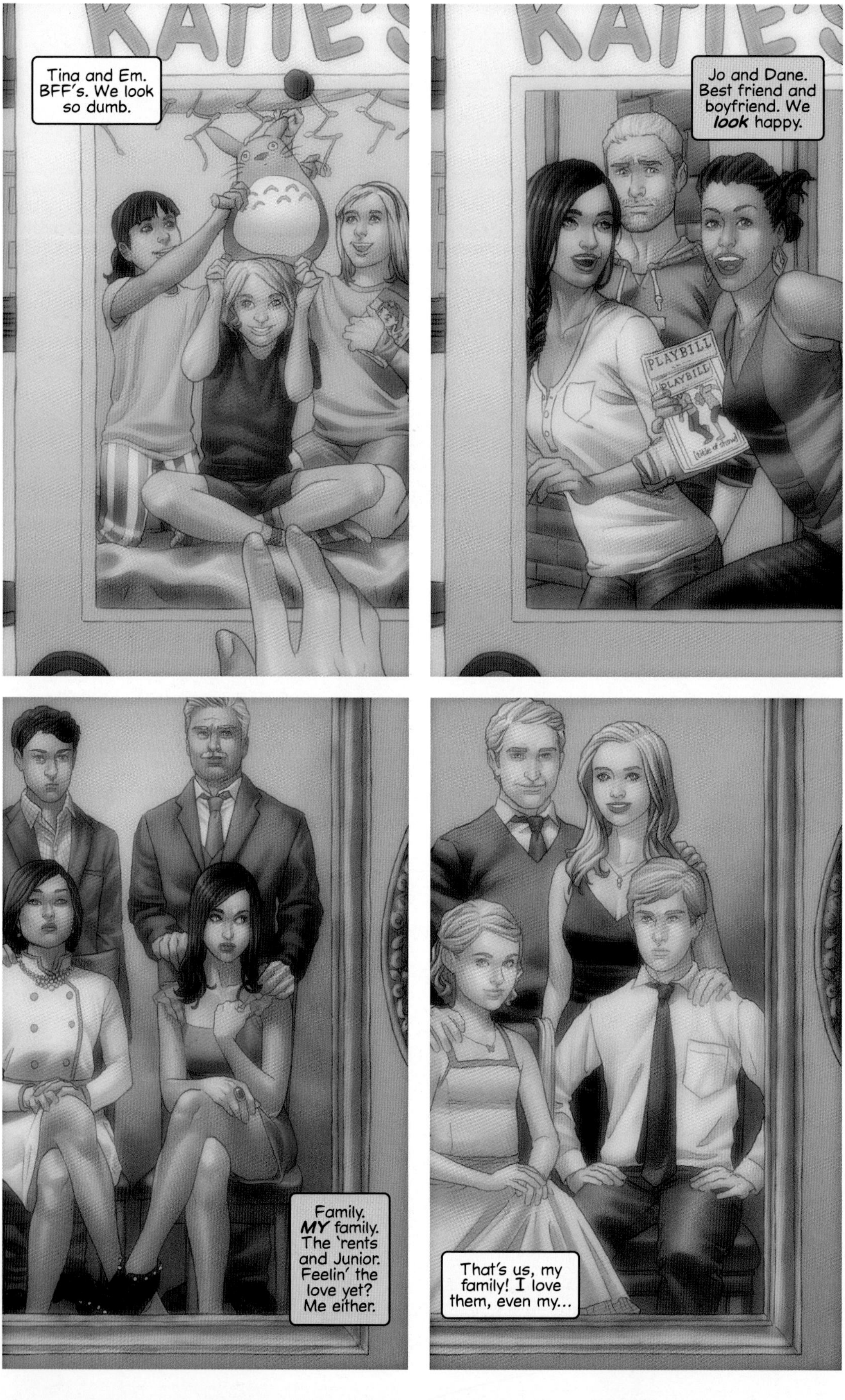
Tina and Em. BFF's. We look so dumb.
Jo and Dane. Best friend and boyfriend. We ***look*** happy.
PLAYBILL
Family. ***MY*** family. The 'rents and Junior. Feelin' the love yet? Me either.
That's us, my family! I love them, even my...

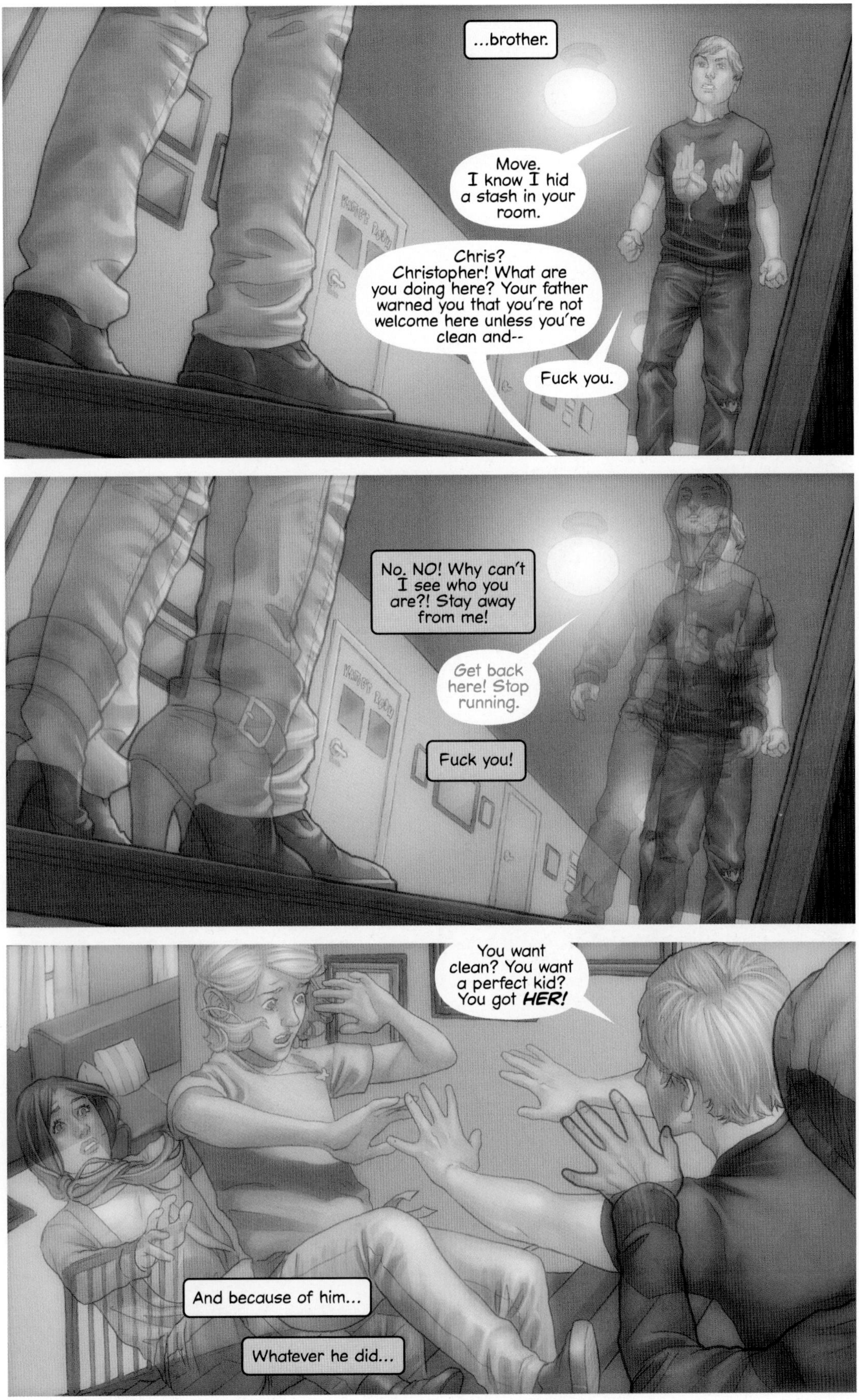
...brother.
Move. I know I hid a stash in your room.
Chris? Christopher! What are you doing here? Your father warned you that you're not welcome here unless you're clean and--
Fuck you.
No. NO! Why can't I see who you are?! Stay away from me!
Get back here! Stop running.
Fuck you!
You want clean? You want a perfect kid? You got HER!
And because of him...
Whatever he did...

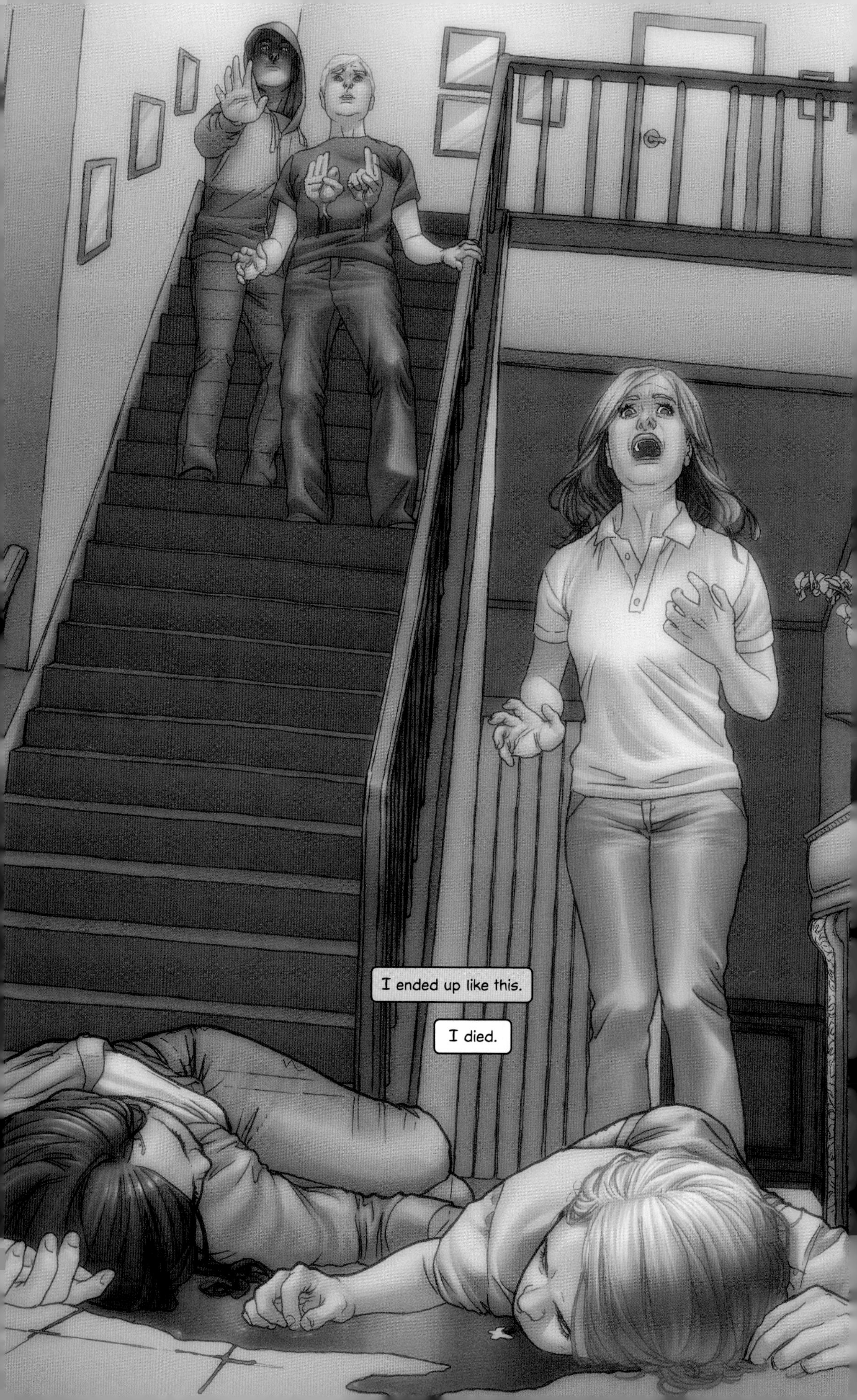
I ended up like this.
I died.

Hi.

Hey.

Now you get it? What I asked you to do?

Yeah, kiddo.

Go down, tell the truth. Which means it's time for you...

...to go... wherever. And you...

...to go down there and do that voodoo only I do...

Only the second time trying this. First time, not so great. *THAT* time I was just trying to say my name. Now...

Shit, I hope I remember all of this when I get...

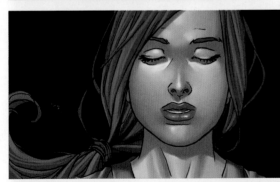

Here.

WISH YOU WERE HERE
PART I
"SLEEP FURIOUSLY"

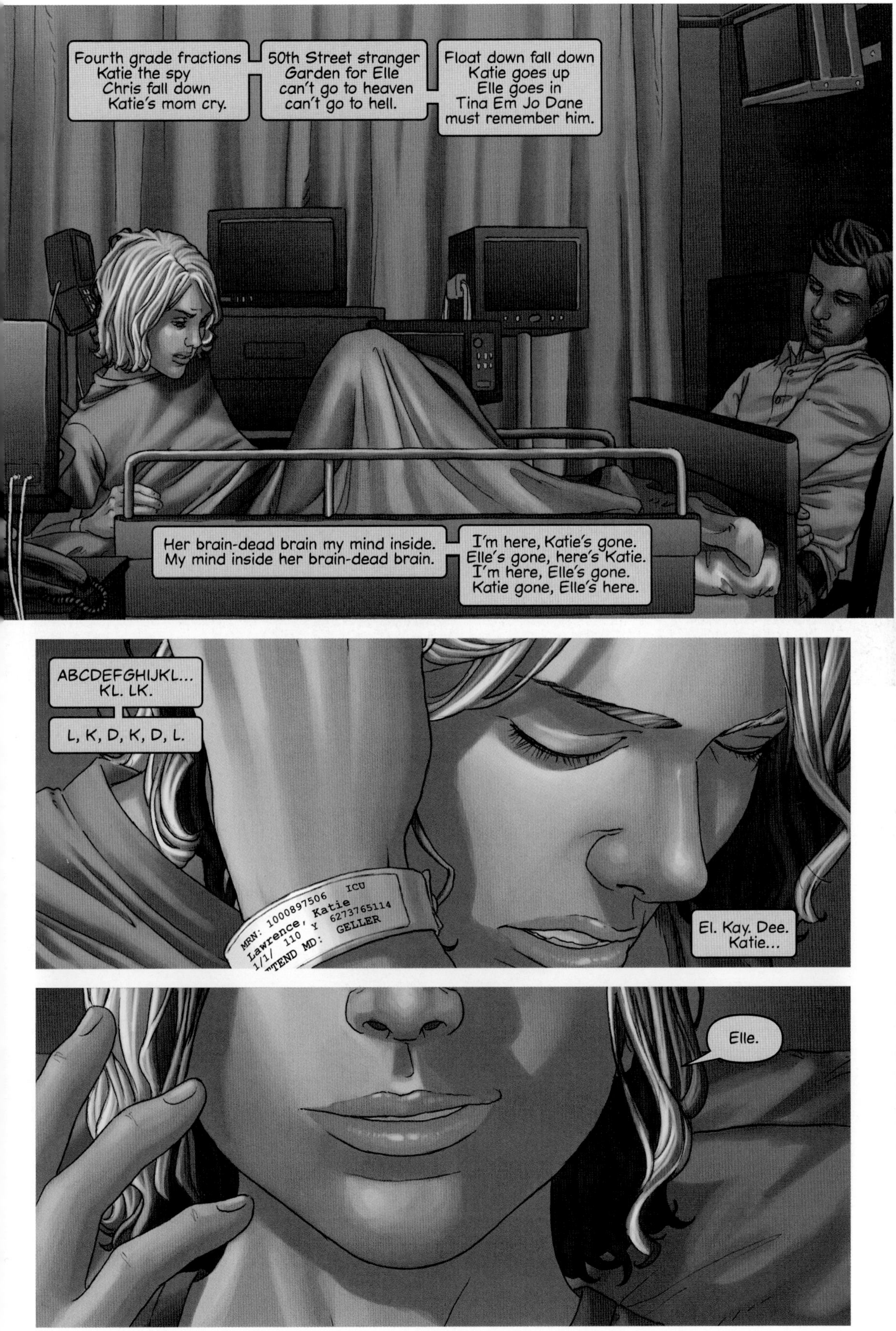
Fourth grade fractions Katie the spy Chris fall down Katie's mom cry.
50th Street stranger Garden for Elle can't go to heaven can't go to hell.
Float down fall down Katie goes up Elle goes in Tina Em Jo Dane must remember him.
Her brain-dead brain my mind inside. My mind inside her brain-dead brain.
I'm here, Katie's gone. Elle's gone, here's Katie. I'm here, Elle's gone. Katie gone, Elle's here.
ABCDEFGHIJKL... KL. LK.
L, K, D, K, D, L.
MRN: 1000897506 ICU
Lawrence, Katie
6273765114
GELLER
El. Kay. Dee. Katie...
Elle.

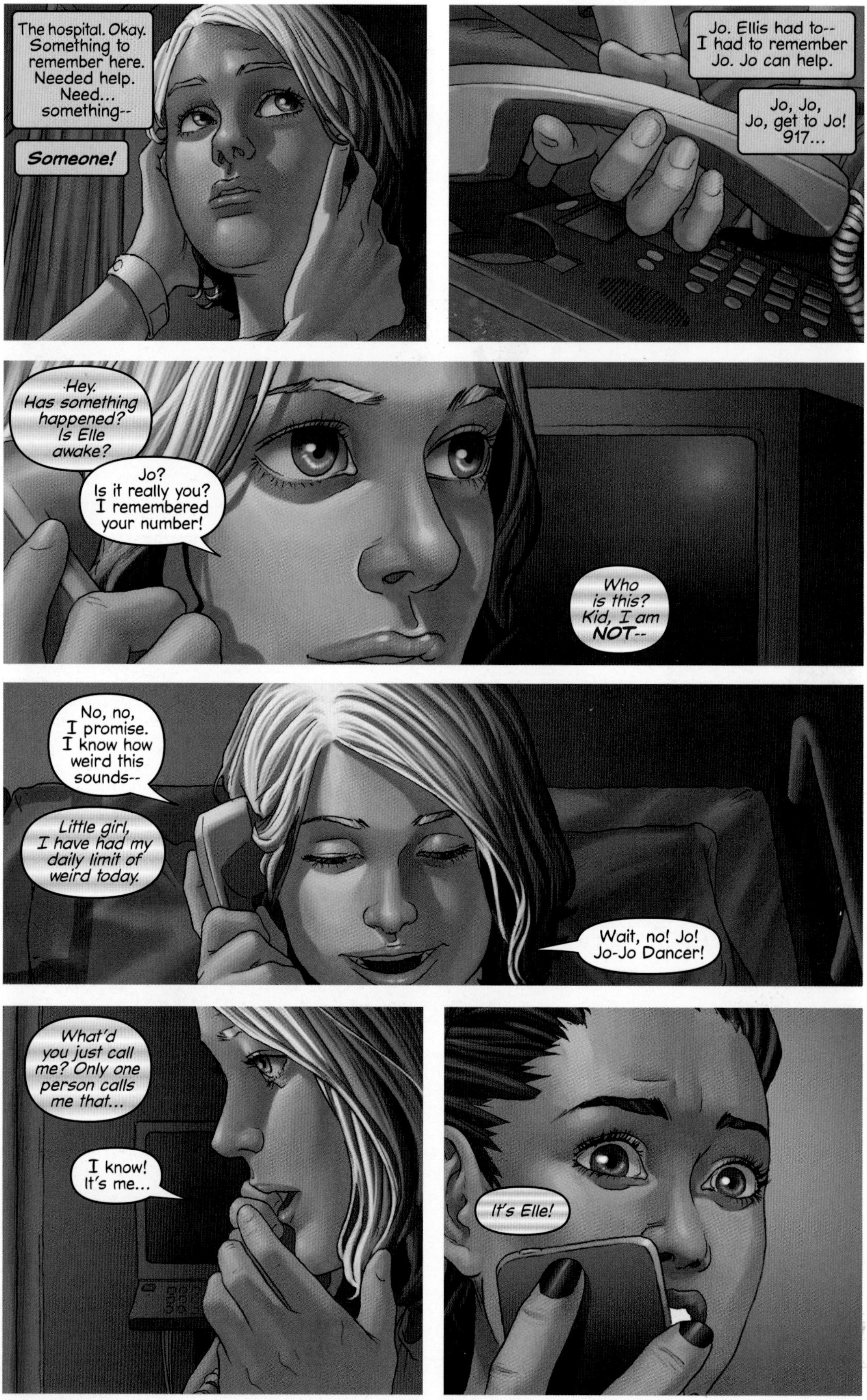
The hospital. Okay. Something to remember here. Needed help. Need... something--
Someone!
Jo. Ellis had to-- I had to remember Jo. Jo can help.
Jo, Jo, Jo, get to Jo! 917...
Hey. Has something happened? Is Elle awake?
Jo? Is it really you? I remembered your number!
Who is this? Kid, I am NOT--
No, no, I promise. I know how weird this sounds--
Little girl, I have had my daily limit of weird today.
Wait, no! Jo! Jo-Jo Dancer!
What'd you just call me? Only one person calls me that...
I know! It's me...
It's Elle!

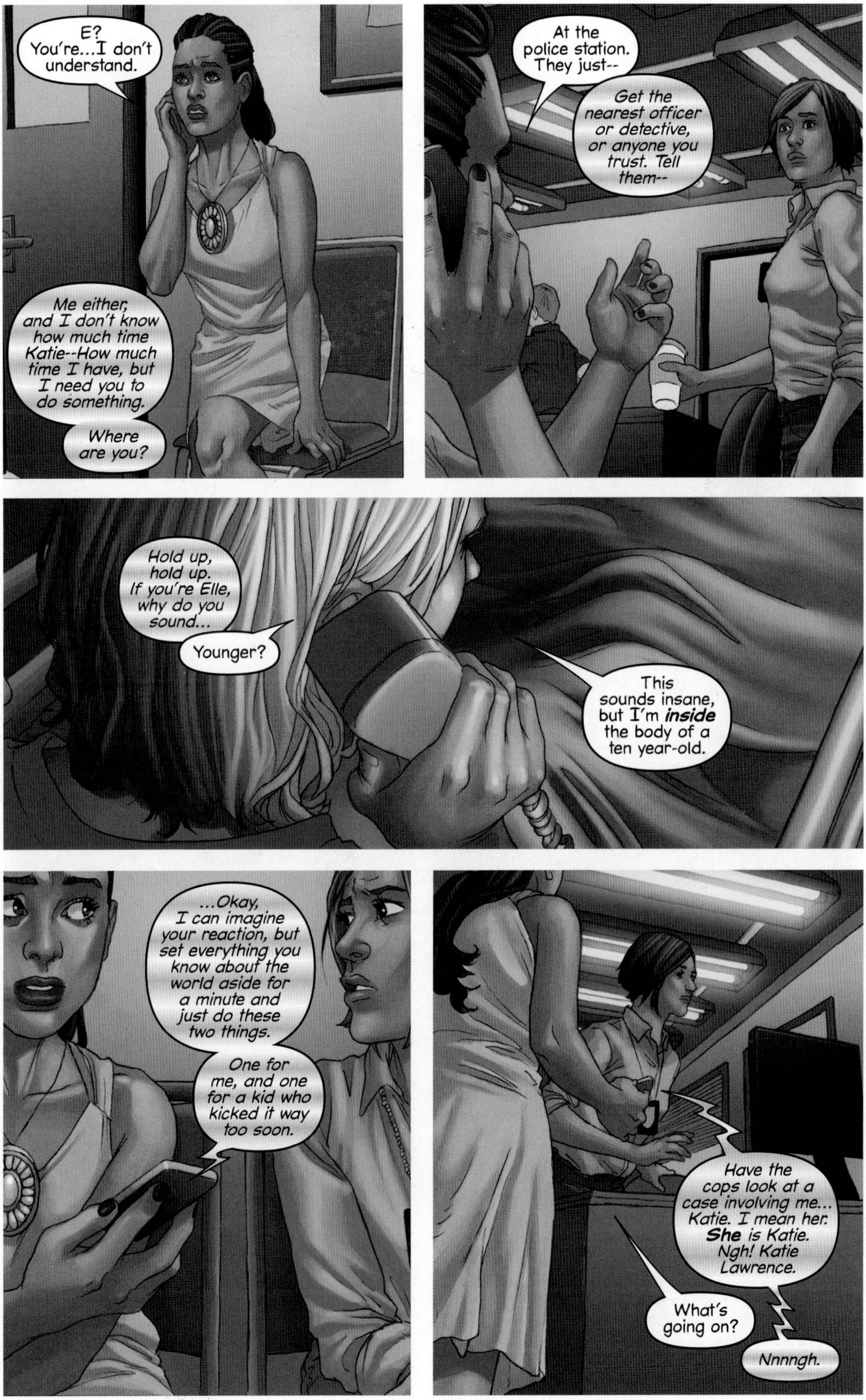
E? You're...I don't understand.
Me either, and I don't know how much time Katie--How much time I have, but I need you to do something.
Where are you?
At the police station. They just--
Get the nearest officer or detective, or anyone you trust. Tell them--
Hold up, hold up. If you're Elle, why do you sound...
Younger?
This sounds insane, but I'm *inside* the body of a ten year-old.
...Okay, I can imagine your reaction, but set everything you know about the world aside for a minute and just do these two things.
One for me, and one for a kid who kicked it way too soon.
Have the cops look at a case involving me... Katie. I mean her. **She** is Katie. Ngh! Katie Lawrence.
What's going on?
Nnnngh.

Harder... than I thought... Fighting to stay me and my mind.

Okay, I'm with a friend. She's got the Lawrence case pulled up, says...okay... uh-huh...

Fell down a flight of stairs, appeared to be accidental, and the kid...

Katie Lawrence was in a coma for two days. Declared brain dead this morning.

You... you're dead?

In between. Trust me, this is *REAL*. I don't know how or when I'll be able to do this again, but you need to look... look...look in her, in my case!

BOTH of us. What happened. They're lying. They're all lying.

Who is?

The people who did this to me... to her...Fuck! Both! He did it! Check the alibi. The brother, the brother. Eddie! No...*Chris!* I mean Chris!

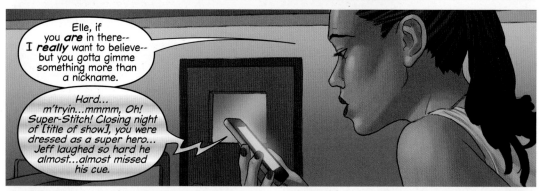

Elle, if you *are* in there-- I *really* want to believe-- but you gotta gimme something more than a nickname.

Hard... m'tryin...mmmm, Oh! Super-Stitch! Closing night of [title of show], you were dressed as a super hero... Jeff laughed so hard he almost...almost missed his cue.

Elle.

Told ya.

KATIE?!

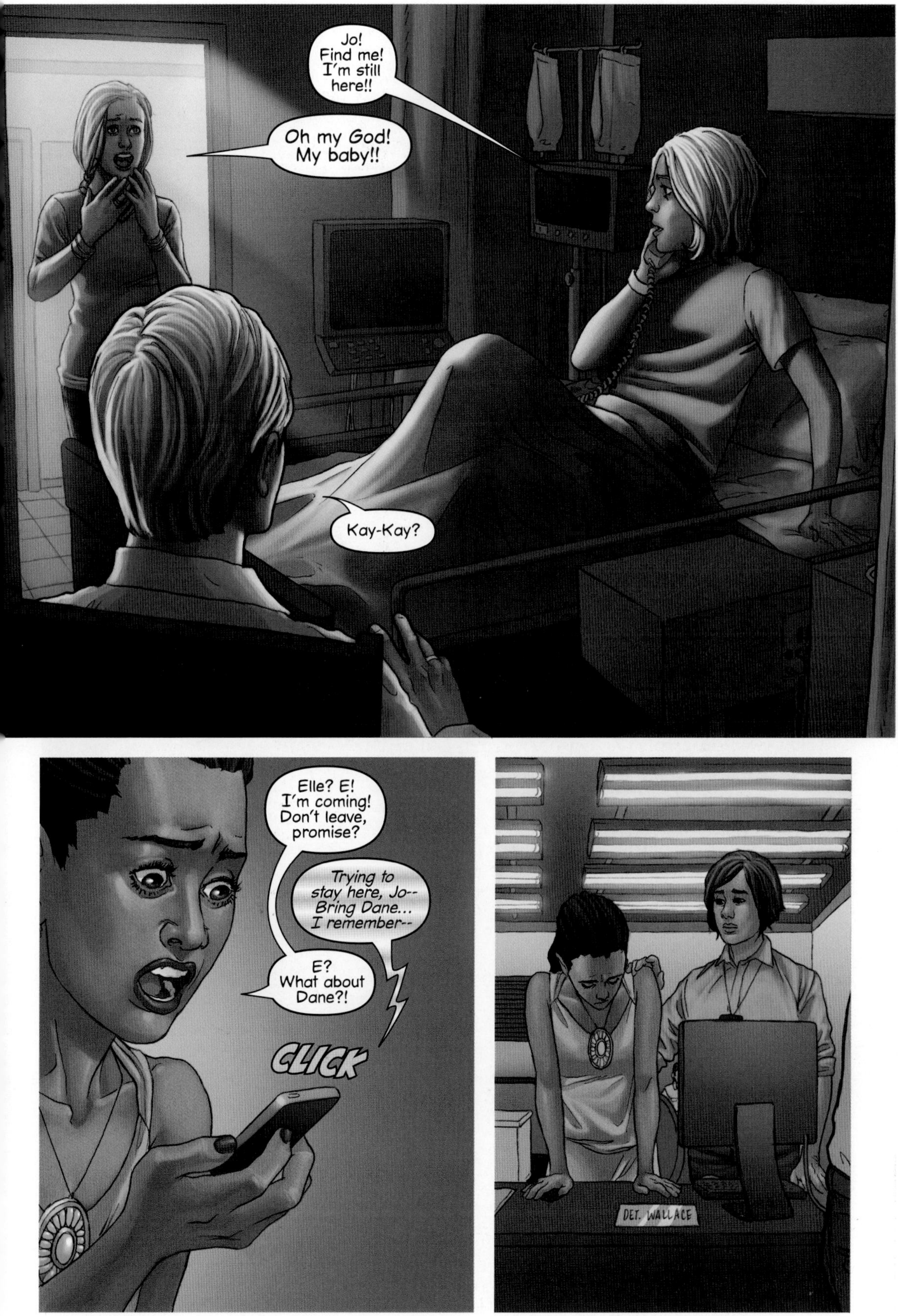
Jo! Find me! I'm still here!!
Oh my God! My baby!!
Kay-Kay?
Elle? E! I'm coming! Don't leave, promise?
Trying to stay here, Jo-- Bring Dane... I remember--
E? What about Dane?!
CLICK
DET. WALLACE

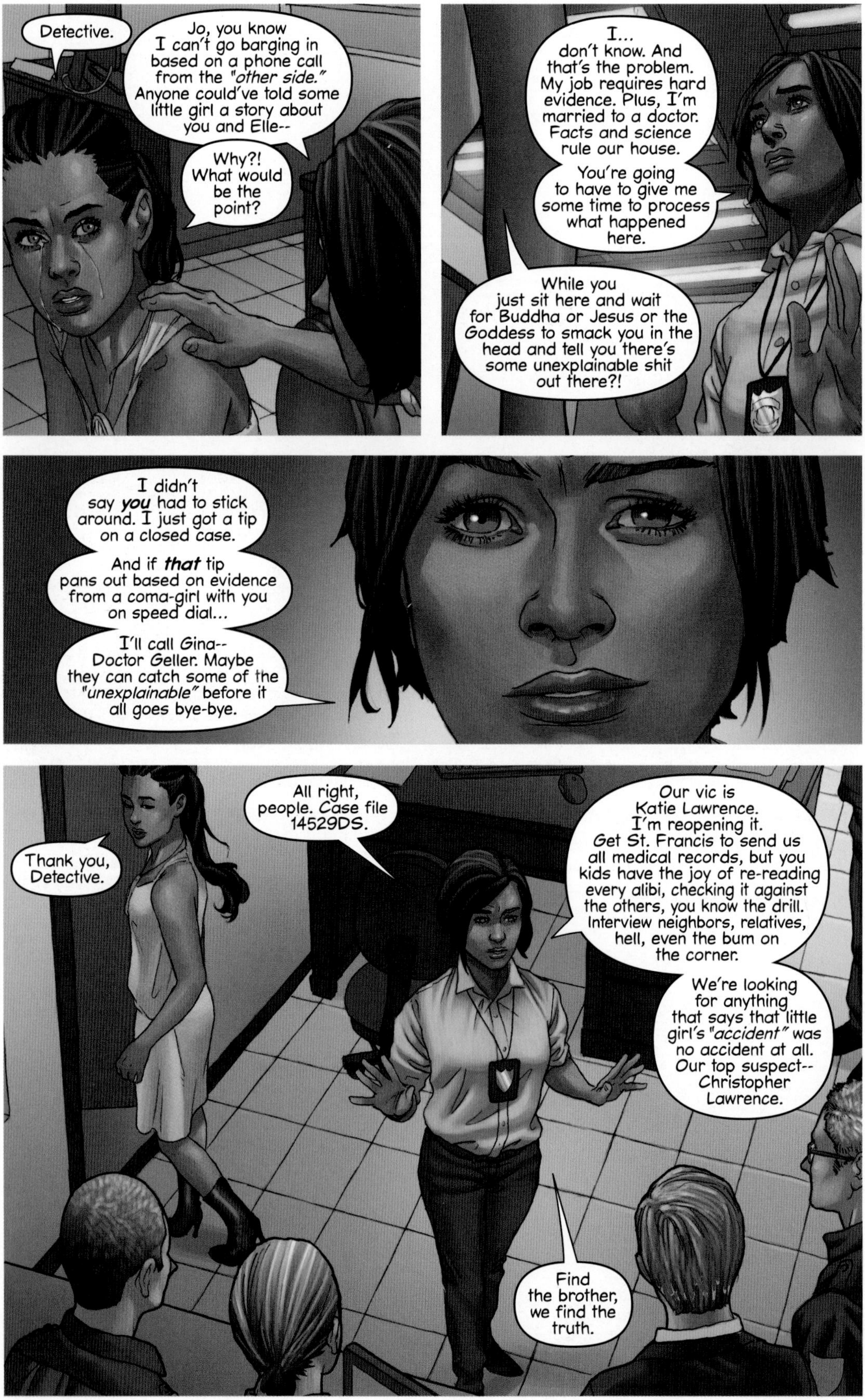
Detective.
Jo, you know I can't go barging in based on a phone call from the *"other side."* Anyone could've told some little girl a story about you and Elle--
Why?! What would be the point?
I... don't know. And that's the problem. My job requires hard evidence. Plus, I'm married to a doctor. Facts and science rule our house.
You're going to have to give me some time to process what happened here.
While you just sit here and wait for Buddha or Jesus or the Goddess to smack you in the head and tell you there's some unexplainable shit out there?!
I didn't say ***you*** had to stick around. I just got a tip on a closed case.
And if ***that*** tip pans out based on evidence from a coma-girl with you on speed dial...
I'll call Gina-- Doctor Geller. Maybe they can catch some of the *"unexplainable"* before it all goes bye-bye.
Thank you, Detective.
All right, people. Case file 14529DS.
Our vic is Katie Lawrence. I'm reopening it. Get St. Francis to send us all medical records, but you kids have the joy of re-reading every alibi, checking it against the others, you know the drill. Interview neighbors, relatives, hell, even the bum on the corner.
We're looking for anything that says that little girl's *"accident"* was no accident at all. Our top suspect-- Christopher Lawrence.
Find the brother, we find the truth.

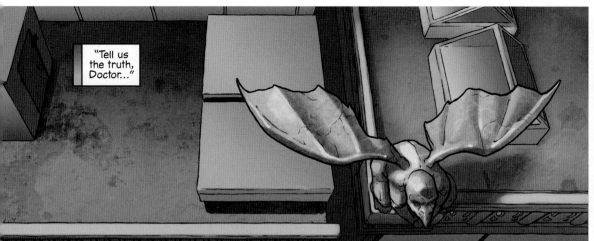

"Tell us the truth, Doctor..."

Did our daughter just come back from the dead?

Depends on your definition.

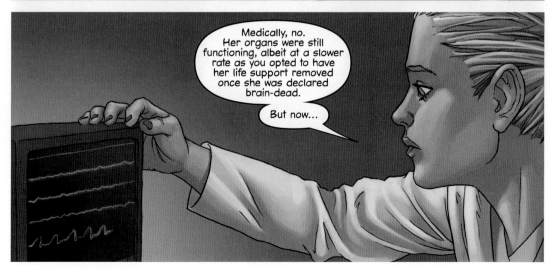

Medically, no. Her organs were still functioning, albeit at a slower rate as you opted to have her life support removed once she was declared brain-dead.

But now...

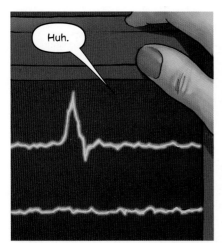

Huh.

"Huh?" That's your medical assessment?

You people told us our daughter was *gone.* Katie would never wake up. And after the decision we had to make, to pull the plug. Say good-bye...

Then my little girl wakes up and all you can say is "*Huh?!*"

You nearly *killed* our daughter! I will *own* this hospital!

Honey, please.

If you would like to waste an inordinate amount of time, effort, and money to level a malpractice suit, as I assume you are thinking, in order to "*own this hospital,*" be my guest.

Or you can let me finish my thought.

"*Huh*" was the beginning of "*Huh, that's strange*"--

--the strange being that your daughter's brain activity shows little to no damage at this moment.

This is in stark contrast to when she was admitted and the EEG showed no activity, indicating massive damage, and by all signs, her brain was dead.

Really most sincerely dead.

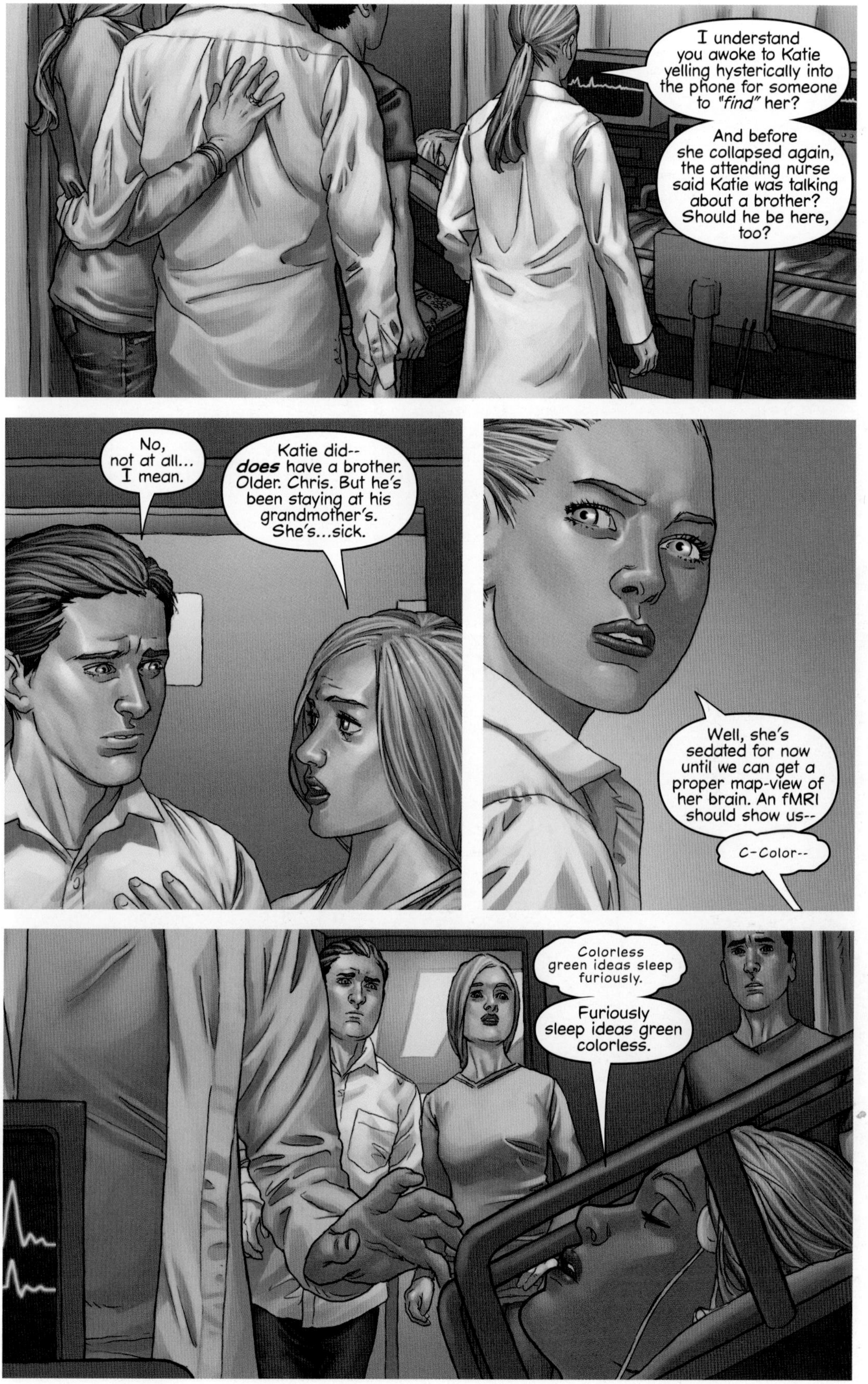
I understand you awoke to Katie yelling hysterically into the phone for someone to "find" her?
And before she collapsed again, the attending nurse said Katie was talking about a brother? Should he be here, too?
No, not at all... I mean.
Katie did-- does have a brother. Older. Chris. But he's been staying at his grandmother's. She's...sick.
Well, she's sedated for now until we can get a proper map-view of her brain. An fMRI should show us--
C-Color--
Colorless green ideas sleep furiously.
Furiously sleep ideas green colorless.

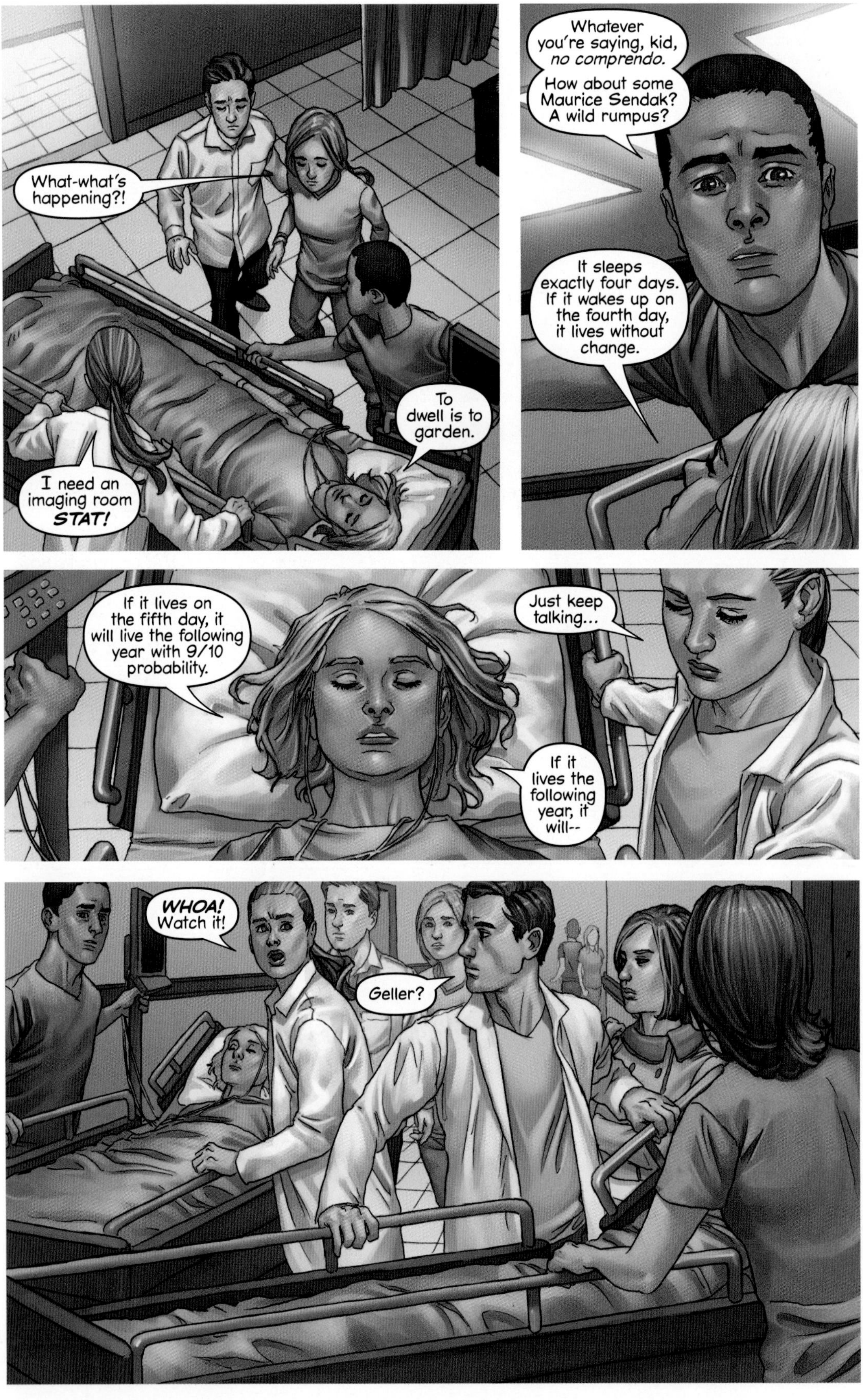
What-what's happening?!
To dwell is to garden.
I need an imaging room *STAT!*
Whatever you're saying, kid, *no comprendo.*
How about some Maurice Sendak? A wild rumpus?
It sleeps exactly four days. If it wakes up on the fourth day, it lives without change.
If it lives on the fifth day, it will live the following year with 9/10 probability.
Just keep talking...
If it lives the following year, it will--
WHOA! Watch it!
Geller?

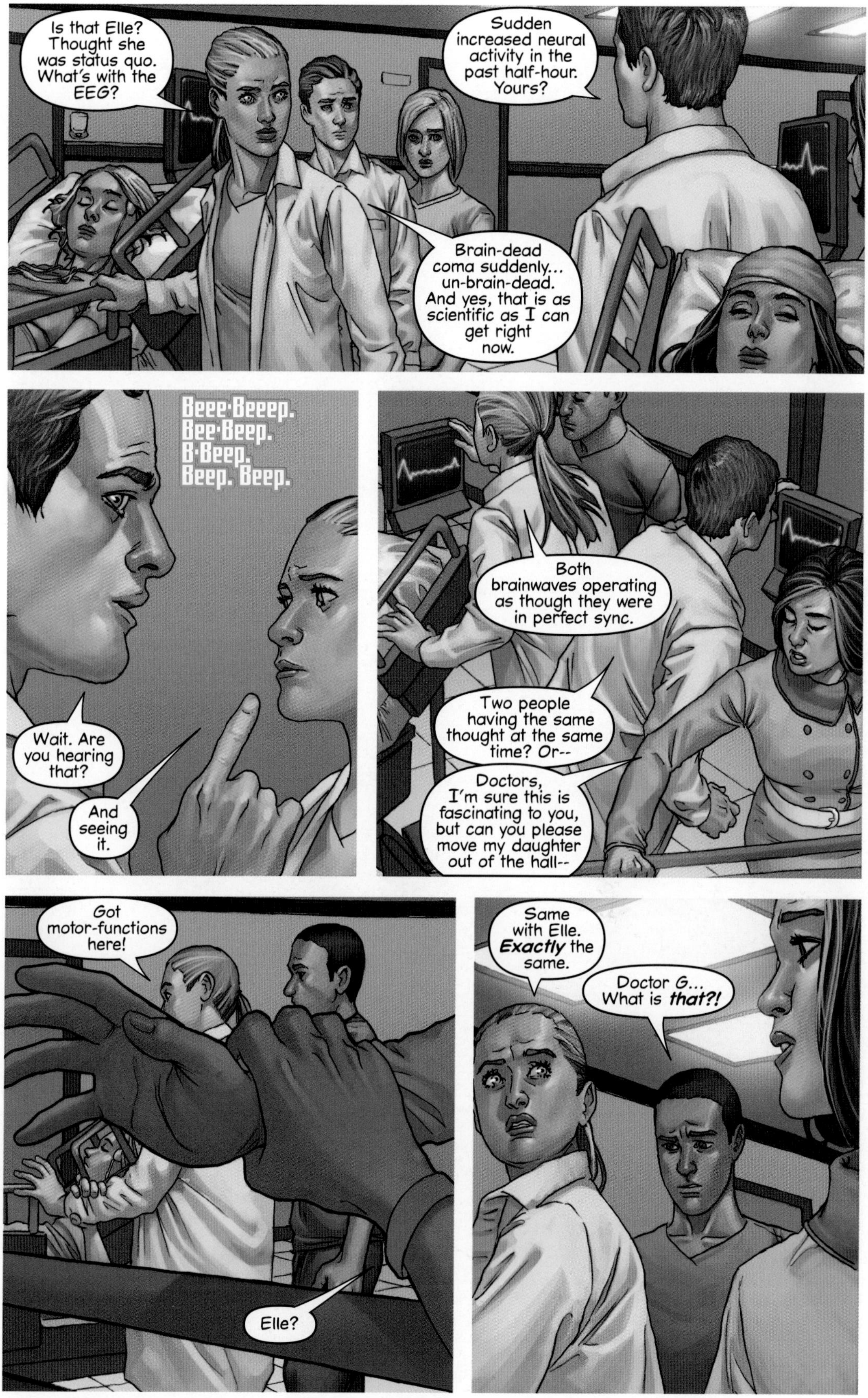
Is that Elle? Thought she was status quo. What's with the EEG?
Sudden increased neural activity in the past half-hour. Yours?
Brain-dead coma suddenly... un-brain-dead. And yes, that is as scientific as I can get right now.
Beee·Beeep. Bee·Beep. B·Beep. Beep. Beep.
Wait. Are you hearing that?
And seeing it.
Both brainwaves operating as though they were in perfect sync.
Two people having the same thought at the same time? Or--
Doctors, I'm sure this is fascinating to you, but can you please move my daughter out of the hall--
Got motor-functions here!
Elle?
Same with Elle. Exactly the same.
Doctor G... What is that?!

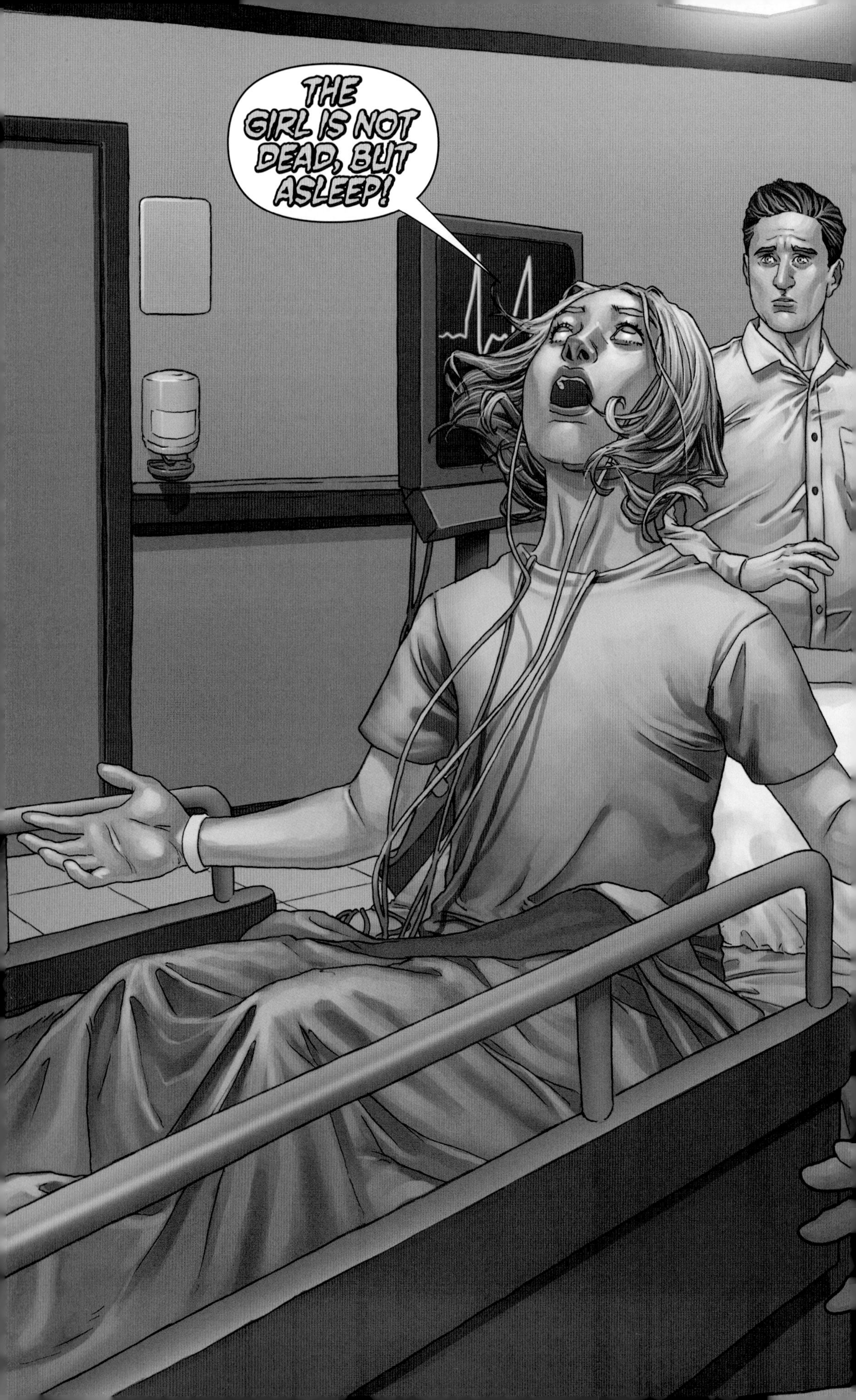
THE GIRL IS NOT DEAD, BUT ASLEEP!

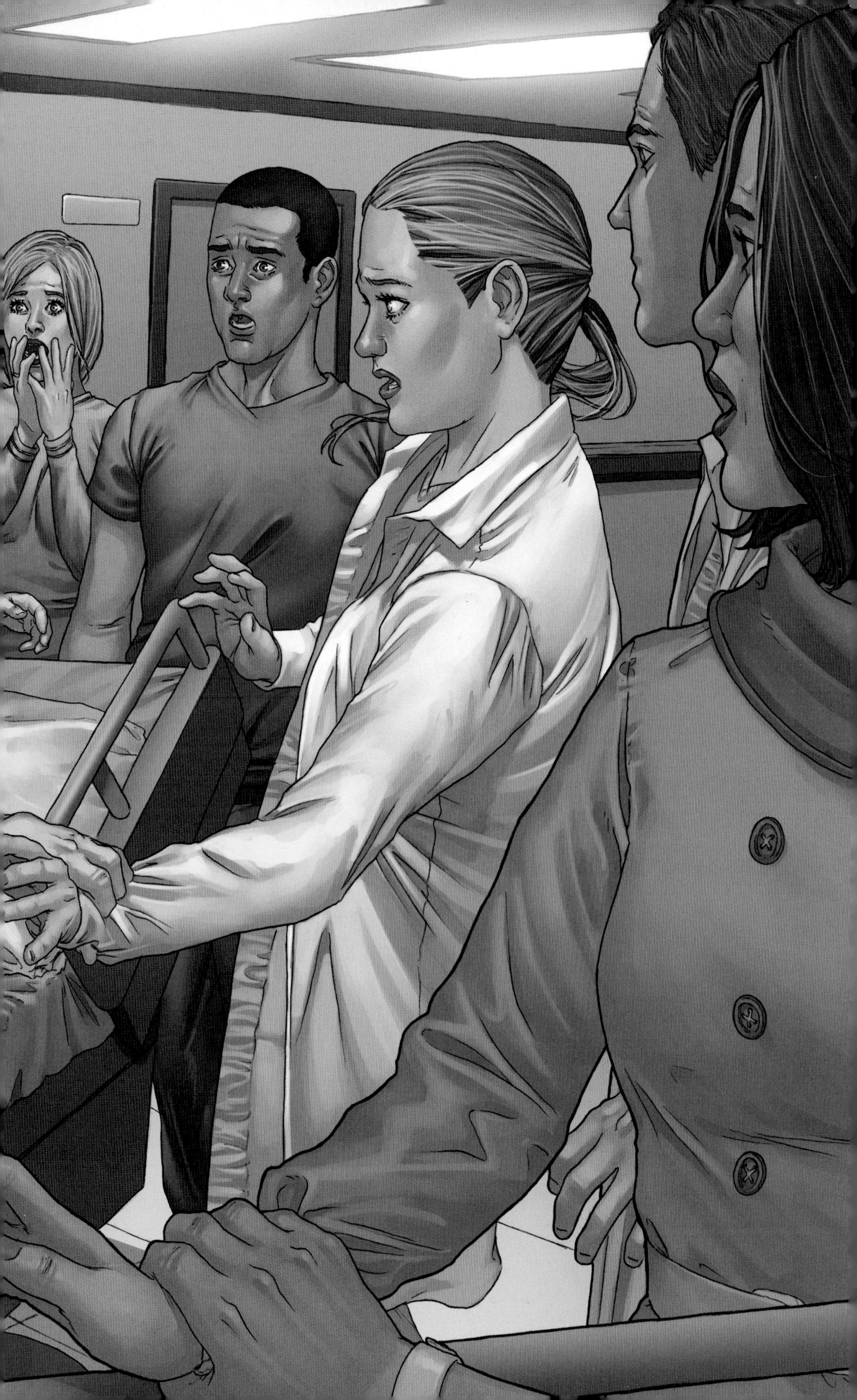

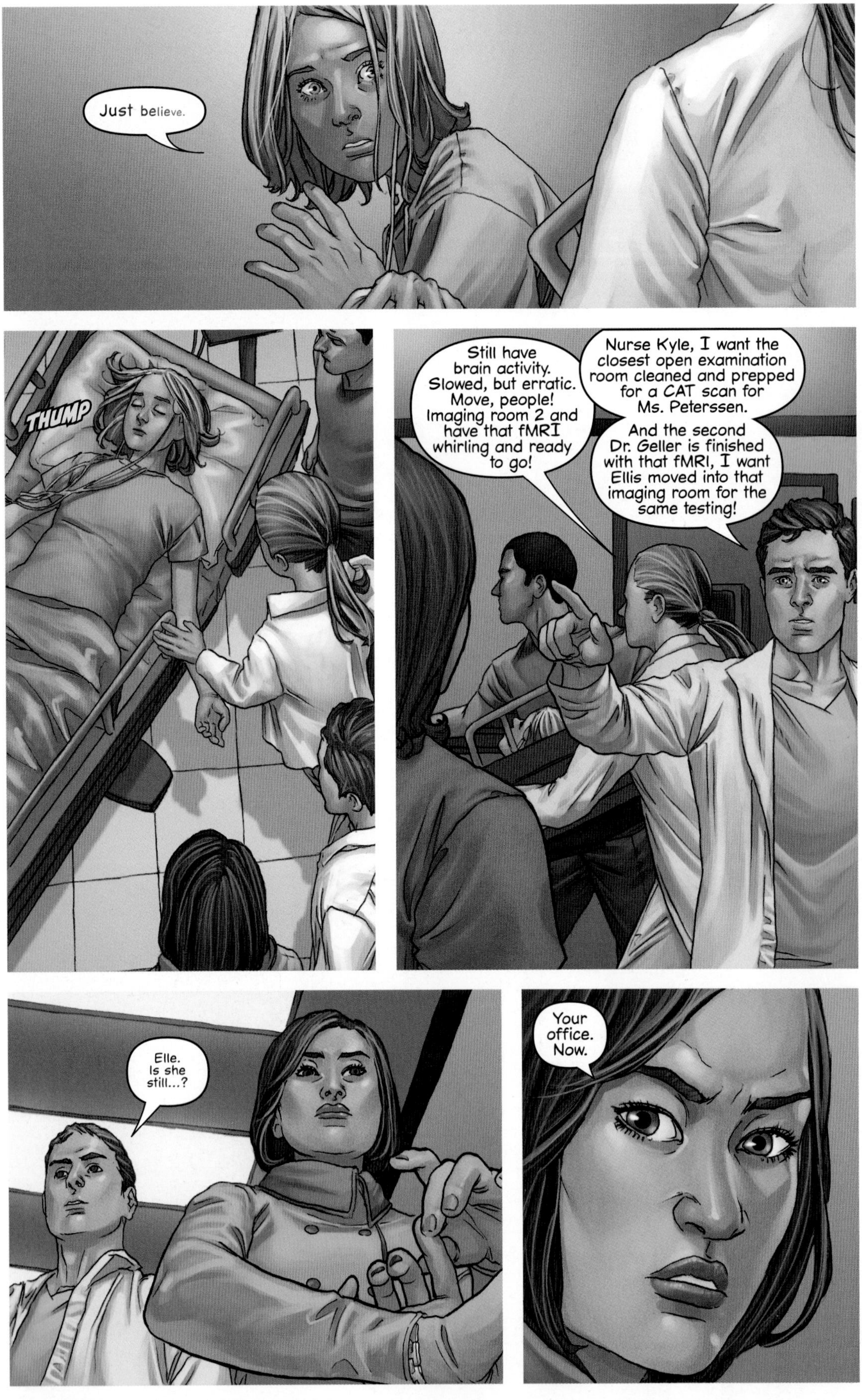
Just believe.
THUMP
Still have brain activity. Slowed, but erratic. Move, people! Imaging room 2 and have that fMRI whirling and ready to go!
Nurse Kyle, I want the closest open examination room cleaned and prepped for a CAT scan for Ms. Peterssen.
And the second Dr. Geller is finished with that fMRI, I want Ellis moved into that imaging room for the same testing!
Elle. Is she still...?
Your office. Now.

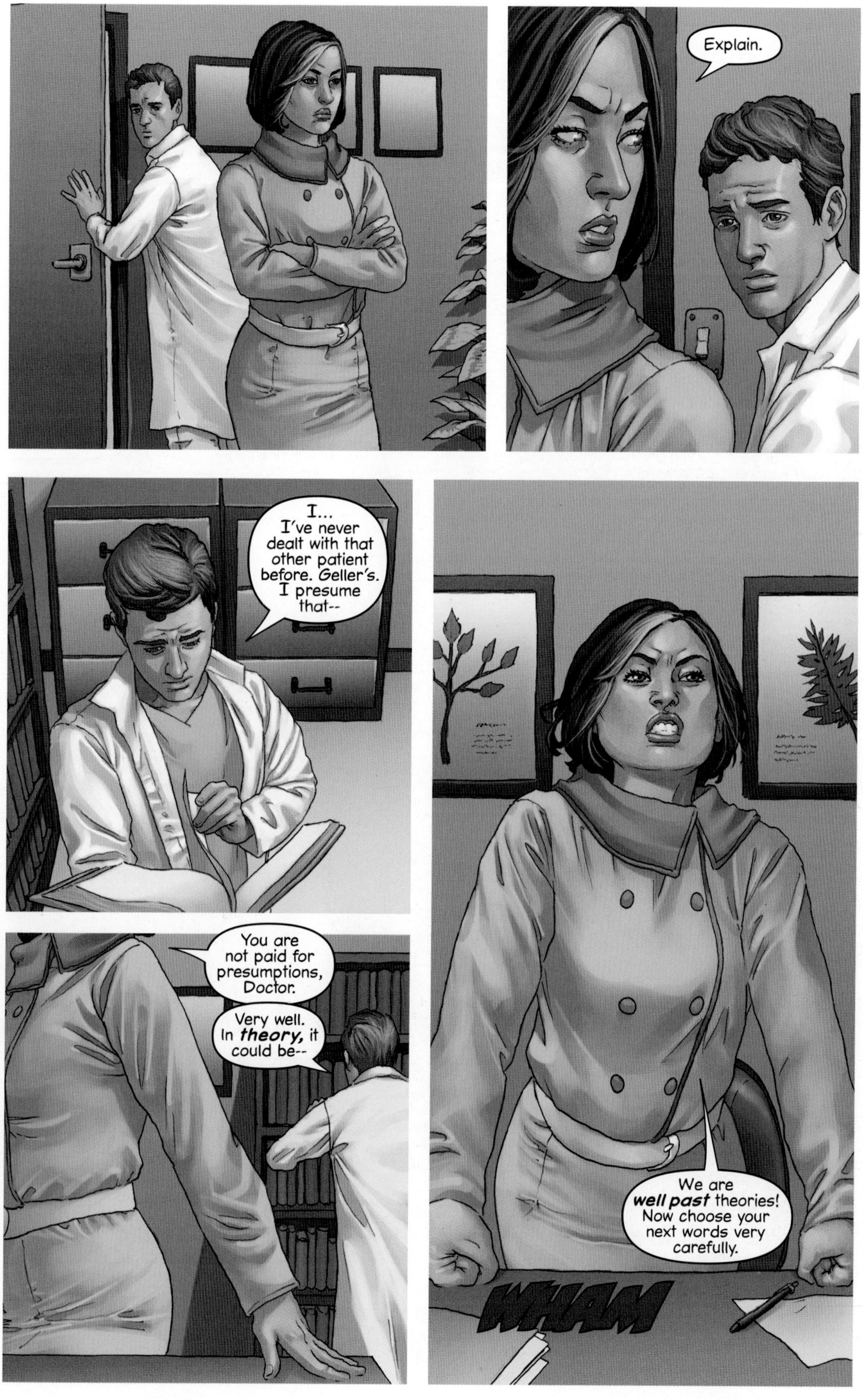
Explain.
I... I've never dealt with that other patient before. Geller's. I presume that--
You are not paid for presumptions, Doctor.
Very well. In *theory,* it could be--
We are ***well past*** theories! Now choose your next words very carefully.
WHAM

We were pushed into untested waters when Ellis was... attacked.

The conditions were not sterile, delivery method inconsistent, and the amount of time it took to bring her from the site to here-- all are variables we must account for.

As you are well aware, the timetable has been accelerated with potential unexpected results.

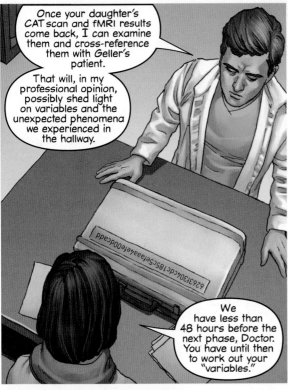

Once your daughter's CAT scan and fMRI results come back, I can examine them and cross-reference them with Geller's patient.

That will, in my professional opinion, possibly shed light on variables and the unexpected phenomena we experienced in the hallway.

62631304cdc185c5efaaa4efe00cdcad

We have less than 48 hours before the next phase, Doctor. You have until then to work out your "variables."

The Fifth, your "Chief," will want answers.

We *all* have our roles in this. Ours is far from over.

If there is so much as an irregular breath between now and Ellis' move to the Facility, you are to notify me immediately.

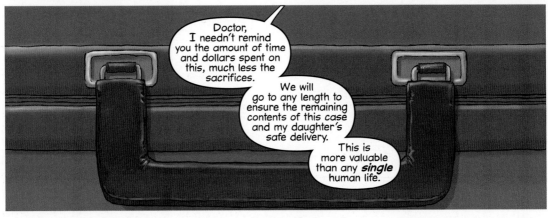

Doctor, I needn't remind you the amount of time and dollars spent on this, much less the sacrifices.

We will go to any length to ensure the remaining contents of this case and my daughter's safe delivery.

This is more valuable than any *single* human life.

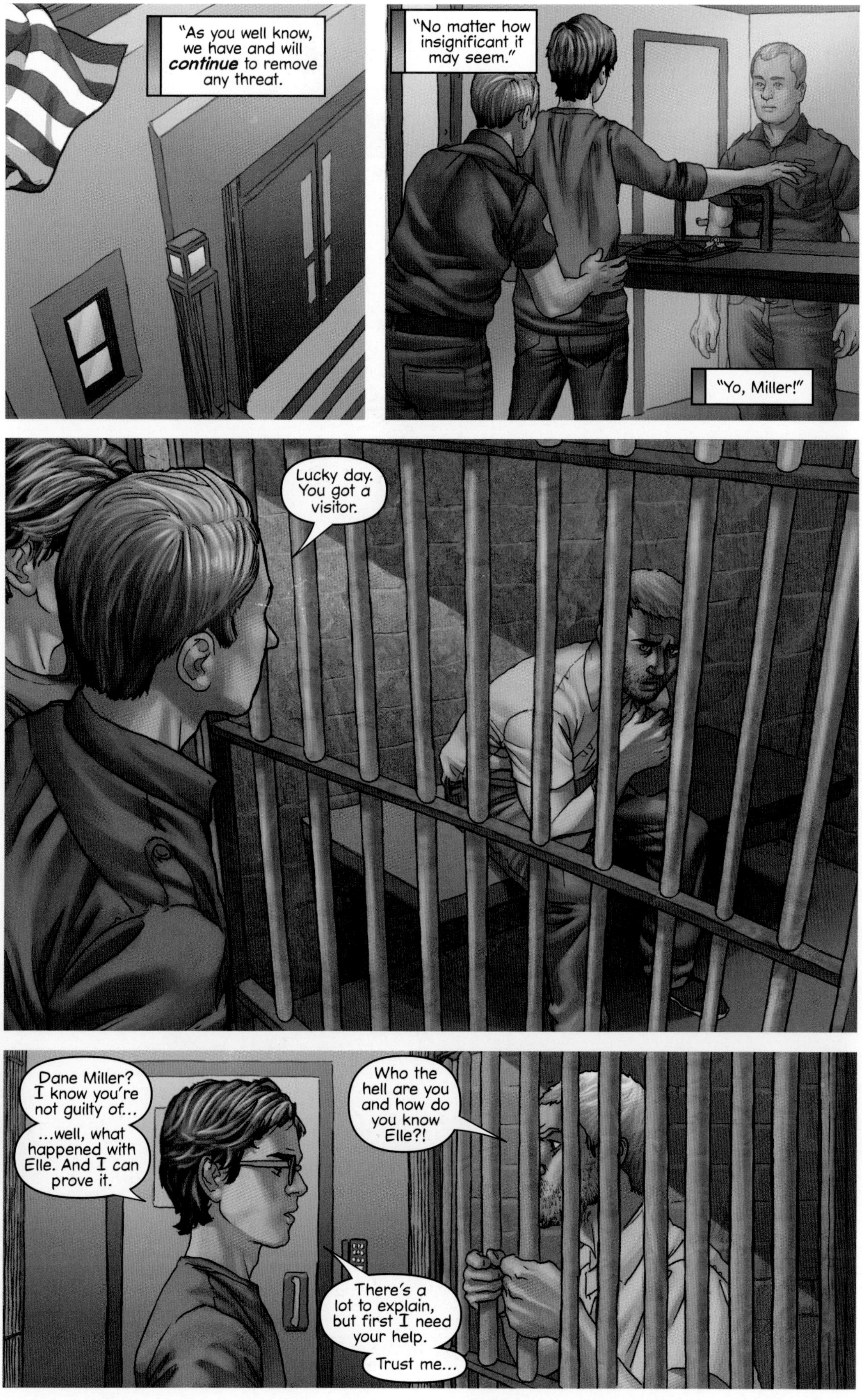
"As you well know, we have and will *continue* to remove any threat.
"No matter how insignificant it may seem."
"Yo, Miller!"
Lucky day. You got a visitor.
Dane Miller? I know you're not guilty of...
...well, what happened with Elle. And I can prove it.
Who the hell are you and how do you know Elle?!
There's a lot to explain, but first I need your help.
Trust me...

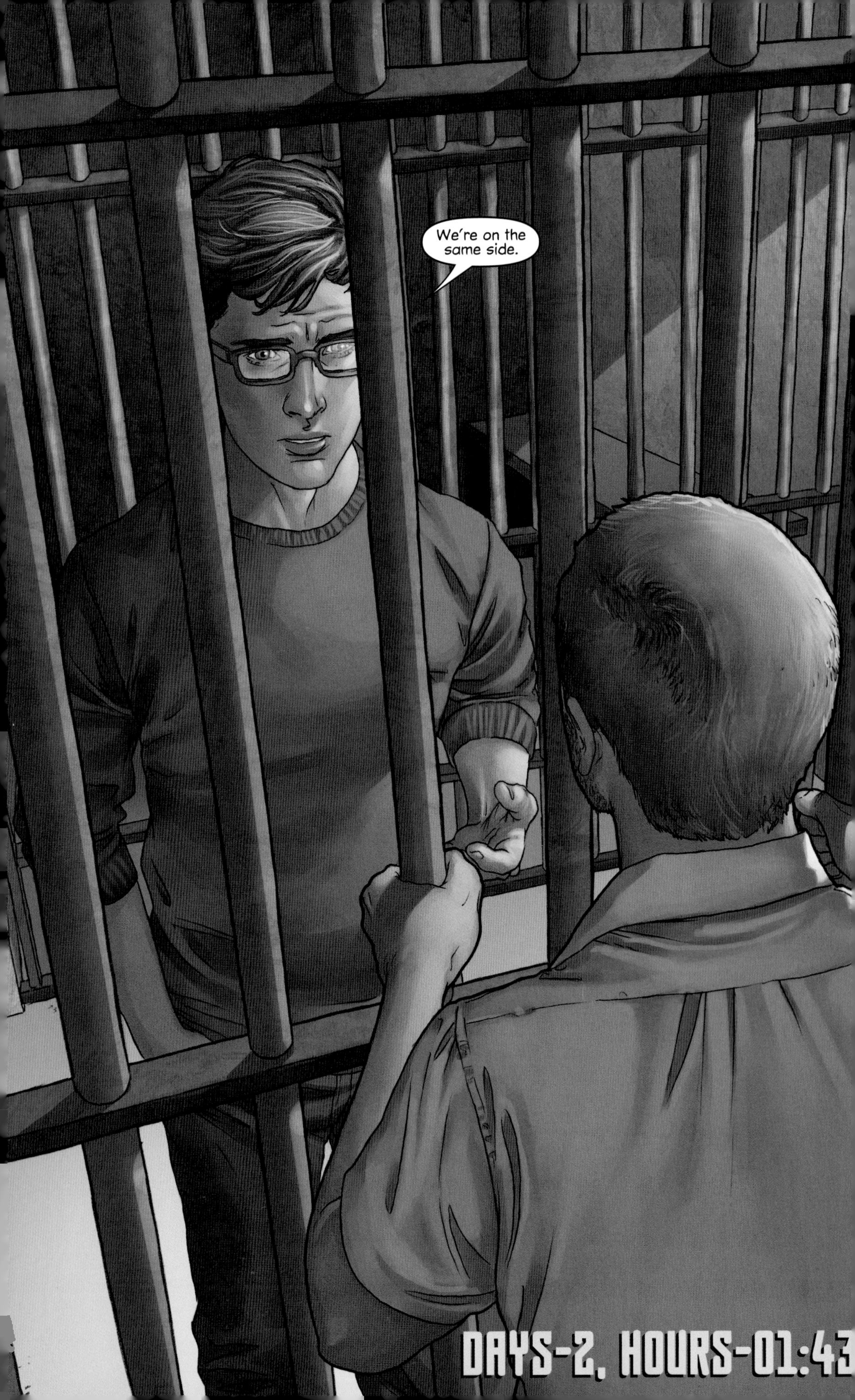
We're on the same side.
DAYS-2, HOURS-01:43

"No mind, however loving, could bear to see plainly into all the recesses of another mind."

-ARNOLD BENNETT

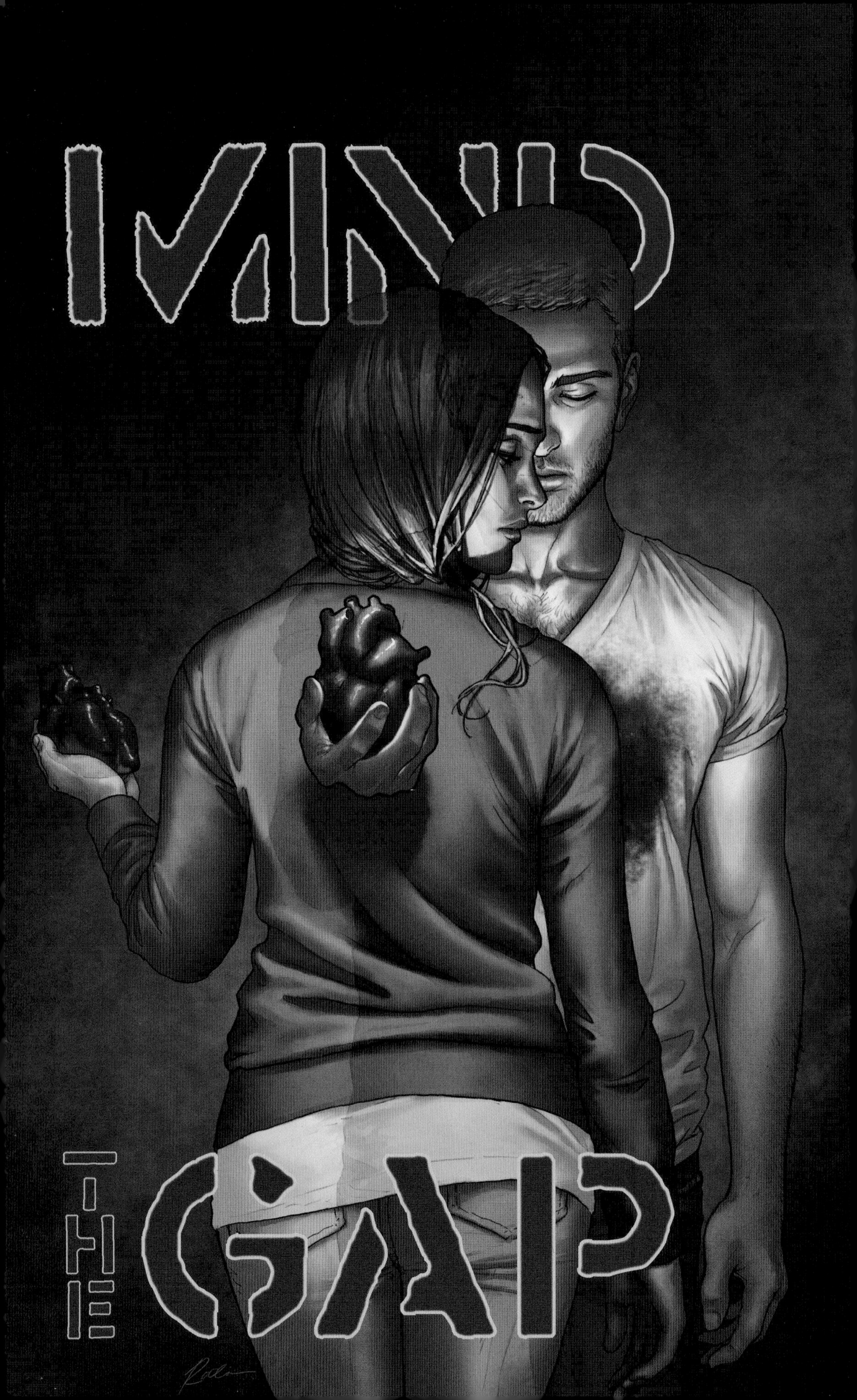
MIND
THE GAP

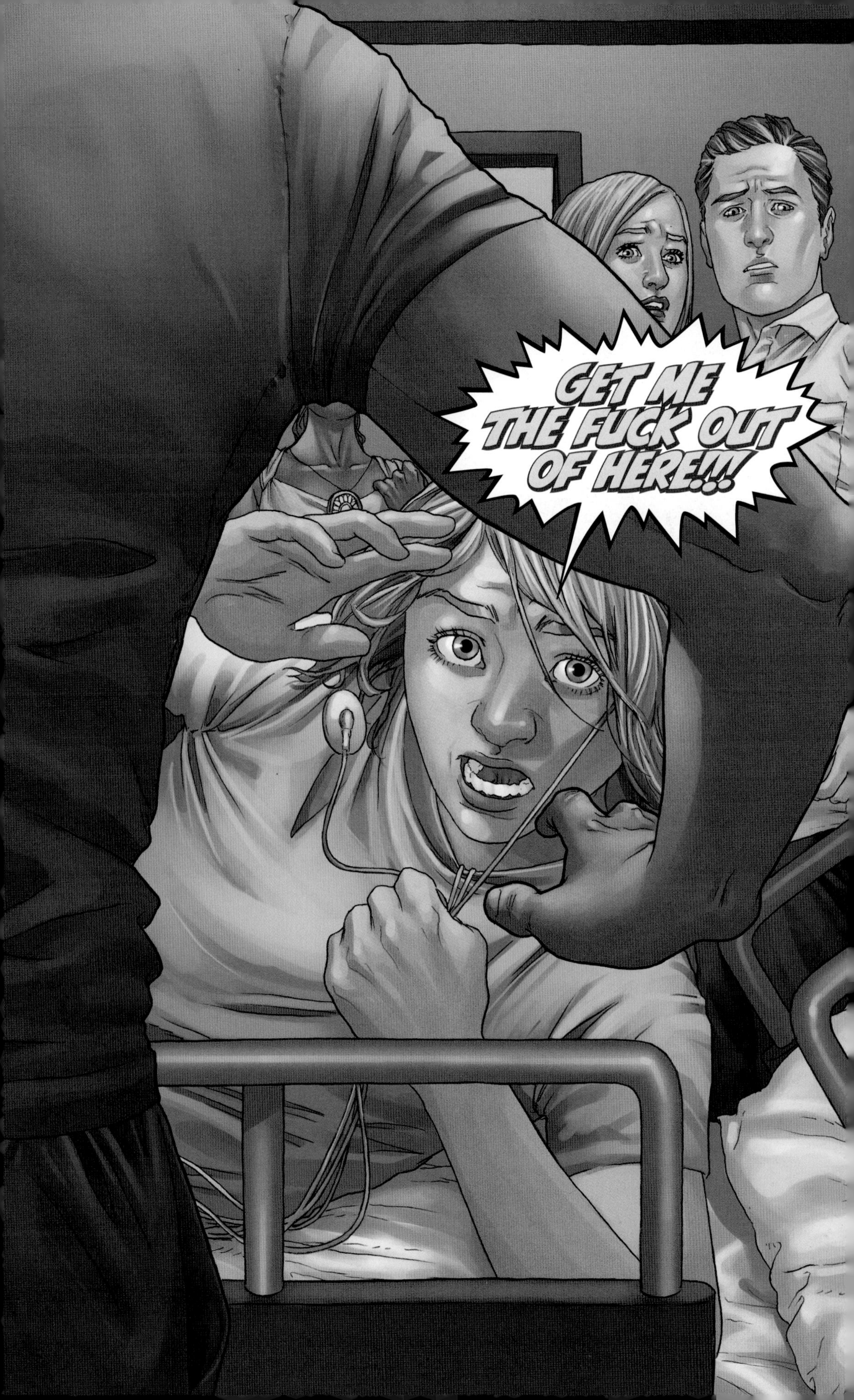
GET ME THE FUCK OUT OF HERE!!!

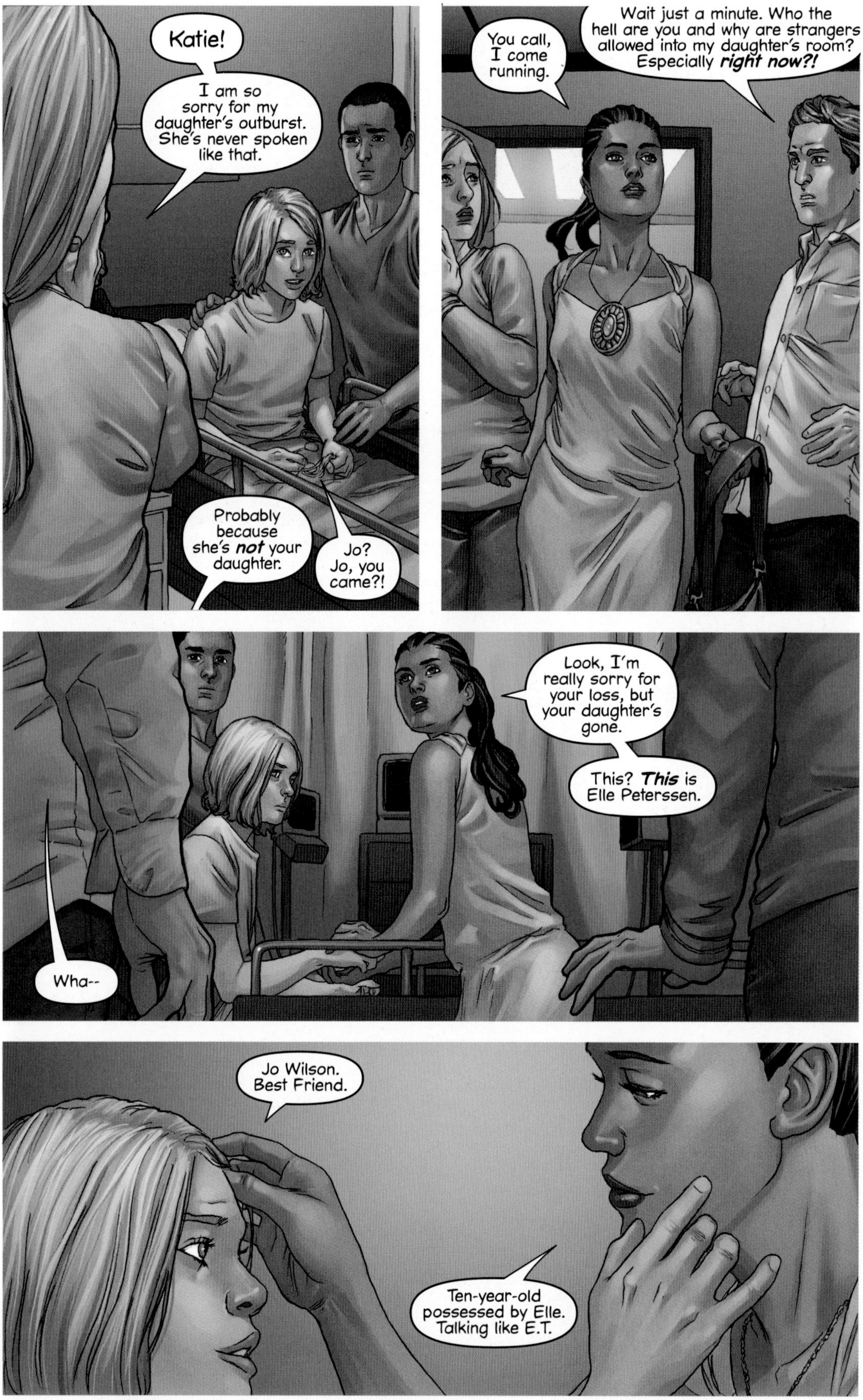

Katie!
I am so sorry for my daughter's outburst. She's never spoken like that.
Probably because she's **not** your daughter.
Jo? Jo, you came?!
You call, I come running.
Wait just a minute. Who the hell are you and why are strangers allowed into my daughter's room? Especially ***right now?!***
Look, I'm really sorry for your loss, but your daughter's gone.
This? ***This*** is Elle Peterssen.
Wha--
Jo Wilson. Best Friend.
Ten-year-old possessed by Elle. Talking like E.T.

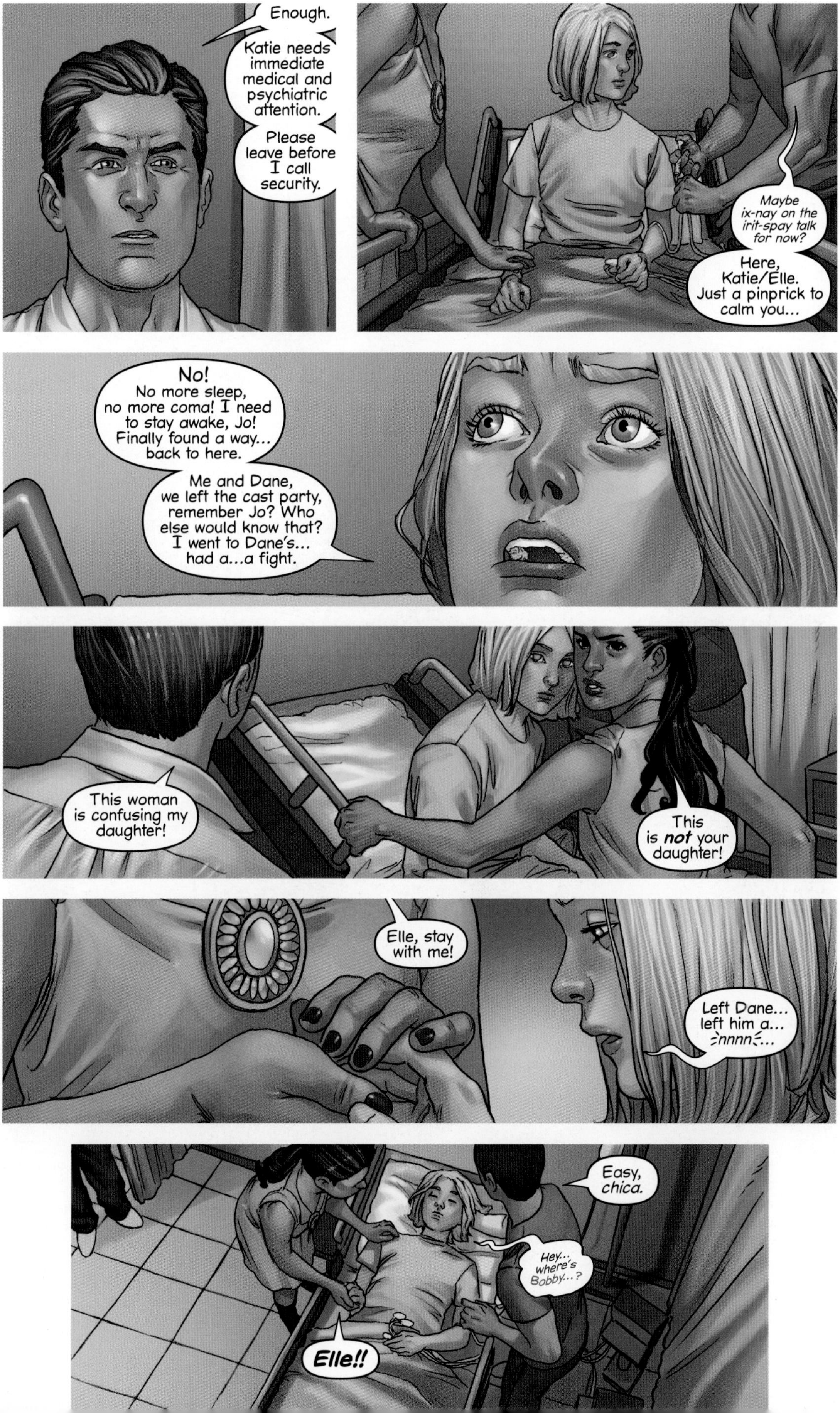

Enough.
Katie needs immediate medical and psychiatric attention.
Please leave before I call security.
Maybe ix-nay on the irit-spay talk for now?
Here, Katie/Elle. Just a pinprick to calm you...
No! No more sleep, no more coma! I need to stay awake, Jo! Finally found a way... back to here.
Me and Dane, we left the cast party, remember Jo? Who else would know that? I went to Dane's... had a...a fight.
This woman is confusing my daughter!
This is *not* your daughter!
Elle, stay with me!
Left Dane... left him a... nnnn...
Easy, chica.
Hey... where's Bobby...?
Elle!!

WISH YOU WERE HERE
PART 2
"CLOUDED EYES, BROKEN HEARTS"

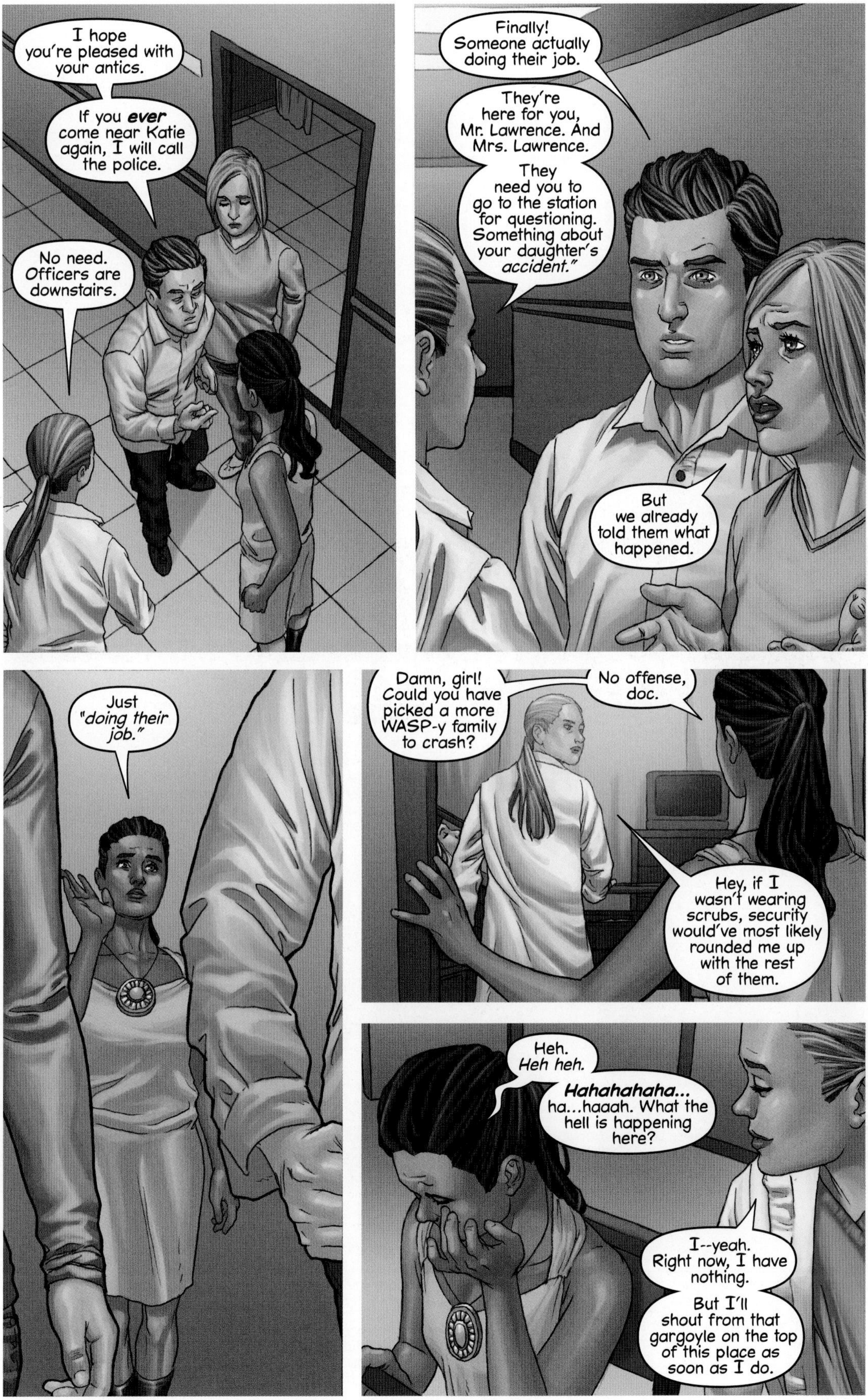
I hope you're pleased with your antics.
If you *ever* come near Katie again, I will call the police.
No need. Officers are downstairs.
Finally! Someone actually doing their job.
They're here for you, Mr. Lawrence. And Mrs. Lawrence.
They need you to go to the station for questioning. Something about your daughter's *accident."*
But we already told them what happened.
Just *"doing their job."*
Damn, girl! Could you have picked a more WASP-y family to crash?
No offense, doc.
Hey, if I wasn't wearing scrubs, security would've most likely rounded me up with the rest of them.
Heh. *Heh heh.*
Hahahahaha... ha...haaah. What the hell is happening here?
I--yeah. Right now, I have nothing.
But I'll shout from that gargoyle on the top of this place as soon as I do.

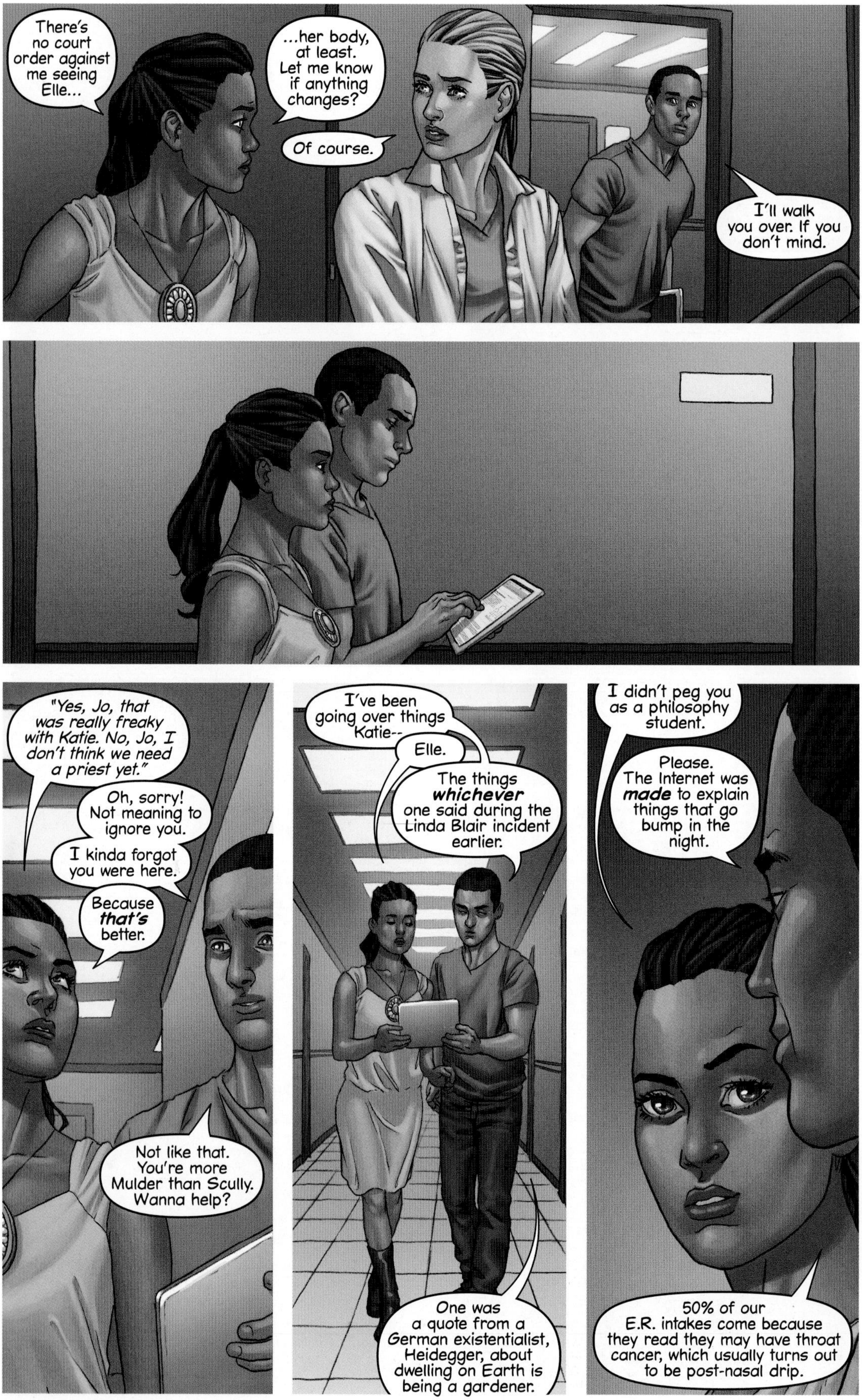
There's no court order against me seeing Elle...
...her body, at least. Let me know if anything changes?
Of course.
I'll walk you over. If you don't mind.
"Yes, Jo, that was really freaky with Katie. No, Jo, I don't think we need a priest yet."
Oh, sorry! Not meaning to ignore you.
I kinda forgot you were here.
Because that's better.
Not like that. You're more Mulder than Scully. Wanna help?
I've been going over things Katie--
Elle.
The things whichever one said during the Linda Blair incident earlier.
One was a quote from a German existentialist, Heidegger, about dwelling on Earth is being a gardener.
I didn't peg you as a philosophy student.
Please. The Internet was made to explain things that go bump in the night.
50% of our E.R. intakes come because they read they may have throat cancer, which usually turns out to be post-nasal drip.

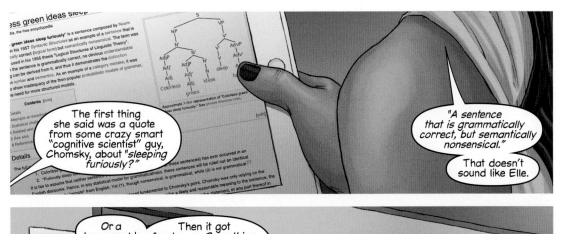

The first thing she said was a quote from some crazy smart "cognitive scientist" guy, Chomsky, about "*sleeping furiously?*"

"*A sentence that is grammatically correct, but semantically nonsensical.*"

That doesn't sound like Elle.

Or a ten-year-old.

Then it got freaky--er. Something with fractions and days something would live. A bunch of "*if/then*"s.

Sounds statistical. What *exactly* did she say?

Something about sleeping four days and waking up on the fourth day it's fine, but if it wakes up on the fifth day "*it will live the following year with a 9/10 probability.*"

Okay, that's *beyond* freaky. It sounds like she was making a Markov chain.

A who-*what*?

Statistical thing. I suck at most left-brain crap, but statistics I got.

And carried Elle's ass that semester. Who do you think she copied off of?

Soooo, another non-Elle-ism.

As for the thing said in her Exorcist moment, all I could find was a Bible story about a rabbi and his daughter--

ELLE!

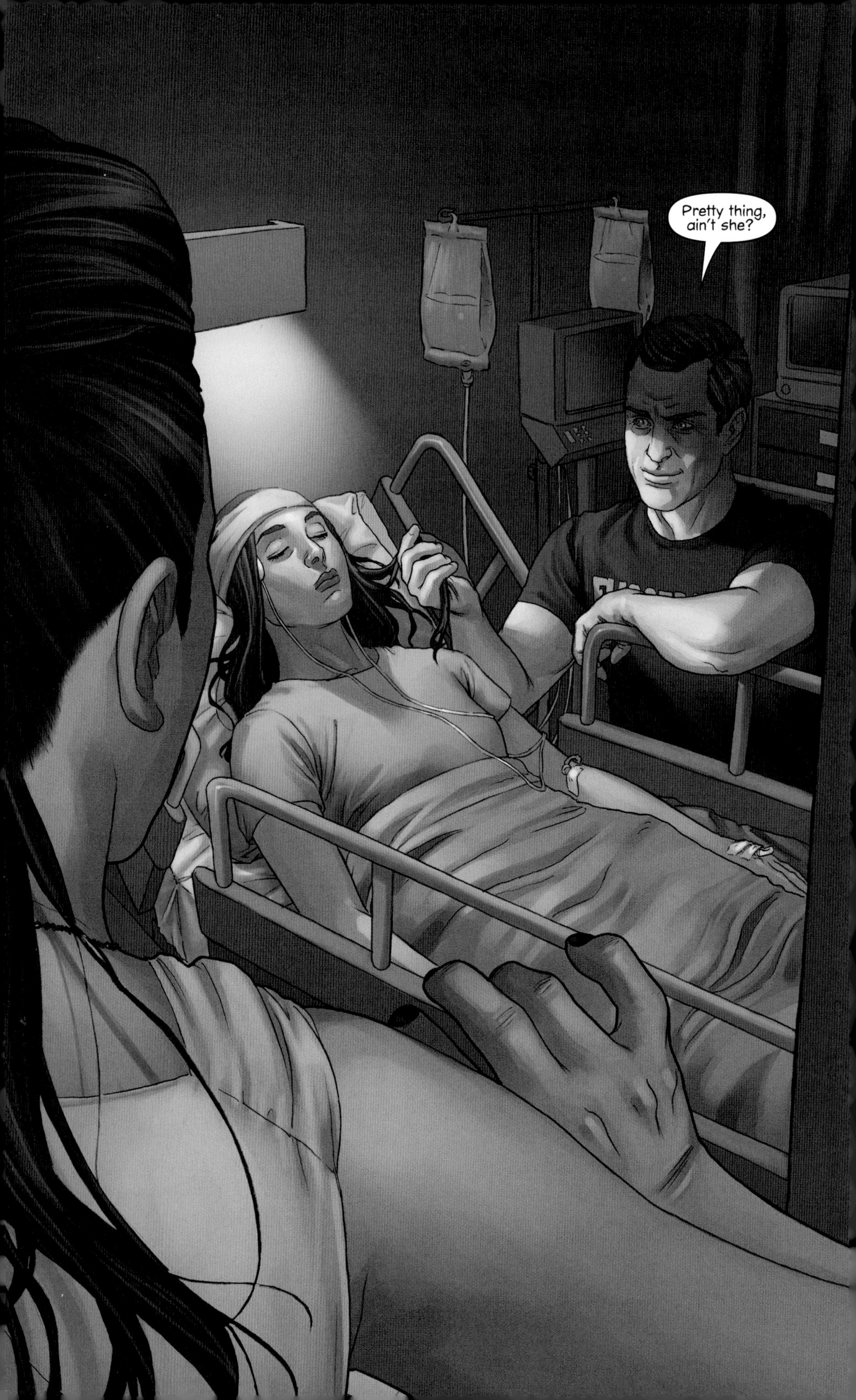
Pretty thing, ain't she?

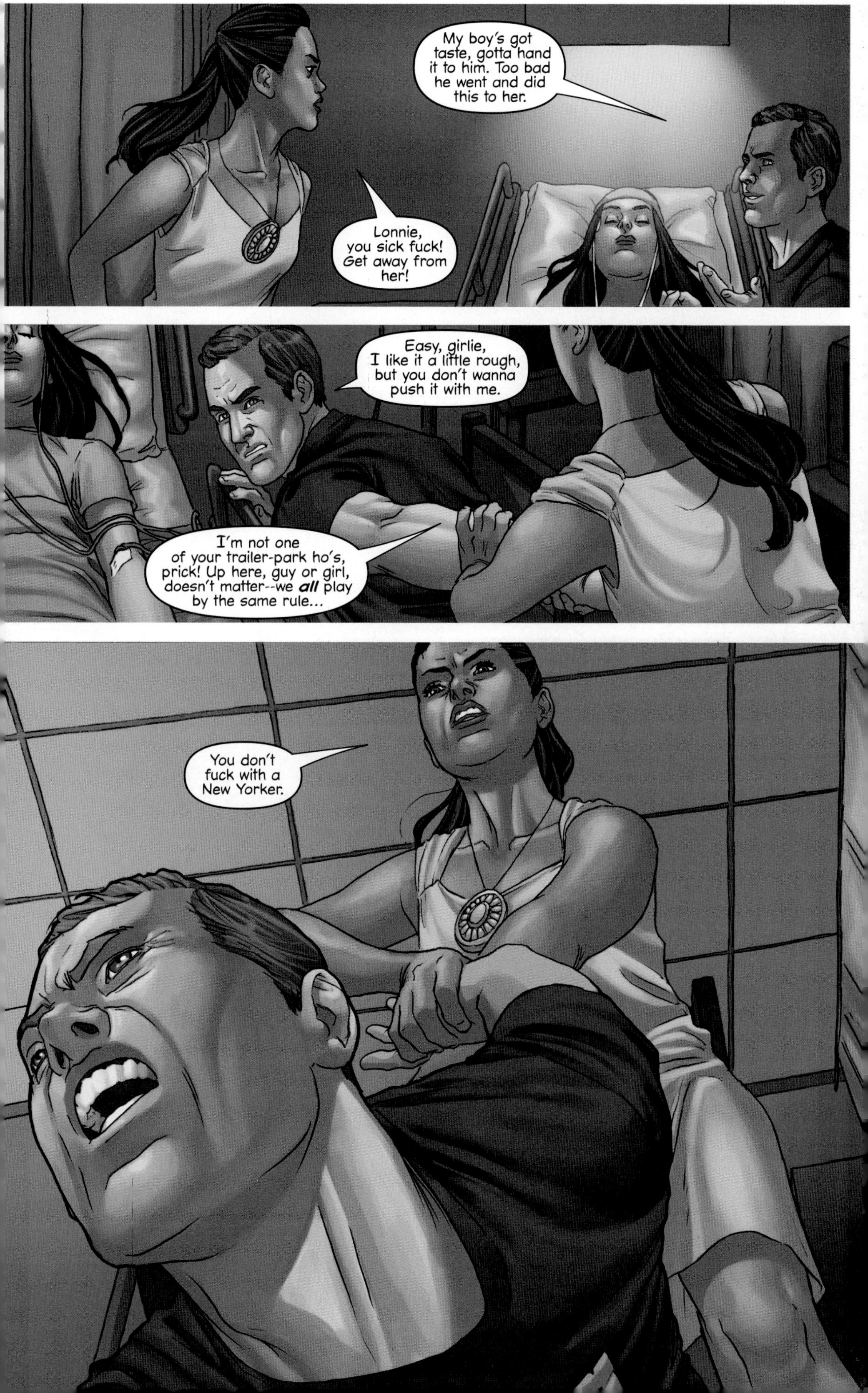
My boy's got taste, gotta hand it to him. Too bad he went and did this to her.
Lonnie, you sick fuck! Get away from her!
Easy, girlie, I like it a little rough, but you don't wanna push it with me.
I'm not one of your trailer-park ho's, prick! Up here, guy or girl, doesn't matter--we ***all*** play by the same rule...
You don't fuck with a New Yorker.

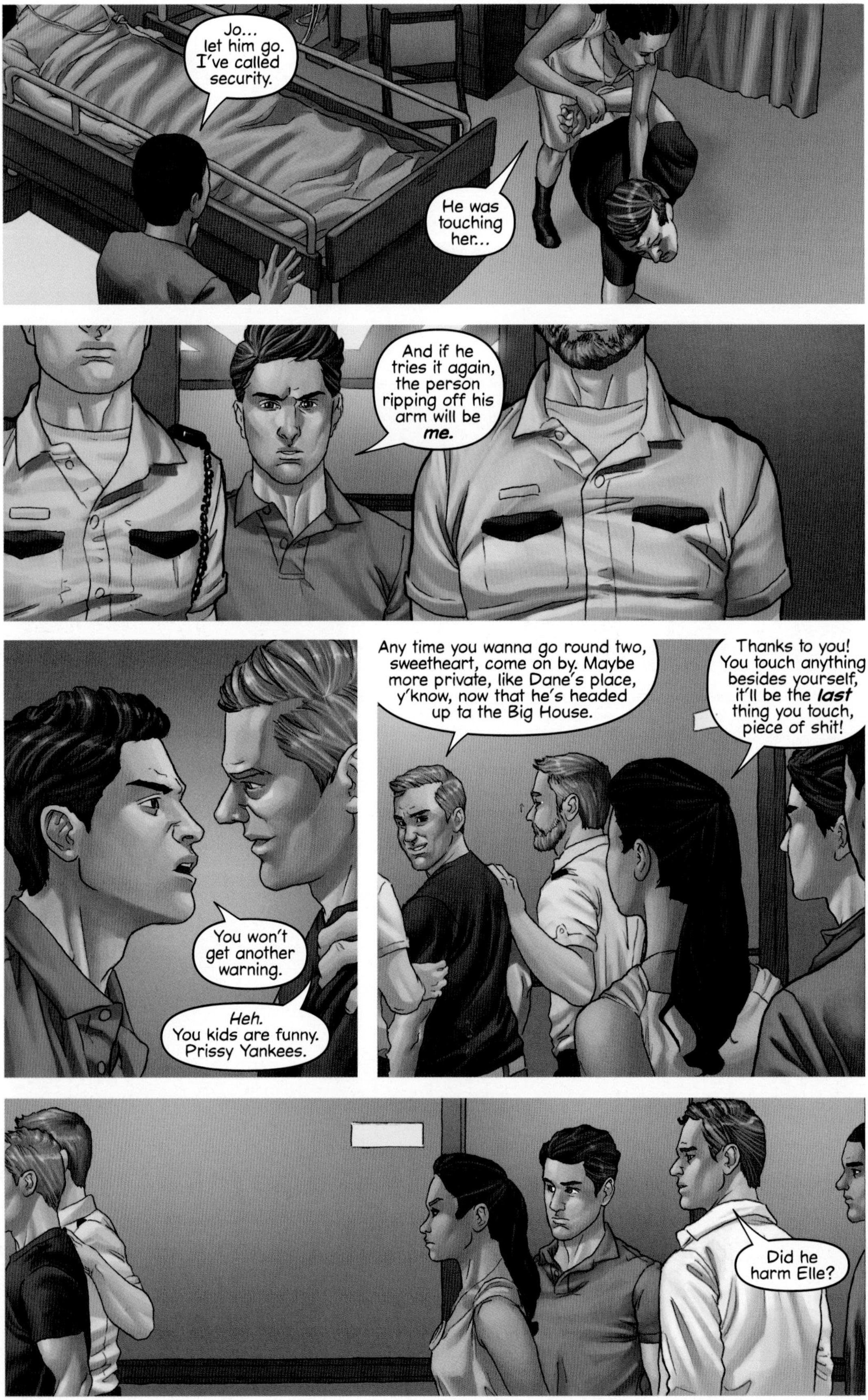
Jo...
let him go.
I've called
security.
He was
touching
her...
And if he
tries it again,
the person
ripping off his
arm will be
me.
You won't
get another
warning.
Heh.
You kids are funny.
Prissy Yankees.
Any time you wanna go round two,
sweetheart, come on by. Maybe
more private, like Dane's place,
y'know, now that he's headed
up ta the Big House.
Thanks to you!
You touch anything
besides yourself,
it'll be the last
thing you touch,
piece of shit!
Did he
harm Elle?

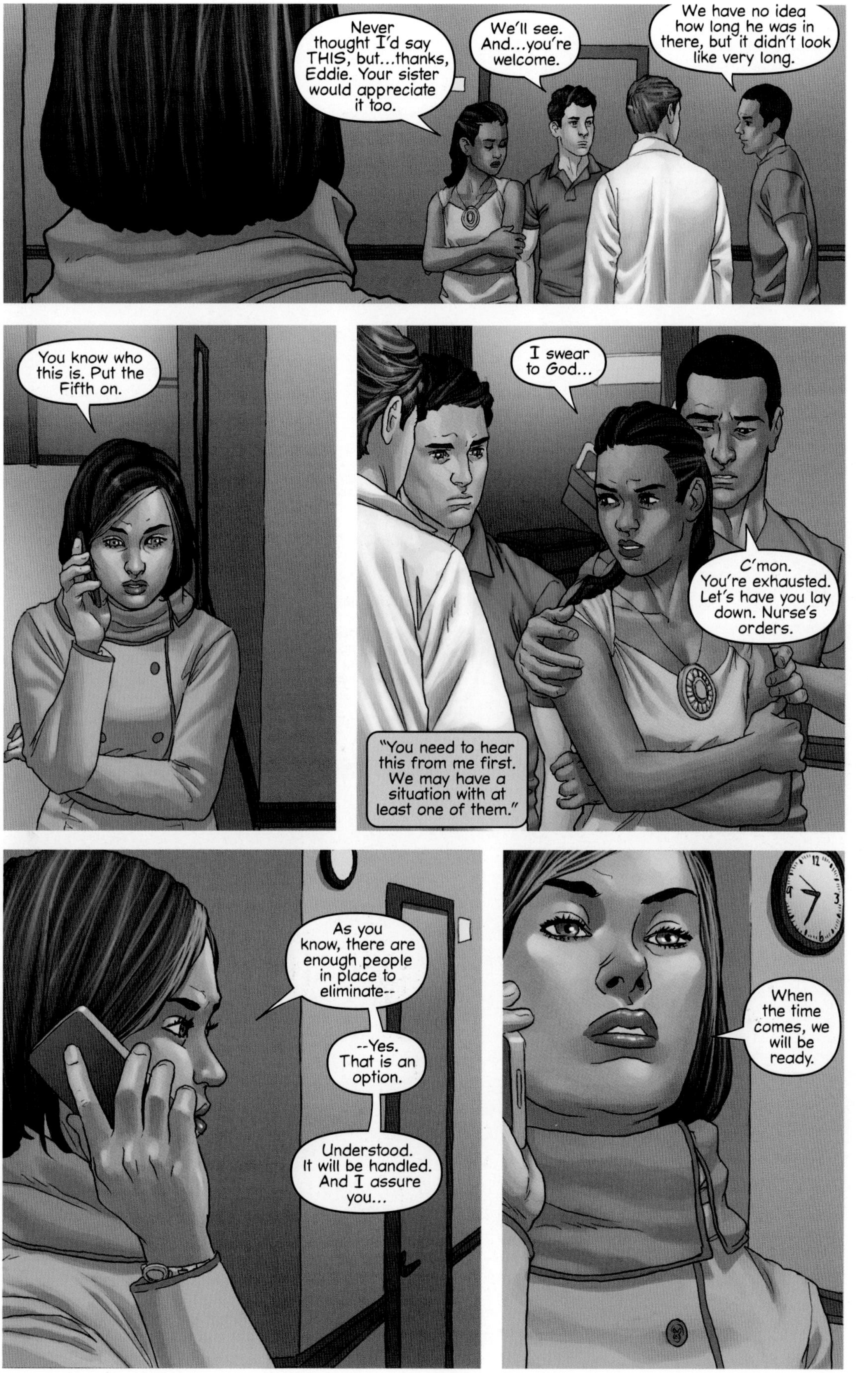
Never thought I'd say THIS, but...thanks, Eddie. Your sister would appreciate it too.
We'll see. And...you're welcome.
We have no idea how long he was in there, but it didn't look like very long.
You know who this is. Put the Fifth on.
I swear to God...
C'mon. You're exhausted. Let's have you lay down. Nurse's orders.
"You need to hear this from me first. We may have a situation with at least one of them."
As you know, there are enough people in place to eliminate--
--Yes. That is an option.
Understood. It will be handled. And I assure you...
When the time comes, we will be ready.

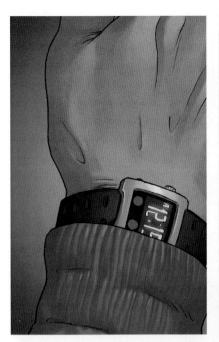

Gethefuckaway!

You are **not** a midnight person, I take it?

Here. Someone named Heidi left this at the nurse's station for you.

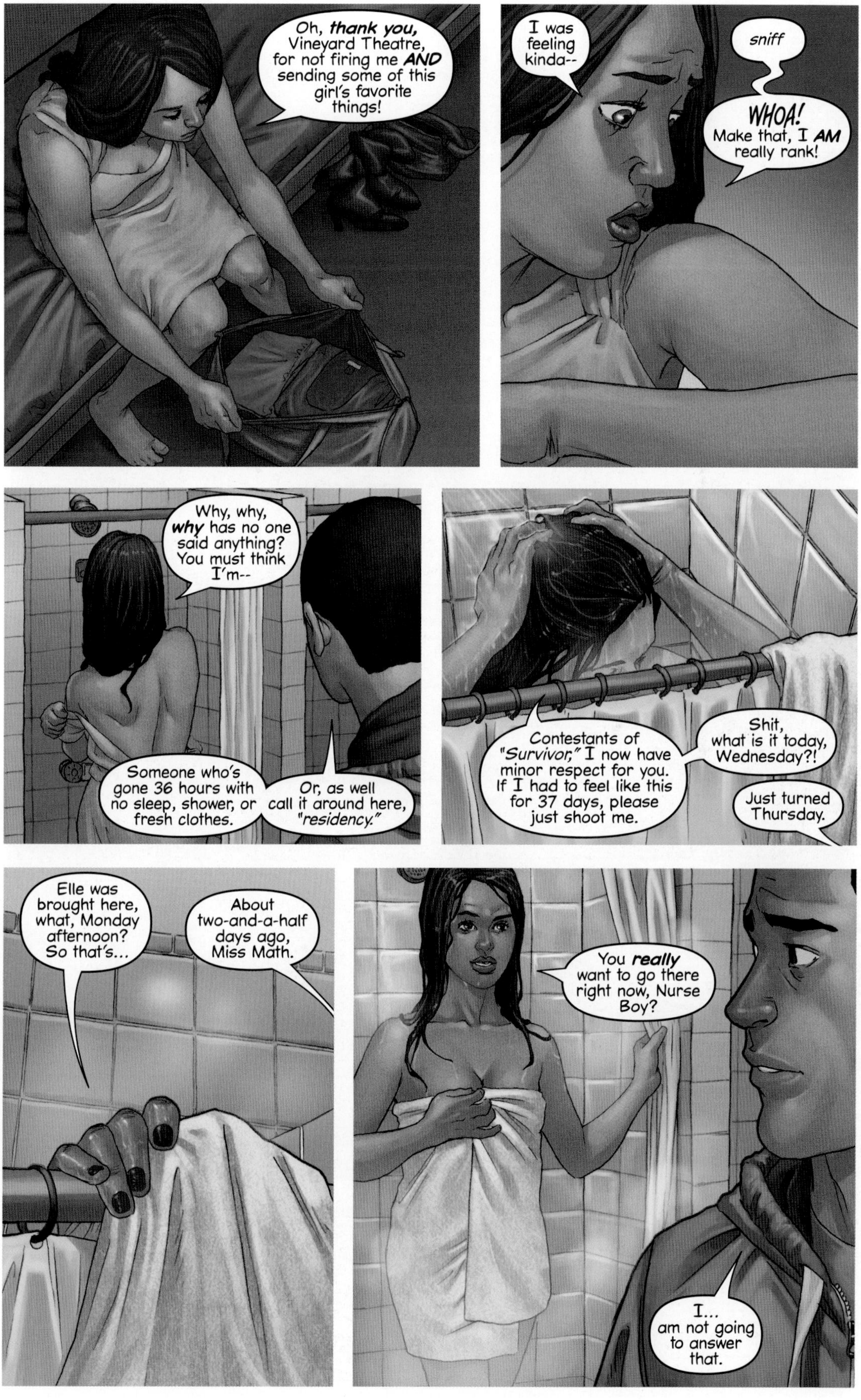
Oh, ***thank you,*** Vineyard Theatre, for not firing me ***AND*** sending some of this girl's favorite things!
I was feeling kinda--
sniff
WHOA! Make that, I ***AM*** really rank!
Why, why, ***why*** has no one said anything? You must think I'm--
Someone who's gone 36 hours with no sleep, shower, or fresh clothes.
Or, as well call it around here, *"residency."*
Contestants of *"Survivor,"* I now have minor respect for you. If I had to feel like this for 37 days, please just shoot me.
Shit, what is it today, Wednesday?!
Just turned Thursday.
Elle was brought here, what, Monday afternoon? So that's...
About two-and-a-half days ago, Miss Math.
You ***really*** want to go there right now, Nurse Boy?
I... am not going to answer that.

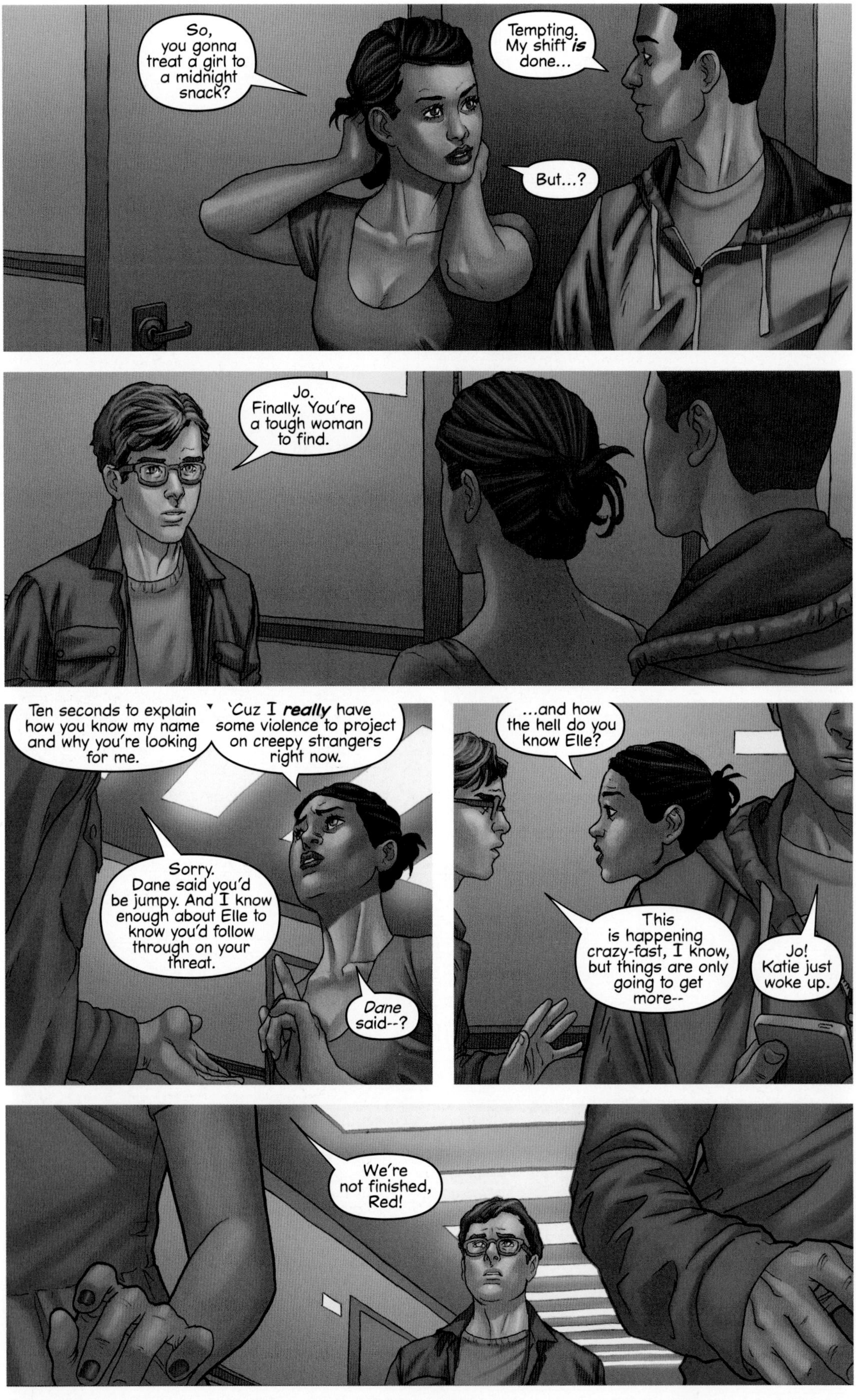
So, you gonna treat a girl to a midnight snack?
Tempting. My shift *is* done...
But...?
Jo. Finally. You're a tough woman to find.
Ten seconds to explain how you know my name and why you're looking for me.
'Cuz I ***really*** have some violence to project on creepy strangers right now.
Sorry. Dane said you'd be jumpy. And I know enough about Elle to know you'd follow through on your threat.
Dane said--?
...and how the hell do you know Elle?
This is happening crazy-fast, I know, but things are only going to get more--
Jo! Katie just woke up.
We're not finished, Red!

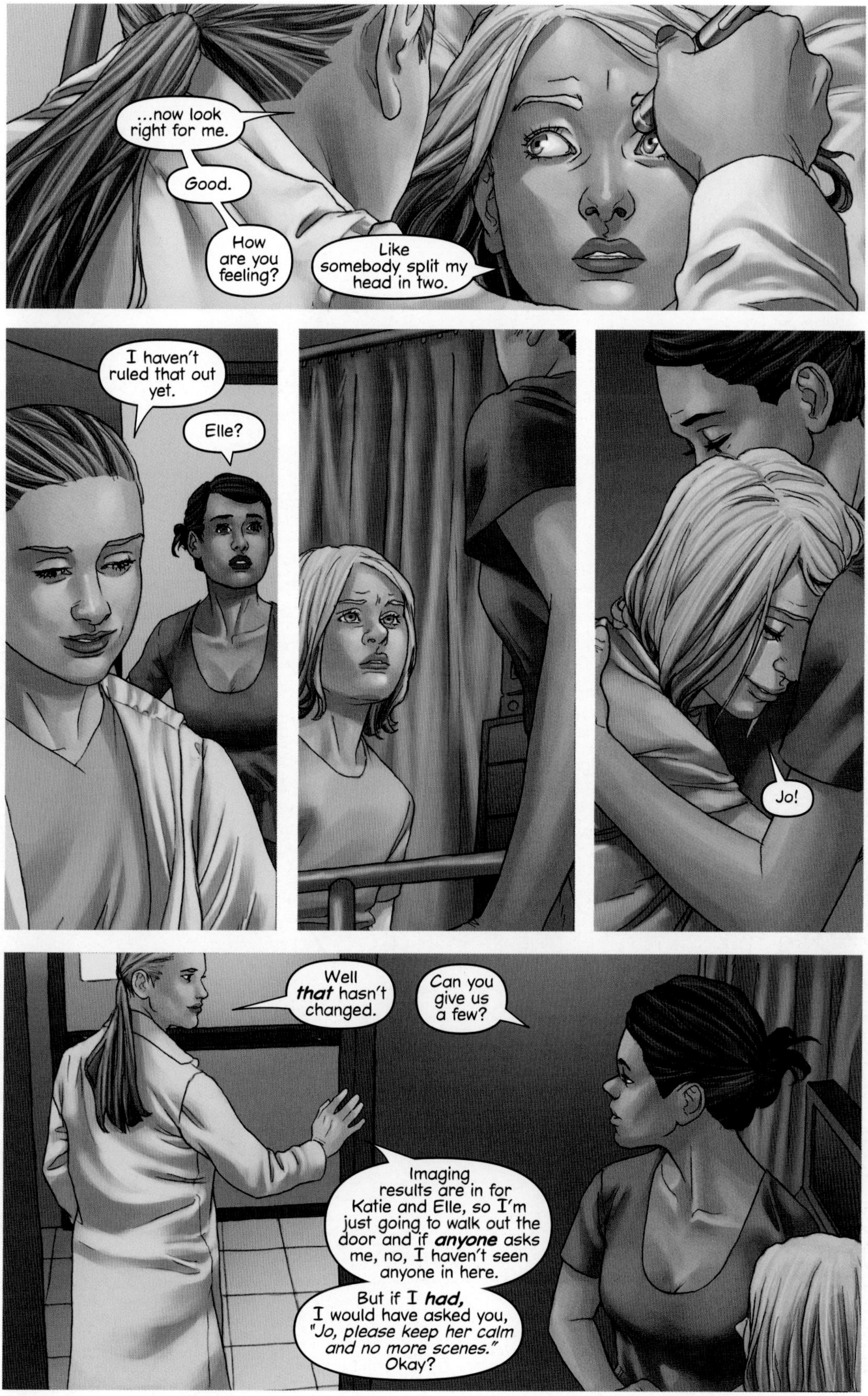

...now look right for me.
Good.
How are you feeling?
Like somebody split my head in two.
I haven't ruled that out yet.
Elle?
Jo!
Well *that* hasn't changed.
Can you give us a few?
Imaging results are in for Katie and Elle, so I'm just going to walk out the door and if *anyone* asks me, no, I haven't seen anyone in here.
But if I *had,* I would have asked you, *"Jo, please keep her calm and no more scenes."* Okay?

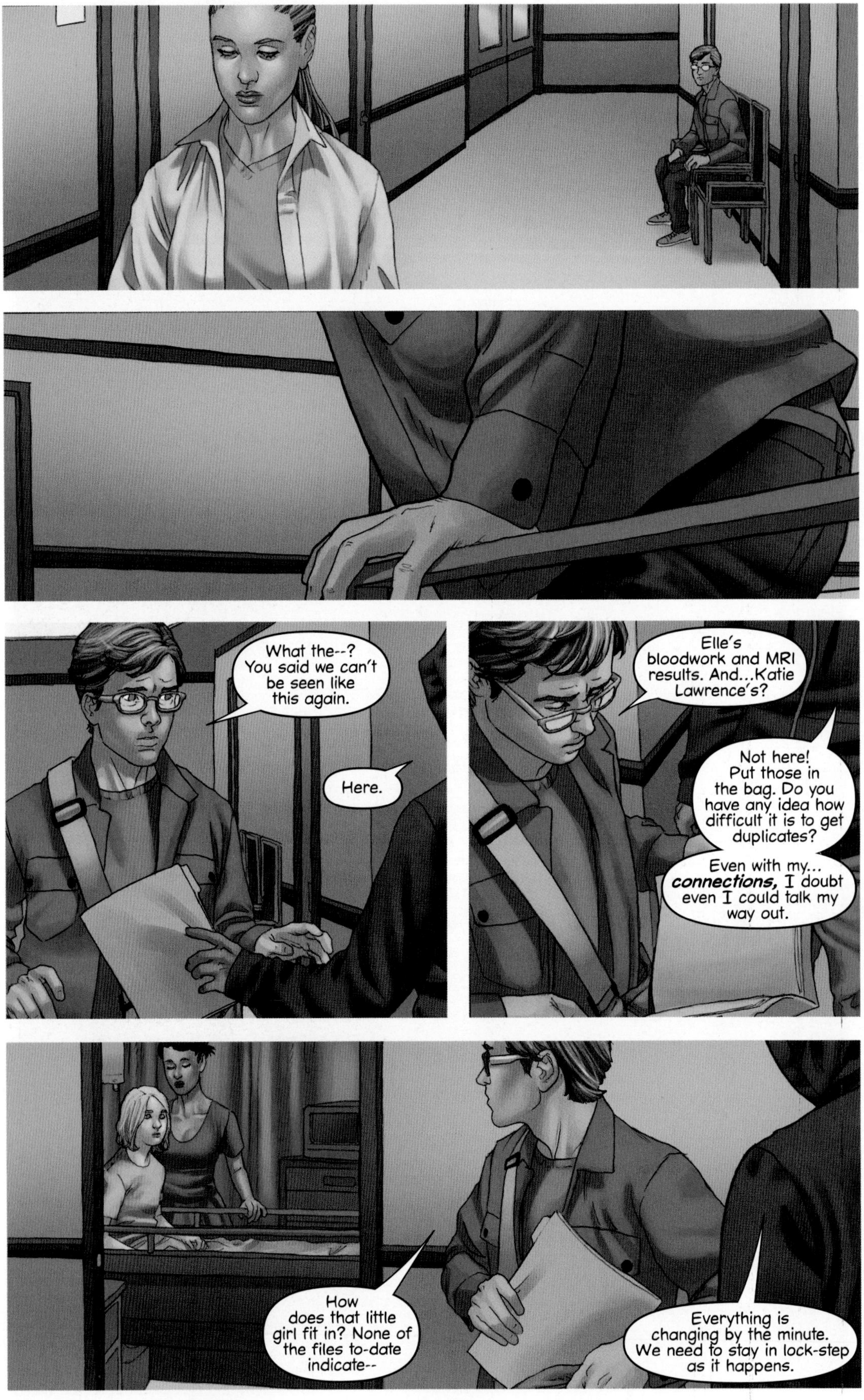
What the--? You said we can't be seen like this again.
Here.
Elle's bloodwork and MRI results. And...Katie Lawrence's?
Not here! Put those in the bag. Do you have any idea how difficult it is to get duplicates?
Even with my... ***connections,*** I doubt even I could talk my way out.
How does that little girl fit in? None of the files to-date indicate--
Everything is changing by the minute. We need to stay in lock-step as it happens.

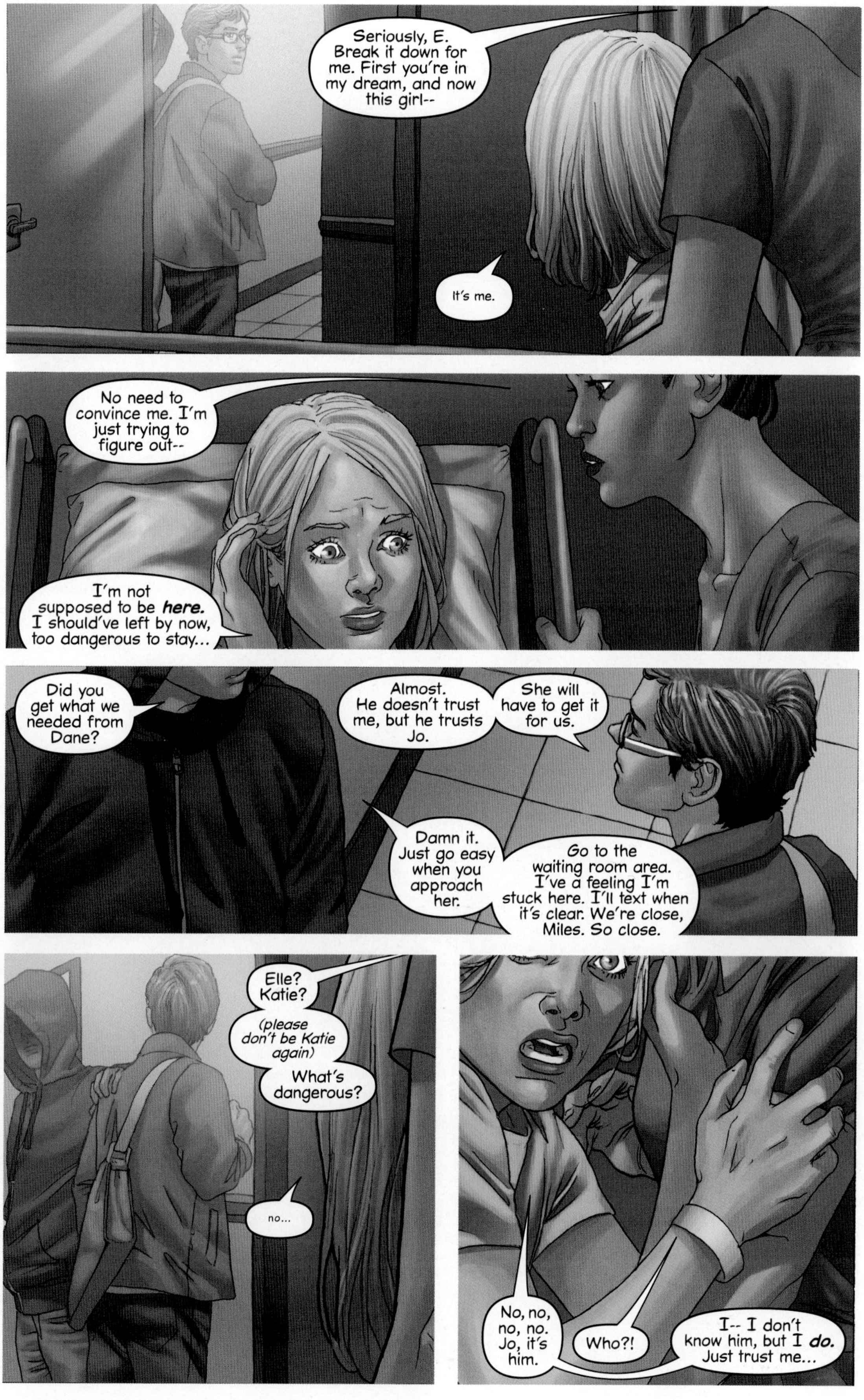
Seriously, E. Break it down for me. First you're in my dream, and now this girl--
It's me.
No need to convince me. I'm just trying to figure out--
I'm not supposed to be ***here.*** I should've left by now, too dangerous to stay...
Did you get what we needed from Dane?
Almost. He doesn't trust me, but he trusts Jo.
She will have to get it for us.
Damn it. Just go easy when you approach her.
Go to the waiting room area. I've a feeling I'm stuck here. I'll text when it's clear. We're close, Miles. So close.
Elle? Katie?
(please don't be Katie again)
What's dangerous?
no...
No, no, no, no. Jo, it's him.
Who?!
I-- I don't know him, but I ***do.*** Just trust me...

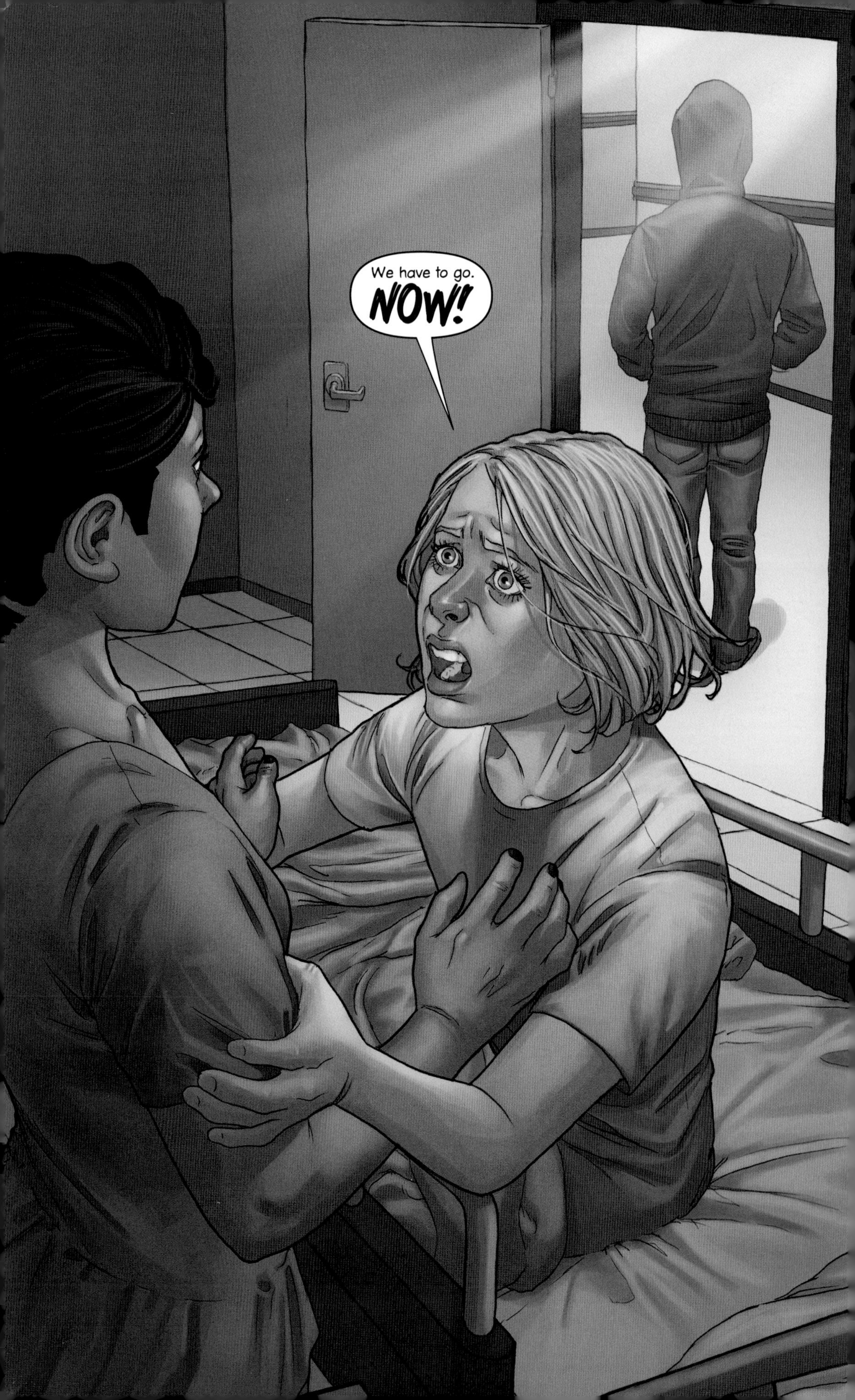
We have to go.
NOW!

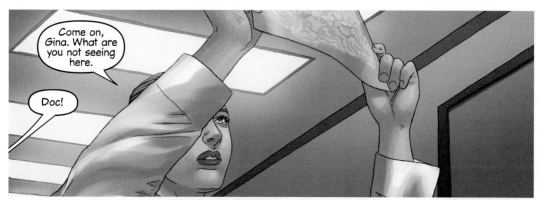

Come on, Gina. What are you not seeing here.

Doc!

You're supposed to be home. The fact that you're not asleep when you have the chance pisses me off.

I've got something to make your day. Night. Whatever.

Elle's labs. *All* of them.

You're welcome?

Good. I'm less pissed off now that I know we're both going to be pulling an extra shift.

In-depth analysis can wait, right now we need to compare and see if there's any match to--

...Katie?

Jo?

"Where the *fuck* did they go?!"

Fifff-- fifty...

50th and Broadway. Hurry.

You sure about that? Yer friend ain't looking so hot back--

I said...

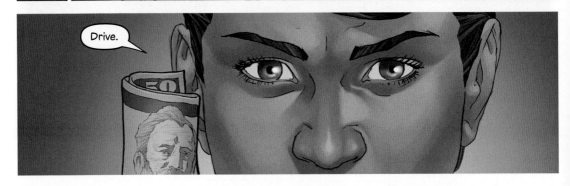

Drive.

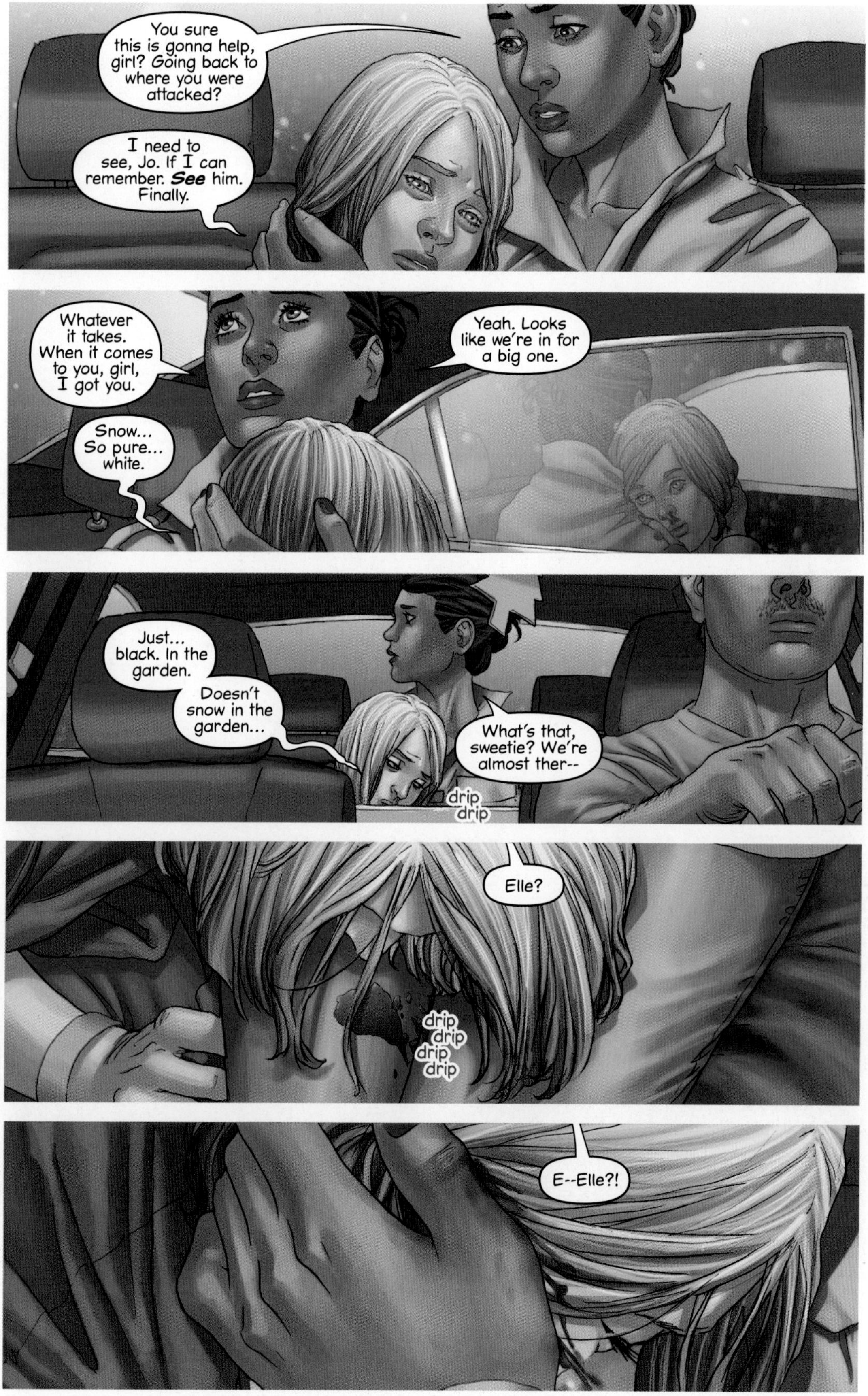
You sure this is gonna help, girl? Going back to where you were attacked?
I need to see, Jo. If I can remember. ***See*** him. Finally.
Whatever it takes. When it comes to you, girl, I got you.
Yeah. Looks like we're in for a big one.
Snow... So pure... white.
Just... black. In the garden.
Doesn't snow in the garden...
What's that, sweetie? We're almost ther--
drip
drip
Elle?
drip
drip
drip
drip
E--Elle?!

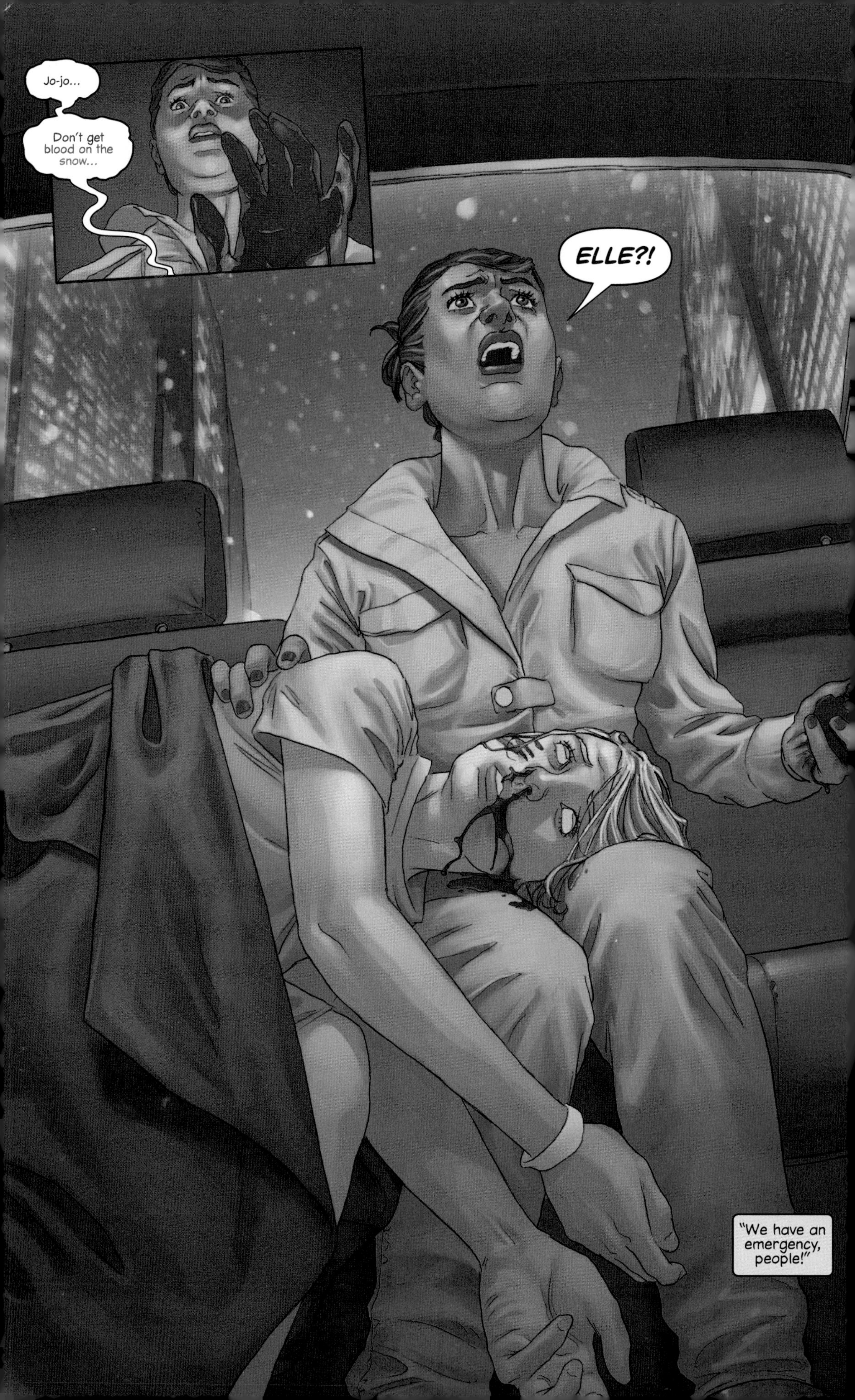
Jo-jo...
Don't get blood on the snow...
ELLE?!
"We have an emergency, people!"

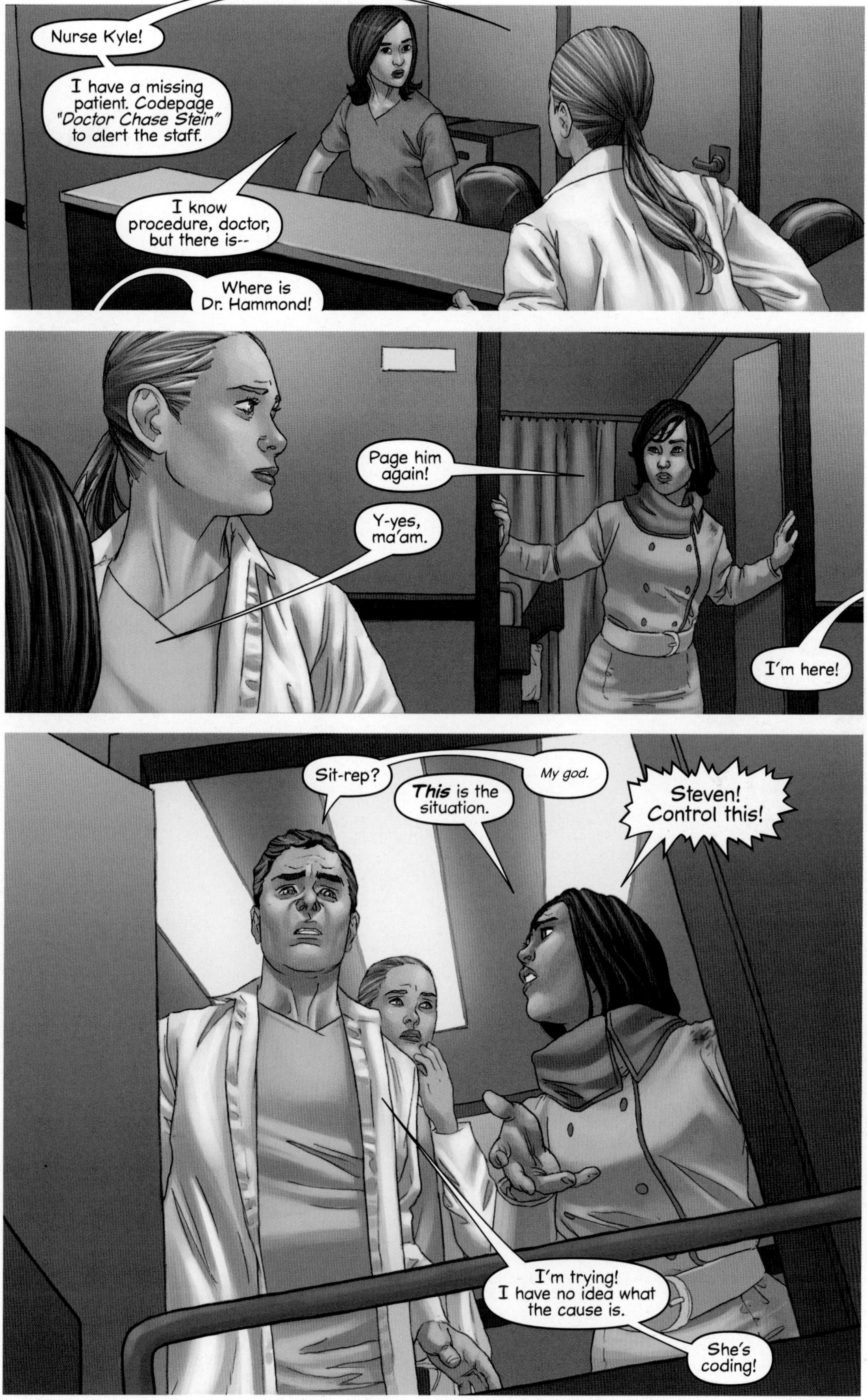
Nurse Kyle!
I have a missing patient. Codepage *"Doctor Chase Stein"* to alert the staff.
I know procedure, doctor, but there is--
Where is Dr. Hammond!
Page him again!
Y-yes, ma'am.
I'm here!
Sit-rep?
My god.
This is the situation.
Steven! Control this!
I'm trying! I have no idea what the cause is.
She's coding!

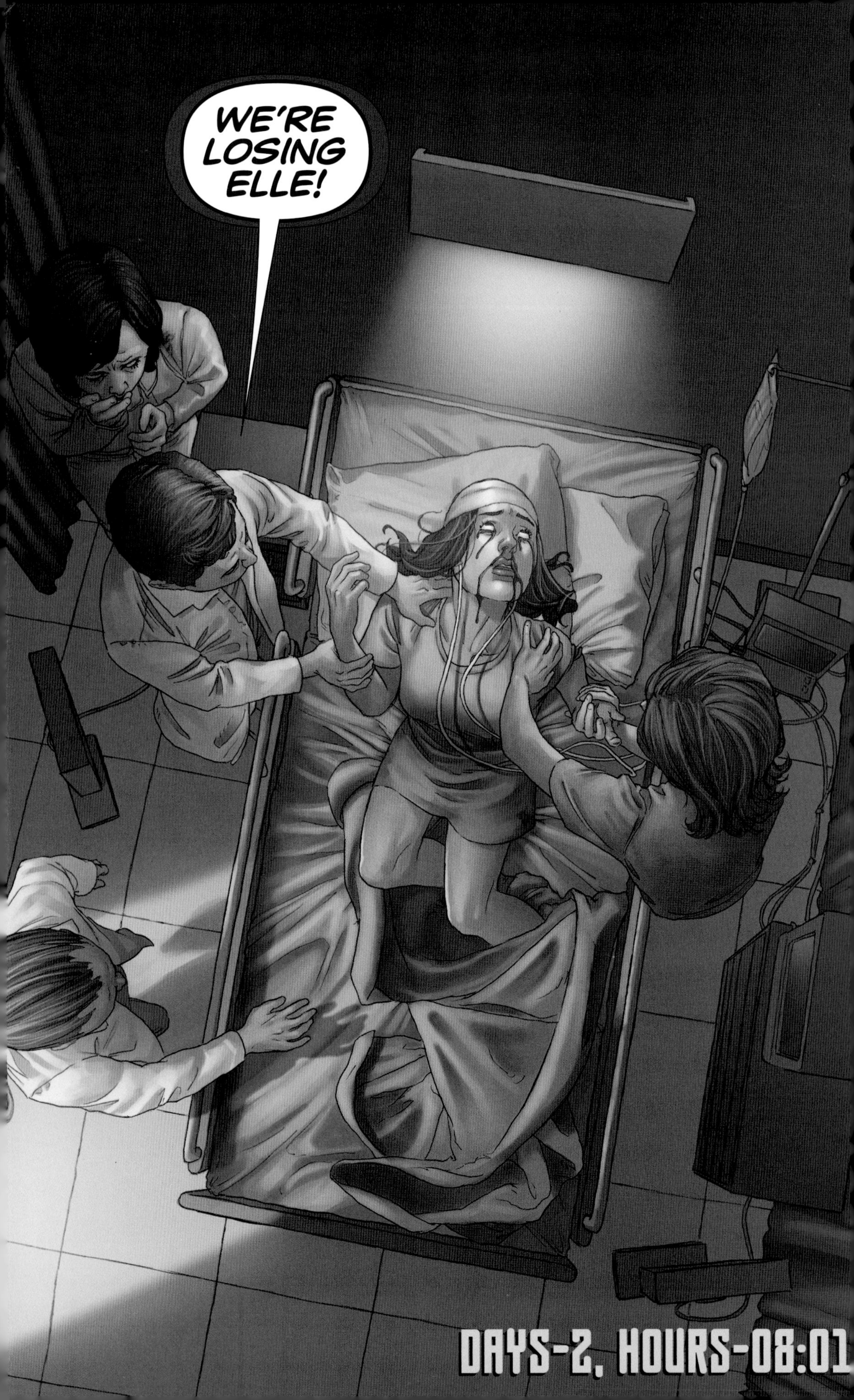
WE'RE LOSING ELLE!
DAYS-2, HOURS-08:01

"When you come back you will not be you. And I may not be I."

— E.M. Forster,
The Life to Come and Other Stories

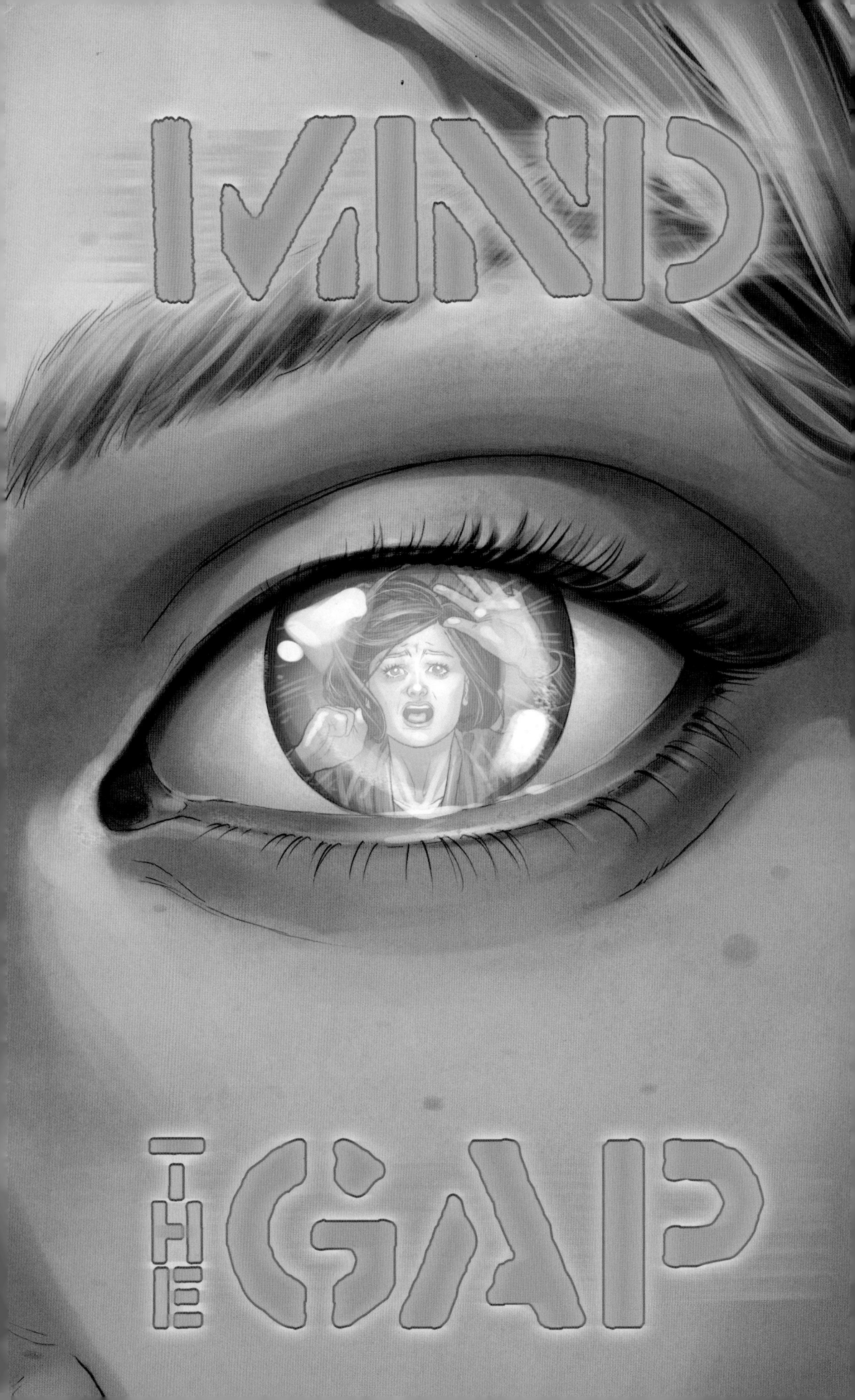
MIND
THE
GAP

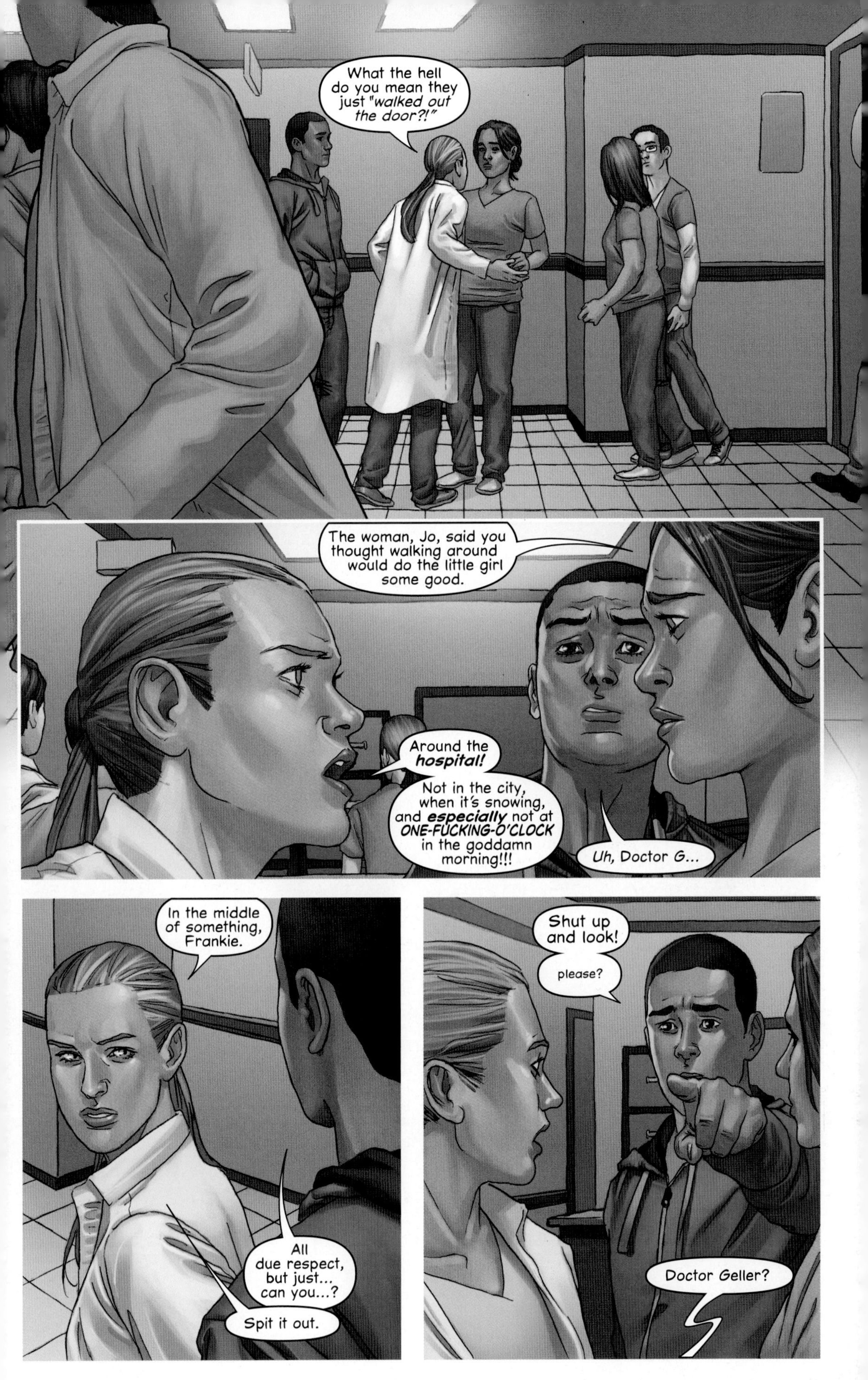
What the hell do you mean they just "*walked out the door?!*"
The woman, Jo, said you thought walking around would do the little girl some good.
Around the **hospital!**
Not in the city, when it's snowing, and **especially** not at ***ONE-FUCKING-O'CLOCK*** in the goddamn morning!!!
Uh, Doctor G...
In the middle of something, Frankie.
All due respect, but just... can you...?
Spit it out.
Shut up and look!
please?
Doctor Geller?

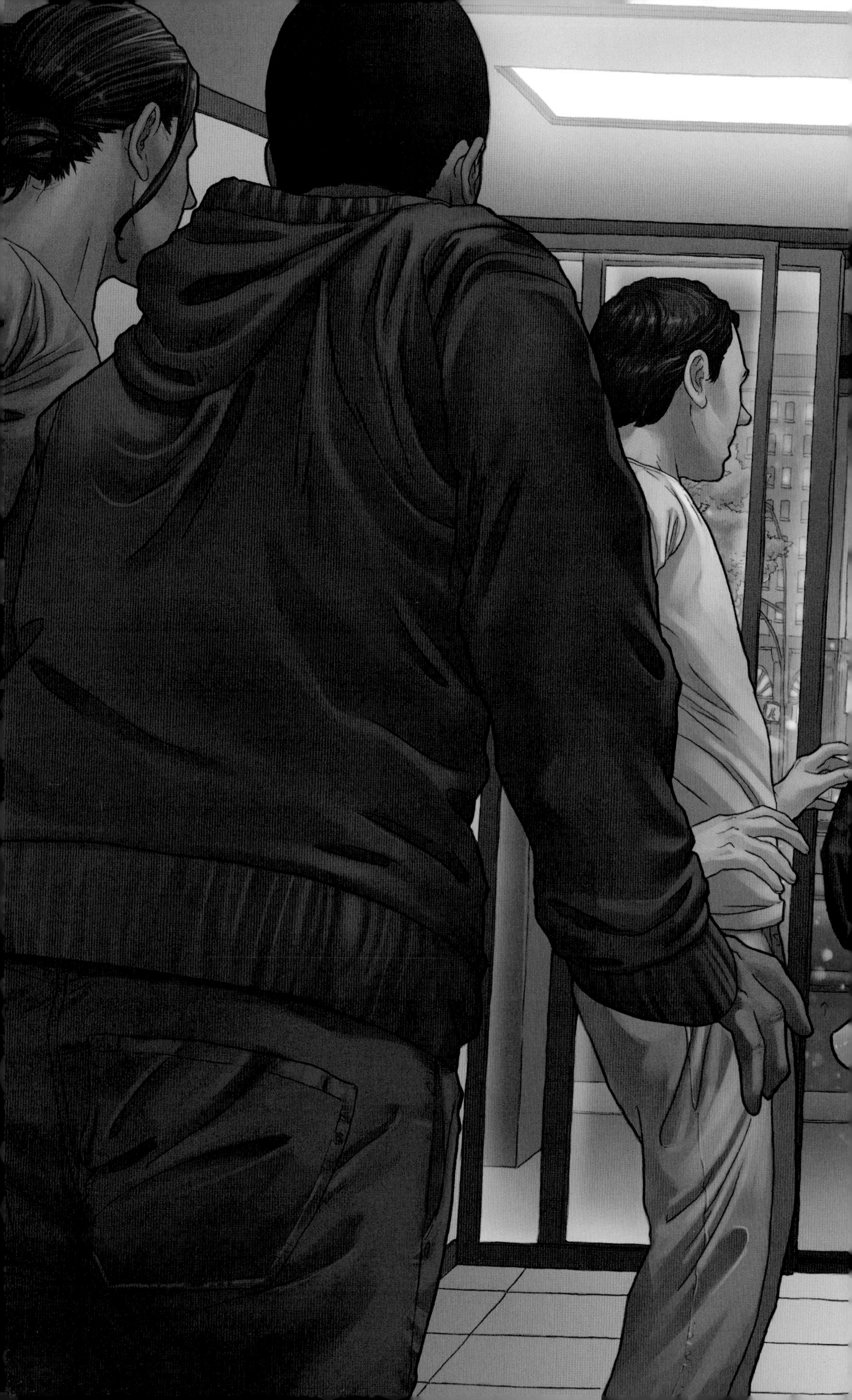

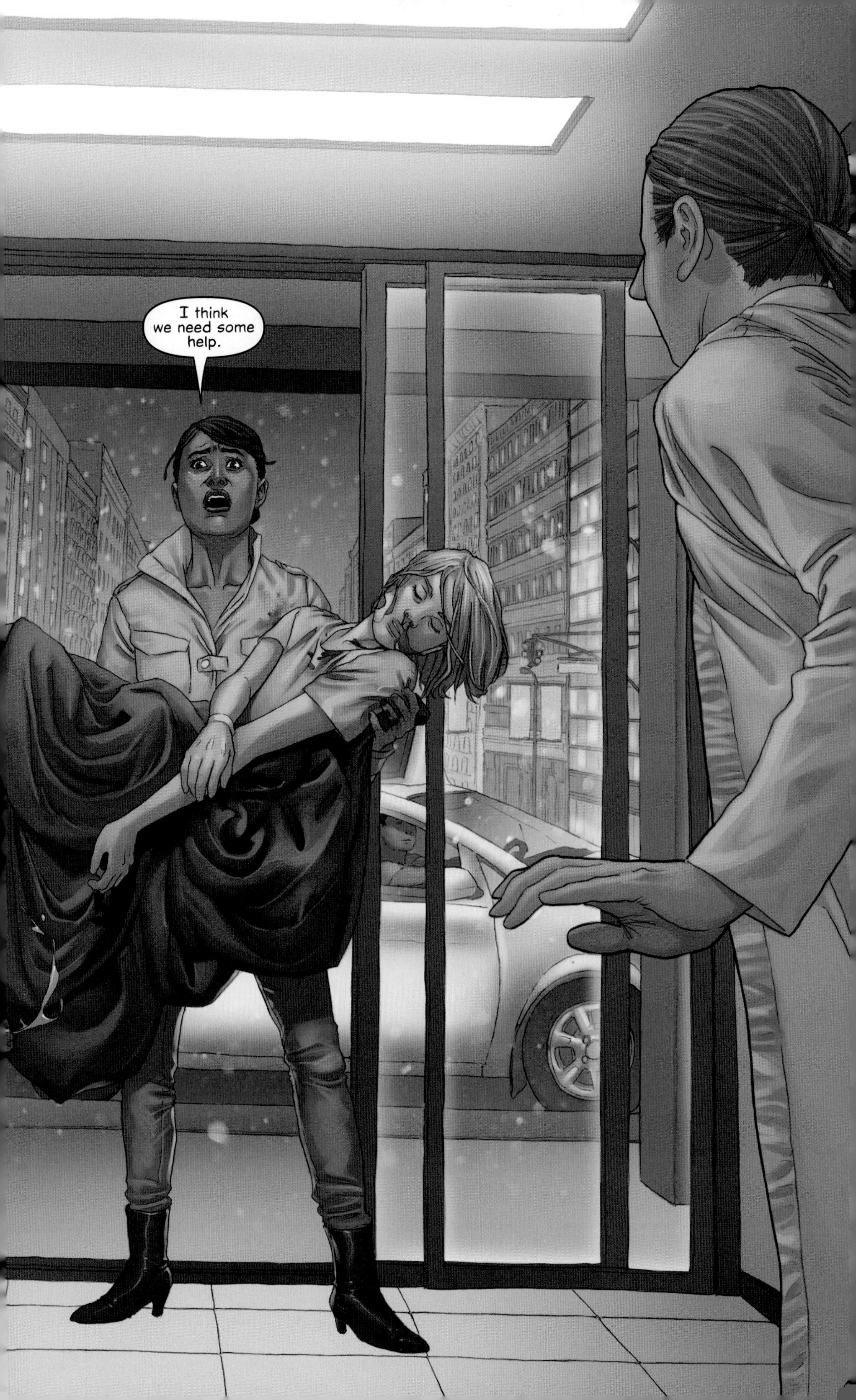
I think we need some help.

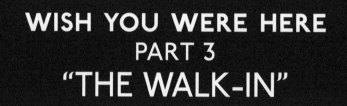

WISH YOU WERE HERE
PART 3
"THE WALK-IN"

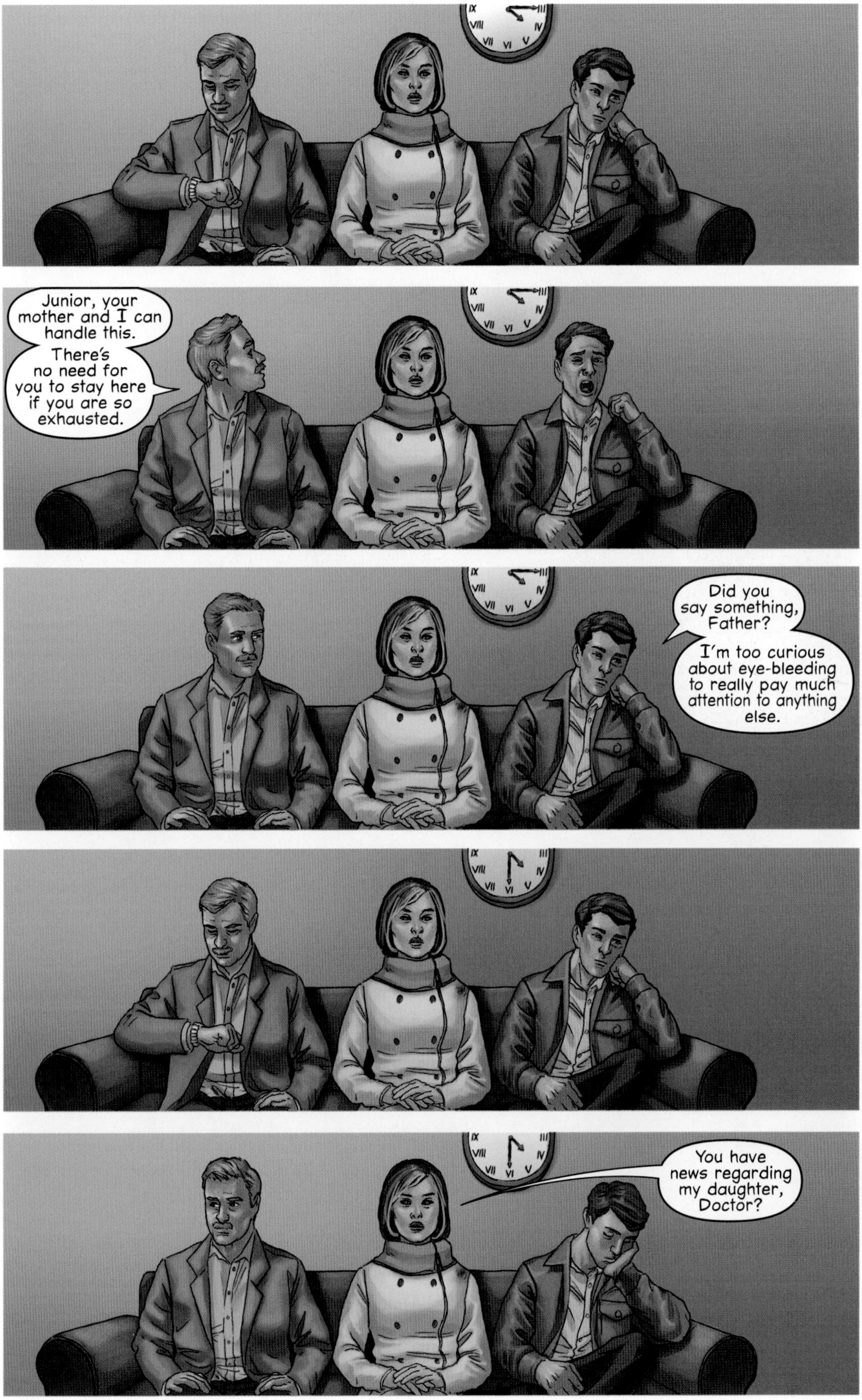
Junior, your mother and I can handle this.
There's no need for you to stay here if you are so exhausted.
Did you say something, Father?
I'm too curious about eye-bleeding to really pay much attention to anything else.
You have news regarding my daughter, Doctor?

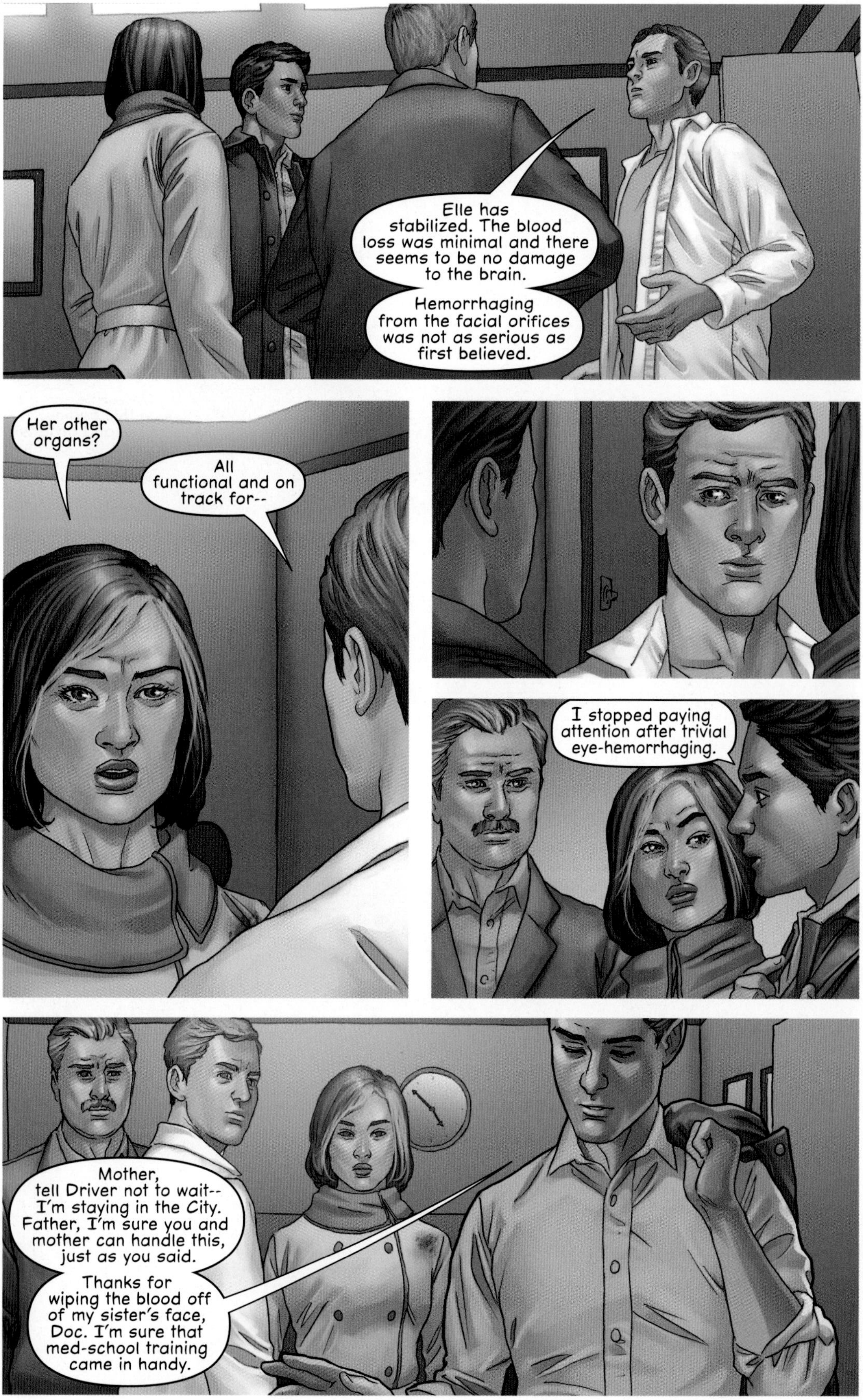
Elle has stabilized. The blood loss was minimal and there seems to be no damage to the brain.
Hemorrhaging from the facial orifices was not as serious as first believed.
Her other organs?
All functional and on track for--
I stopped paying attention after trivial eye-hemorrhaging.
Mother, tell Driver not to wait-- I'm staying in the City. Father, I'm sure you and mother can handle this, just as you said.
Thanks for wiping the blood off of my sister's face, Doc. I'm sure that med-school training came in handy.

Continue.

Her organs and tissue are all on par for what we've theorized.

Her brain functions appeared to dip just prior to the hemorrhaging, but I'm ruling that as circumstantial at the moment.

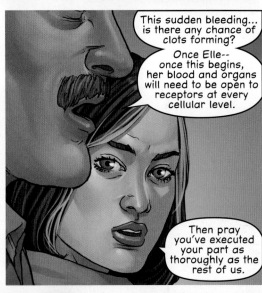

This sudden bleeding... is there any chance of clots forming?

Once Elle-- once this begins, her blood and organs will need to be open to receptors at every cellular level.

Then pray you've executed your part as thoroughly as the rest of us.

Thorough? *YOU*, Hammond, the rest of your lackeys, and the madness of *"The Fifth"* are *delusional!*

It is a delusion of grandeur to think *yourself* above anything but a so-called "lackey!"

I wanted no part of this. I had *no idea* I even was until *you*--

Mr. and Mrs. Peterssen, please. We're too exposed here. Perhaps we can take this to my office?

I agree. Your office would be a much better setting, Dr. Hammond.

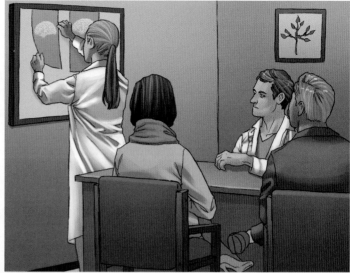

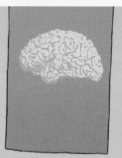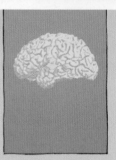

These results are from the fMRI taken after the simultaneous brain activity between Katie Lawrence, here on the right, and Elle Peterssen, on the left.

Who authorized your access to my daughter's medical records, Doctor?

Your daughter's doctor. Given the unusual nature, we agreed it best to cross-reference as quickly as possible.

Elle is a grown woman, there was no need for parental consent.

Now, may I continue?

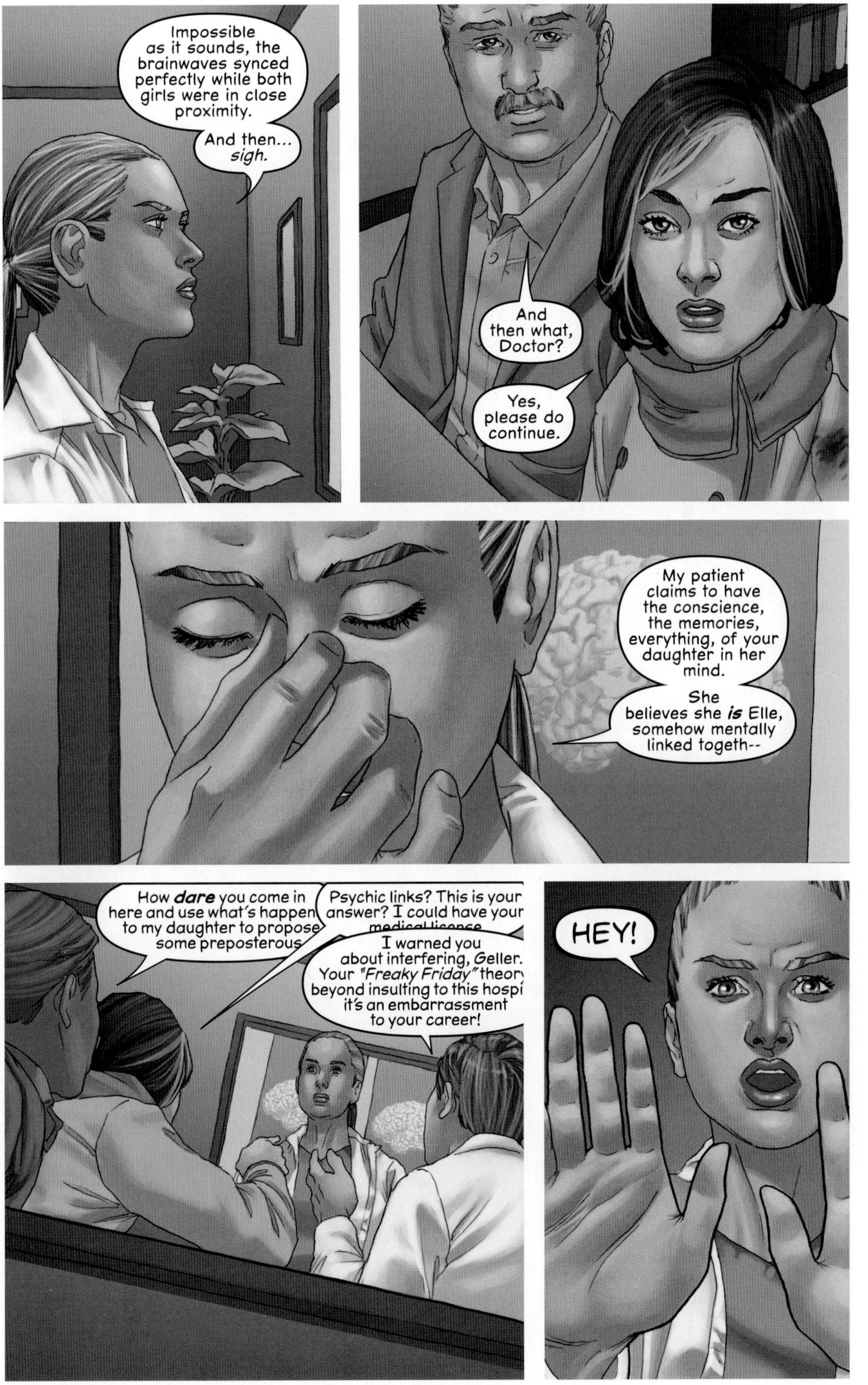

Impossible as it sounds, the brainwaves synced perfectly while both girls were in close proximity.
And then... *sigh.*
And then what, Doctor?
Yes, please do continue.
My patient claims to have the conscience, the memories, everything, of your daughter in her mind.
She believes she ***is*** Elle, somehow mentally linked togeth--
How ***dare*** you come in here and use what's happen to my daughter to propose some preposterous
Psychic links? This is your answer? I could have your
I warned you about interfering, Geller. Your *"Freaky Friday"* theory beyond insulting to this hospi it's an embarrassment to your career!
HEY!

Four hours ago, Katie Lawrence suffered superficial hemorrhaging from cranial orifices. She had a spike in mental acuity just before collapsing.

She was four blocks away from the hospital.

FOUR blocks?

I felt she needed fresh air.

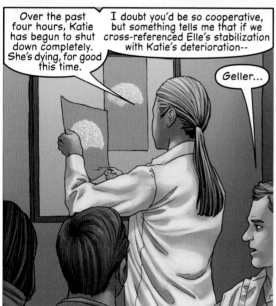

Over the past four hours, Katie has begun to shut down completely. She's dying, for good this time.

I doubt you'd be so cooperative, but something tells me that if we cross-referenced Elle's stabilization with Katie's deterioration--

Geller...

Save it. It's impossible for the cases to be related, right?

We only deal with science here.

CLICK

Please try and live up to your honorific and check on Ellis' condition, doctor.

Once the Lawrence girl has... departed, retrieve her records for comparisons on the off chance that lunatic's ramblings have validity.

Doctor Geller is too public a figure here, *and* married to a detective, so we must tread lightly on how best we deal with her.

Edward, go attend to--

I have *plenty* to attend to right here, "*my love.*"

Things are escalating beyond your control. You've pulled strings and played some sort of sick game with our daughter's life for *God* knows how many years now--

You knew if you had wanted to look close--

Shut up! You think you are controlling things? What about Dane? Elle's boyfriend you set up? I hear his father was here earlier, *alone,* with her. Because of *you.*

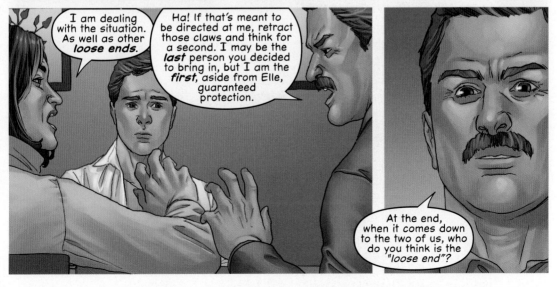

I am dealing with the situation. As well as other *loose ends.*

Ha! If that's meant to be directed at me, retract those claws and think for a second. I may be the *last* person you decided to bring in, but I am the *first,* aside from Elle, guaranteed protection.

At the end, when it comes down to the two of us, who do you think is the "*loose end*"?

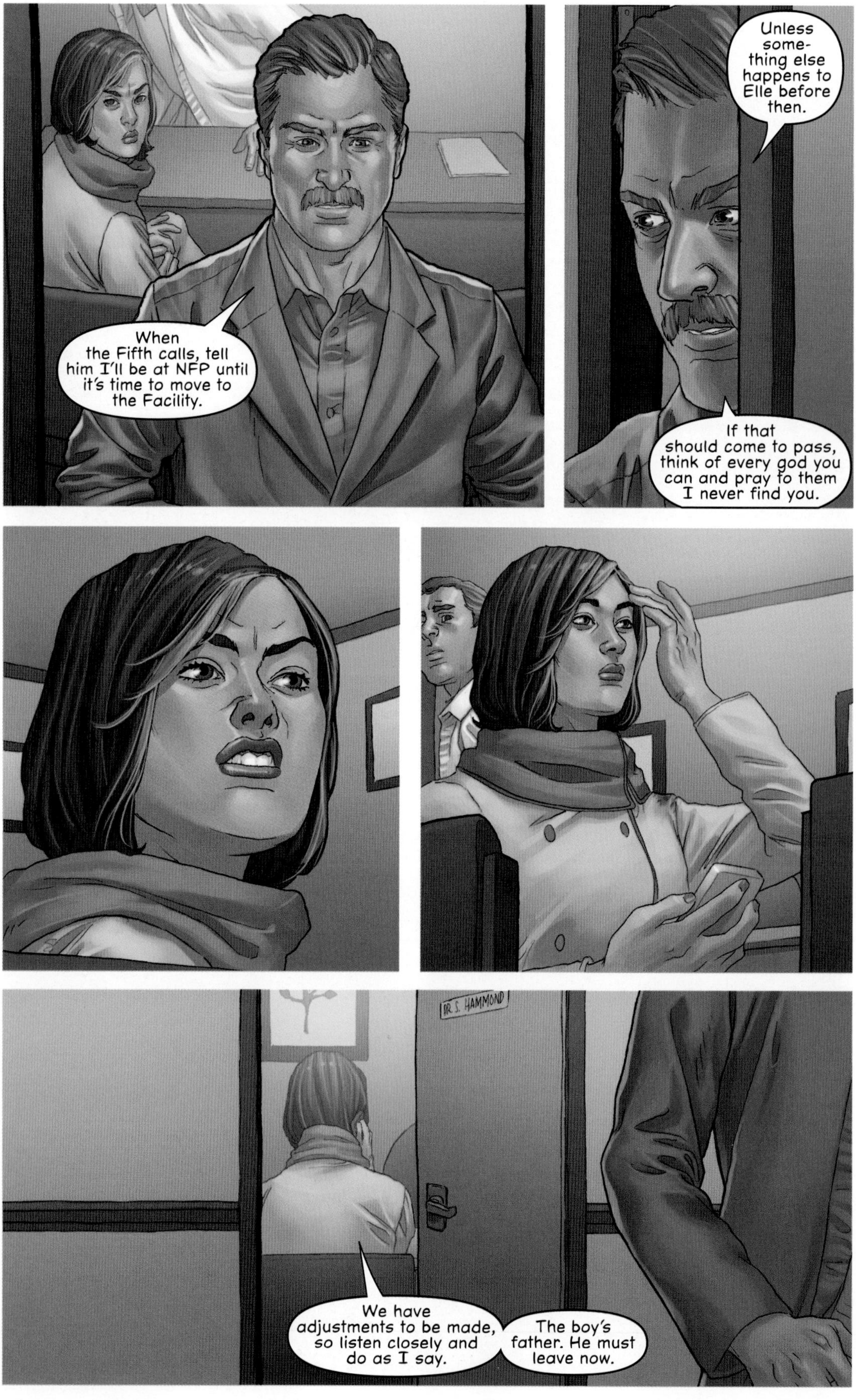
When the Fifth calls, tell him I'll be at NFP until it's time to move to the Facility.
Unless some-thing else happens to Elle before then.
If that should come to pass, think of every god you can and pray to them I never find you.
DR. S. HAMMOND
We have adjustments to be made, so listen closely and do as I say.
The boy's father. He must leave now.

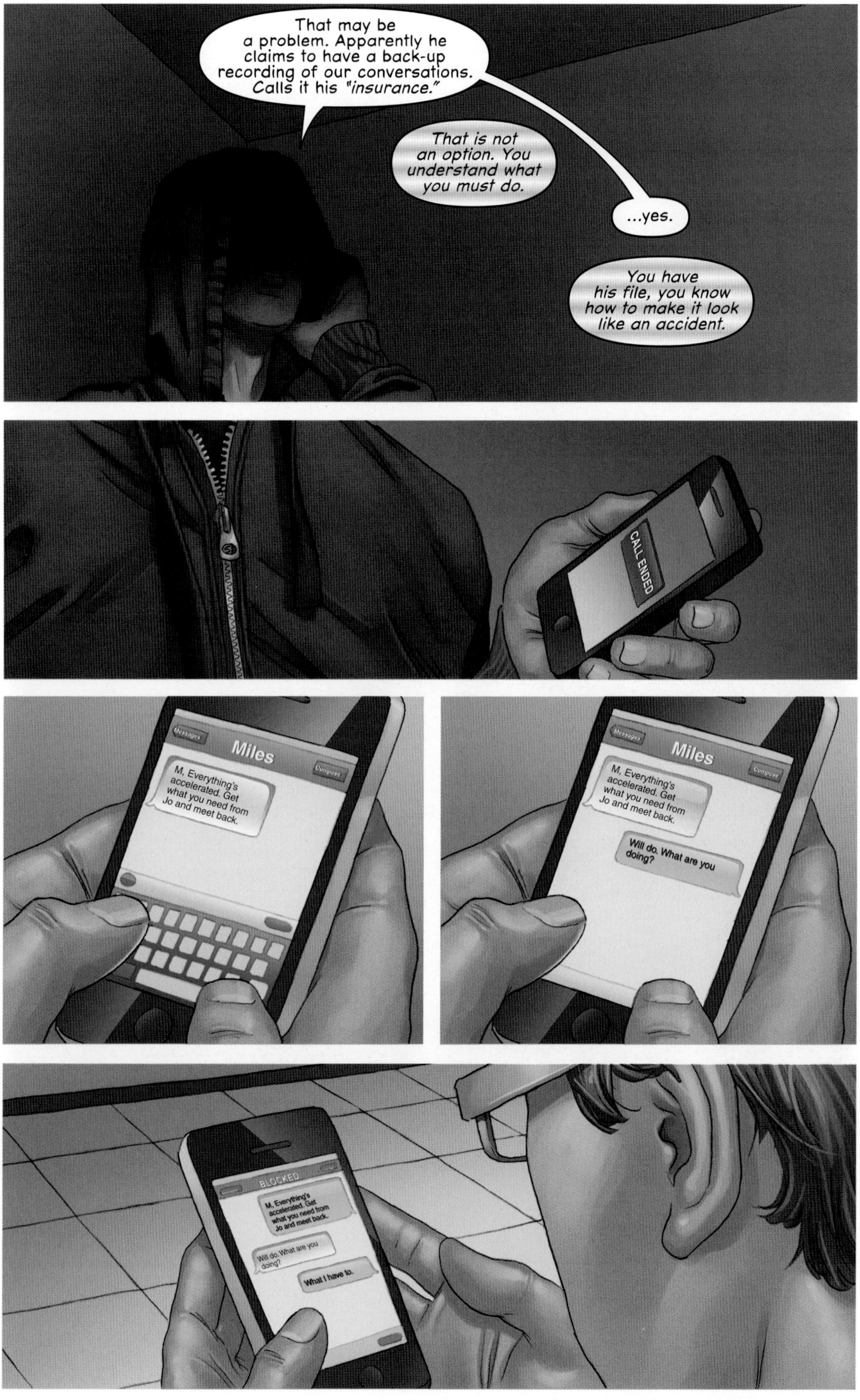
That may be a problem. Apparently he claims to have a back-up recording of our conversations. Calls it his "insurance."
That is not an option. You understand what you must do.
...yes.
You have his file, you know how to make it look like an accident.
CALL ENDED
Messages
Miles
Compose
M, Everything's accelerated. Get what you need from Jo and meet back.
Messages
Miles
Compose
M, Everything's accelerated. Get what you need from Jo and meet back.
Will do. What are you doing?
BLOCKED
M, Everything's accelerated. Get what you need from Jo and meet back.
Will do. What are you doing?
What I have to.

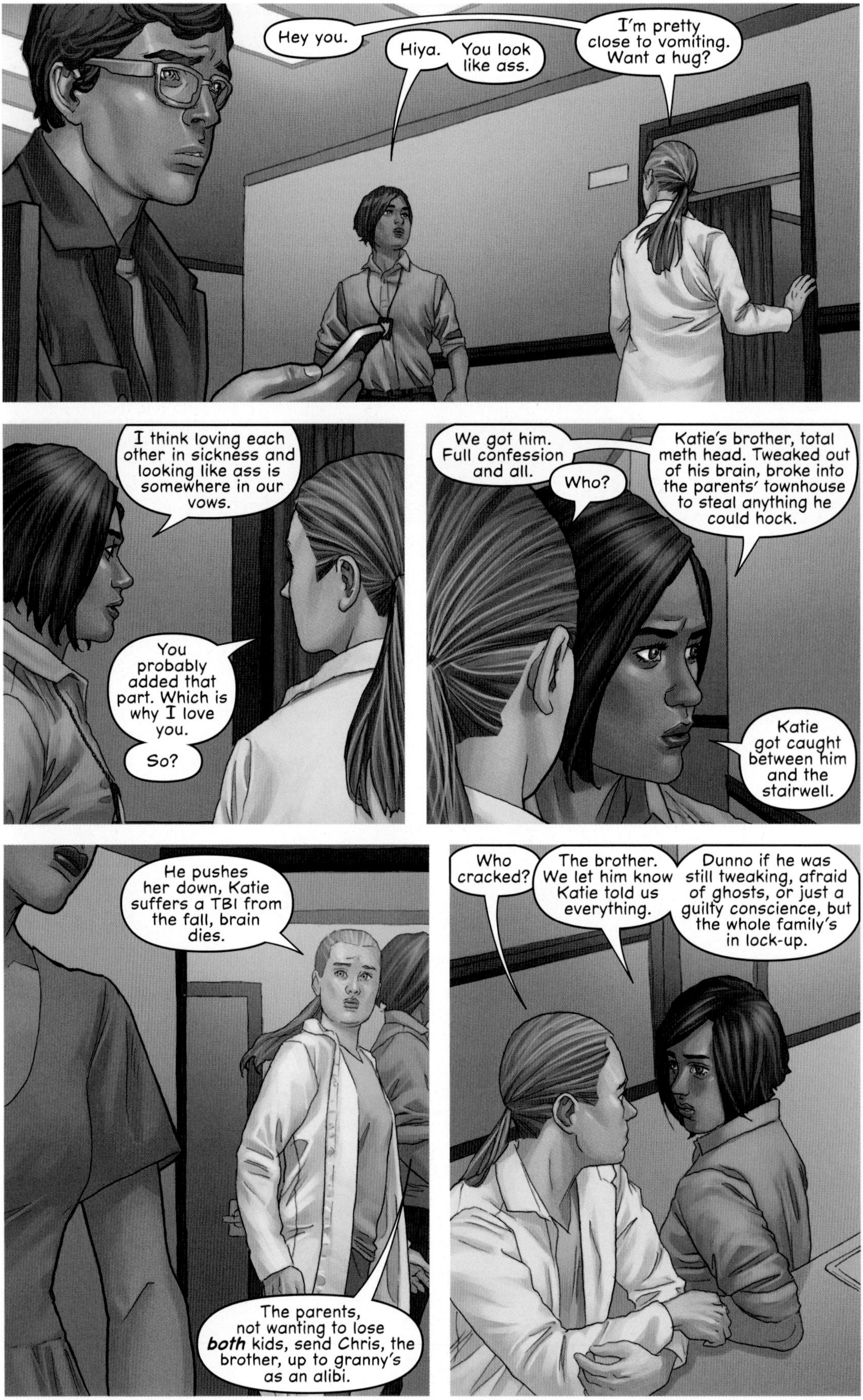
Hey you.
Hiya.
You look like ass.
I'm pretty close to vomiting. Want a hug?
I think loving each other in sickness and looking like ass is somewhere in our vows.
You probably added that part. Which is why I love you.
So?
We got him. Full confession and all.
Who?
Katie's brother, total meth head. Tweaked out of his brain, broke into the parents' townhouse to steal anything he could hock.
Katie got caught between him and the stairwell.
He pushes her down, Katie suffers a TBI from the fall, brain dies.
The parents, not wanting to lose *both* kids, send Chris, the brother, up to granny's as an alibi.
Who cracked?
The brother. We let him know Katie told us everything.
Dunno if he was still tweaking, afraid of ghosts, or just a guilty conscience, but the whole family's in lock-up.

Which *also* means Katie was a ward of the hospital when Jo took her on that joyride. No kidnapping charges.

For anyone.

That saves us *one* awkward situation.

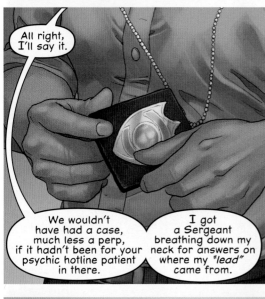

All right, I'll say it.

We wouldn't have had a case, much less a perp, if it hadn't been for your psychic hotline patient in there.

I got a Sergeant breathing down my neck for answers on where my *"lead"* came from.

Trust me, I know.

I basically argued *in favor* of the same theory to a colleague who I already hate and the parents of the patient on the other side of the... whatever.

Maybe it was a one-time thing? No need to break out ECTO-1 yet, Gina.

Yeah, maybe.

I don't like squishy science, Annie.

I like your squishy cheeks.

I'm serious. Exhausted, but serious. And without any brain power to comprehend what's happening right now.

All I know is, after what those two girls have been through, they deserve a private goodbye.

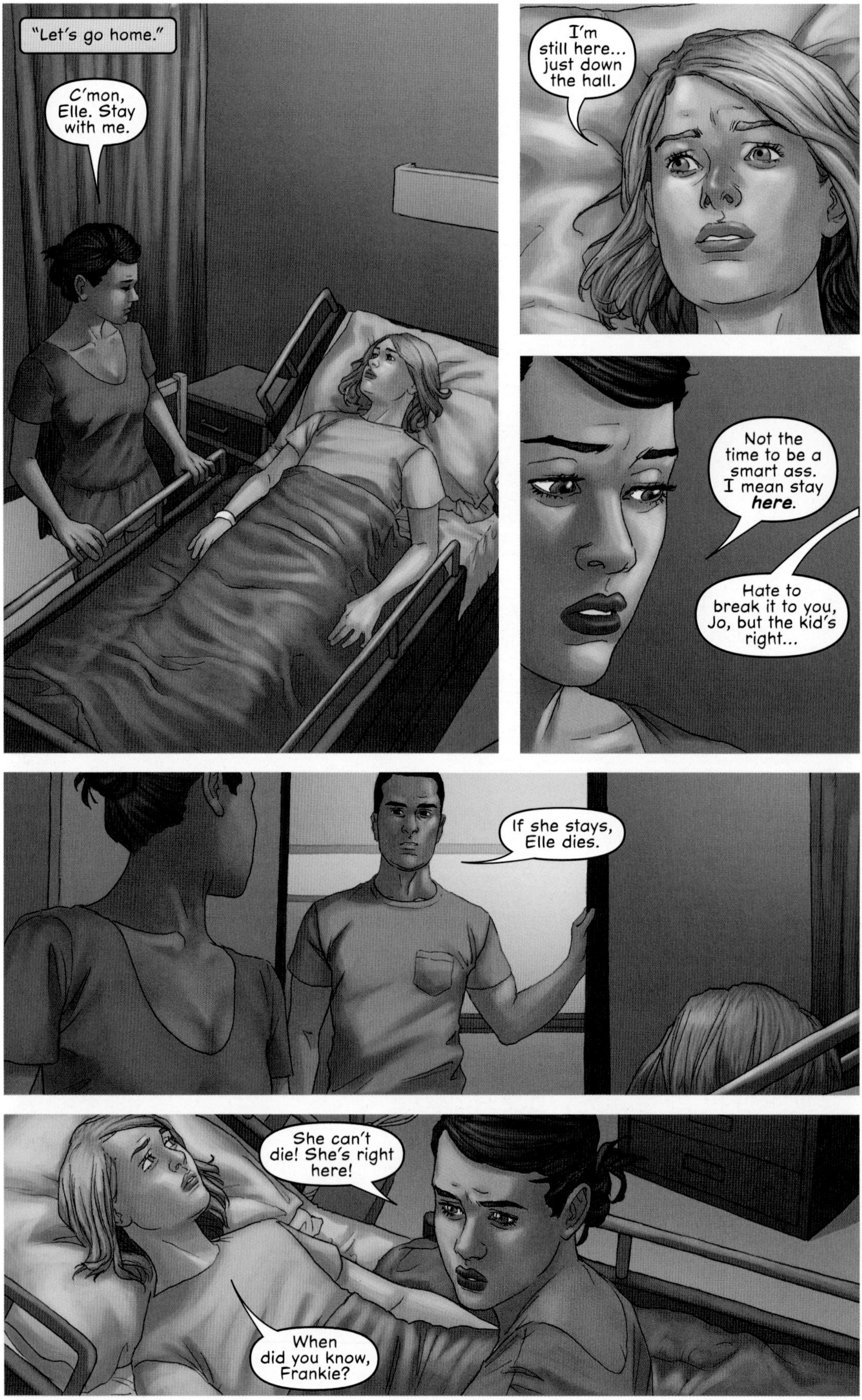
"Let's go home."
C'mon, Elle. Stay with me.
I'm still here... just down the hall.
Not the time to be a smart ass. I mean stay **here**.
Hate to break it to you, Jo, but the kid's right...
If she stays, Elle dies.
She can't die! She's right here!
When did you know, Frankie?

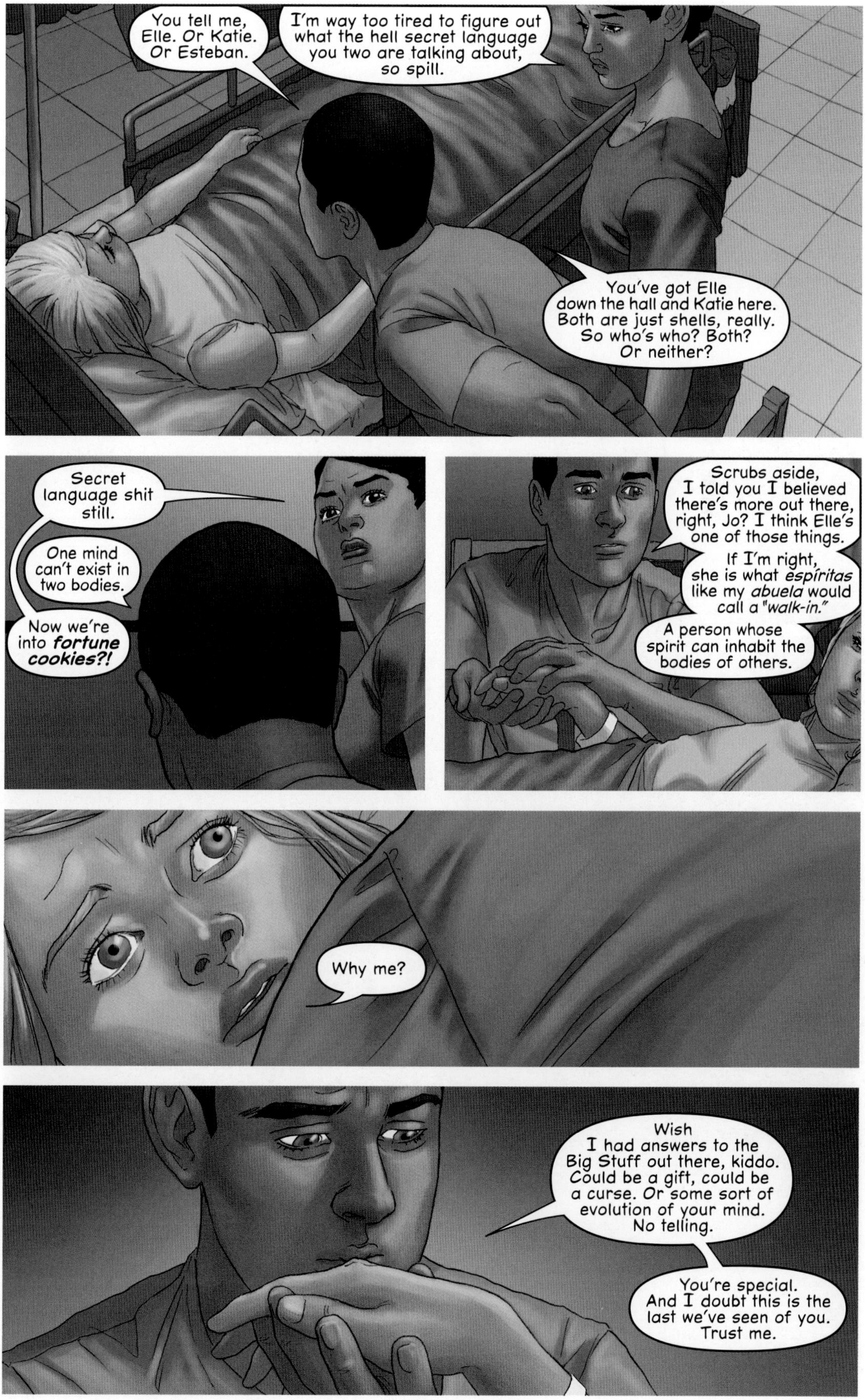
You tell me, Elle. Or Katie. Or Esteban.
I'm way too tired to figure out what the hell secret language you two are talking about, so spill.
You've got Elle down the hall and Katie here. Both are just shells, really. So who's who? Both? Or neither?
Secret language shit still.
One mind can't exist in two bodies.
Now we're into **fortune cookies?!**
Scrubs aside, I told you I believed there's more out there, right, Jo? I think Elle's one of those things.
If I'm right, she is what *espíritas* like my *abuela* would call a "*walk-in.*"
A person whose spirit can inhabit the bodies of others.
Why me?
Wish I had answers to the Big Stuff out there, kiddo. Could be a gift, could be a curse. Or some sort of evolution of your mind. No telling.
You're special. And I doubt this is the last we've seen of you. Trust me.

So why doesn't she just walk herself back into her own damn body?

I can't

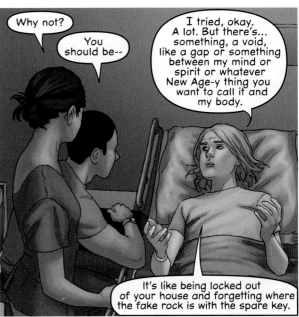

Why not?

You should be--

I tried, okay. A lot. But there's... something, a void, like a gap or something between my mind or spirit or whatever New Age-y thing you want to call it and my body.

It's like being locked out of your house and forgetting where the fake rock is with the spare key.

Hey, Shaman, can't you call your gran and ask what's going on?

It's possible that Elle still has things to learn before awakening. Or it may not be the right time.

All this is me spitballing ideas. Don't expect me to have all the answers, okay?

Great, then if that's it, do you mind giving us some privacy?

No problem. See you around, Elle.

And Jo, that Miles kid is still hanging around when you're done.

Miles?

Some kid, red-head, glasses, says he knows you and Dane?

Miles...

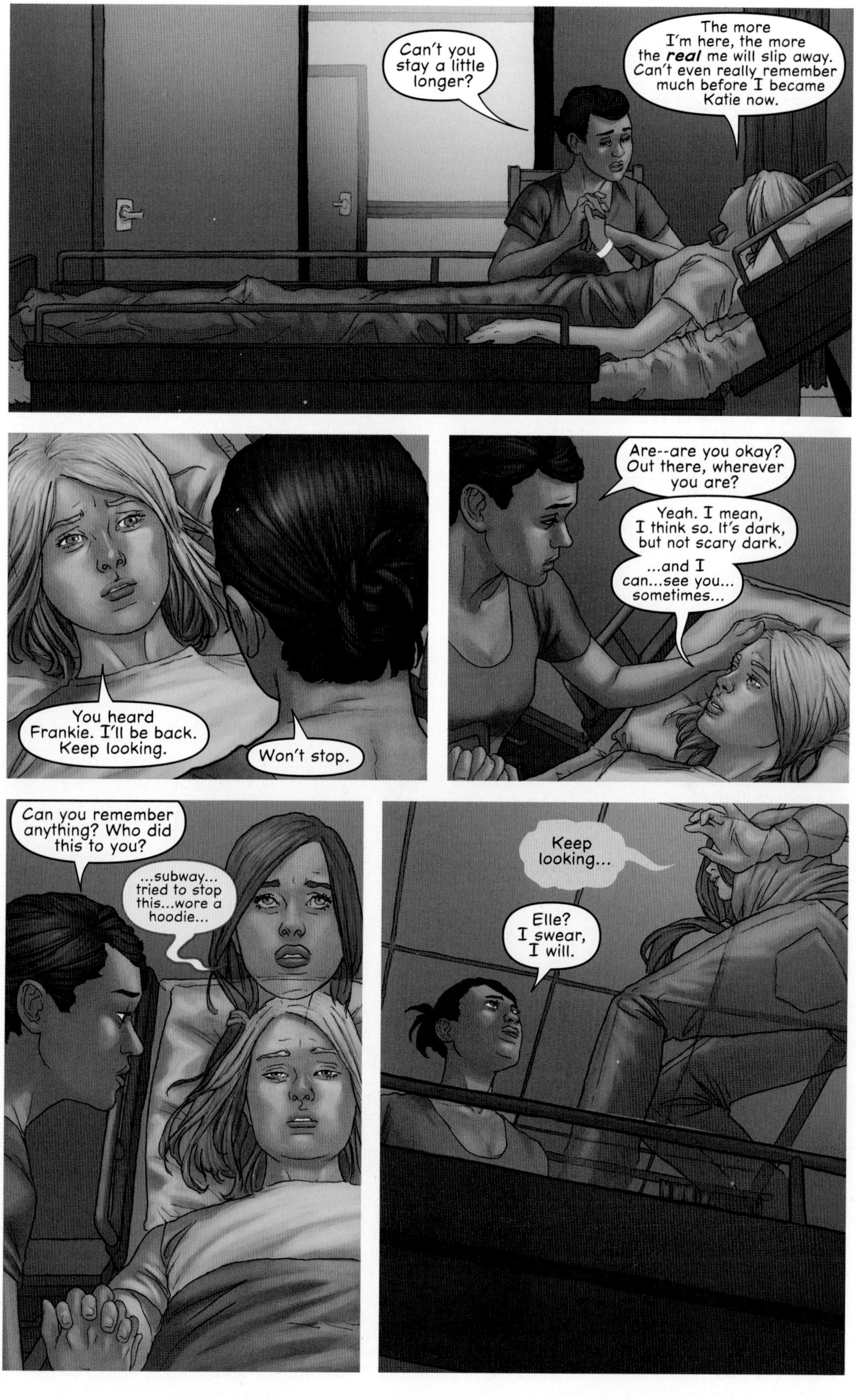
Can't you stay a little longer?
The more I'm here, the more the ***real*** me will slip away. Can't even really remember much before I became Katie now.
You heard Frankie. I'll be back. Keep looking.
Won't stop.
Are--are you okay? Out there, wherever you are?
Yeah. I mean, I think so. It's dark, but not scary dark.
...and I can...see you... sometimes...
Can you remember anything? Who did this to you?
...subway... tried to stop this...wore a hoodie...
Keep looking...
Elle? I swear, I will.

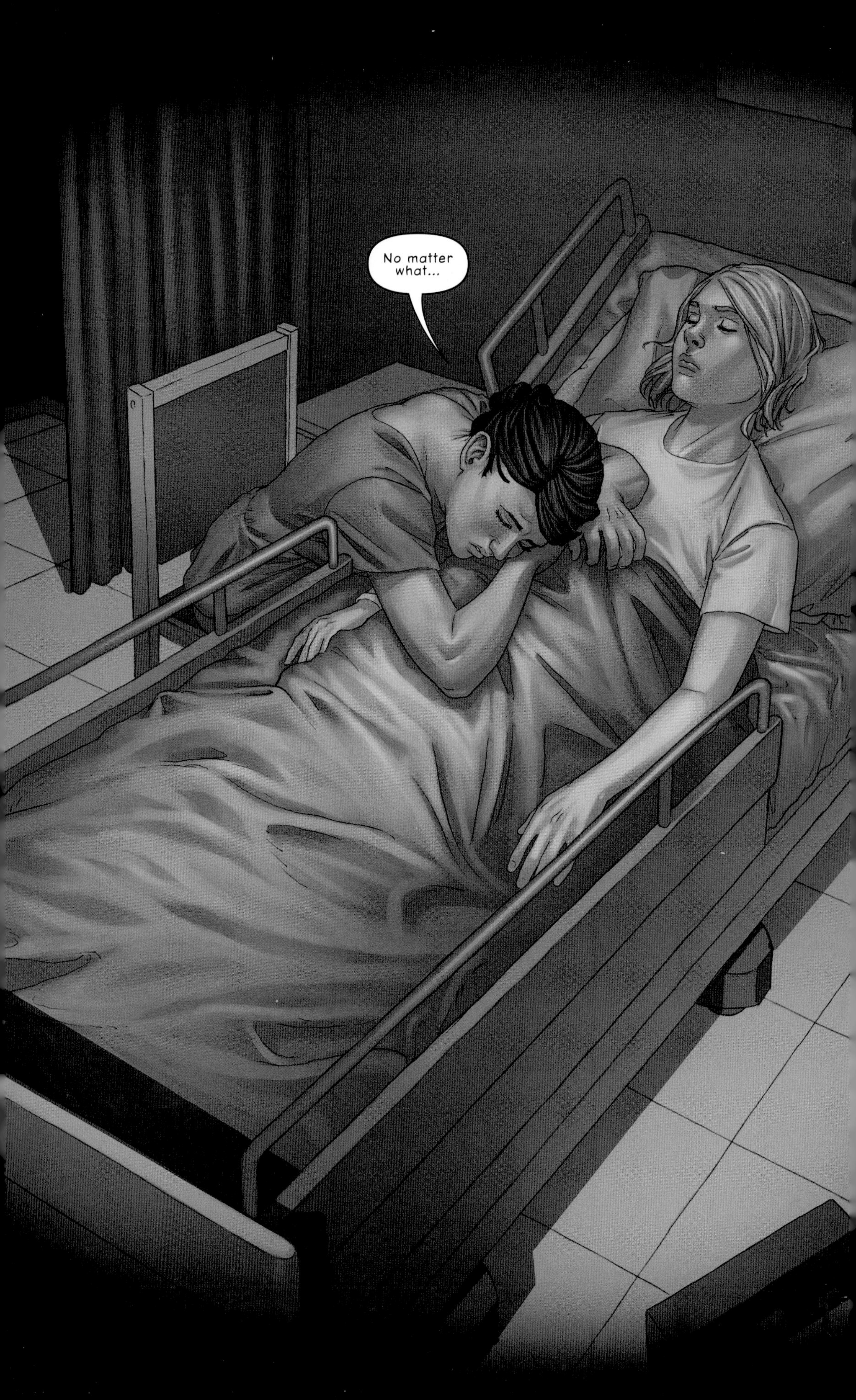
No matter what...

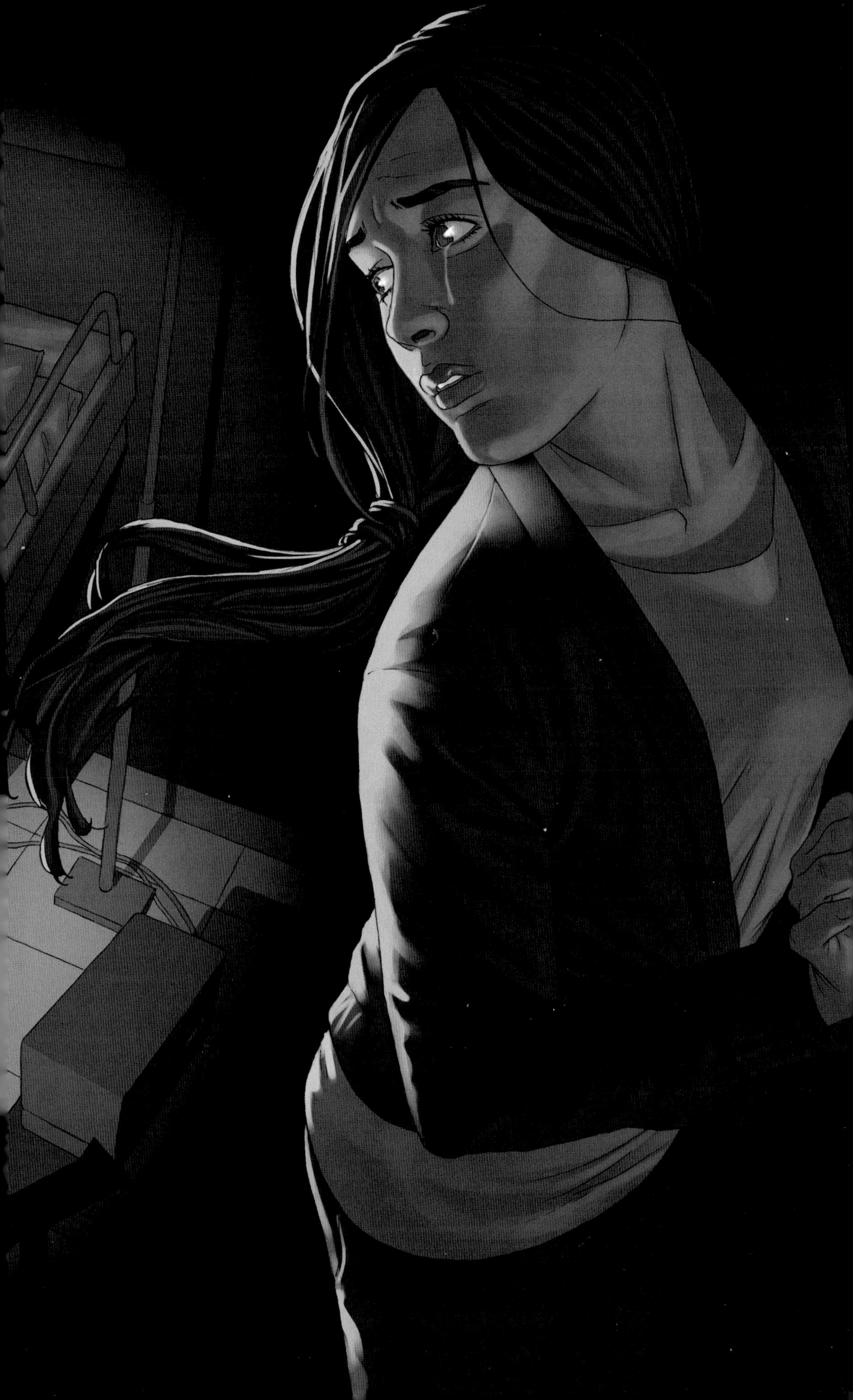

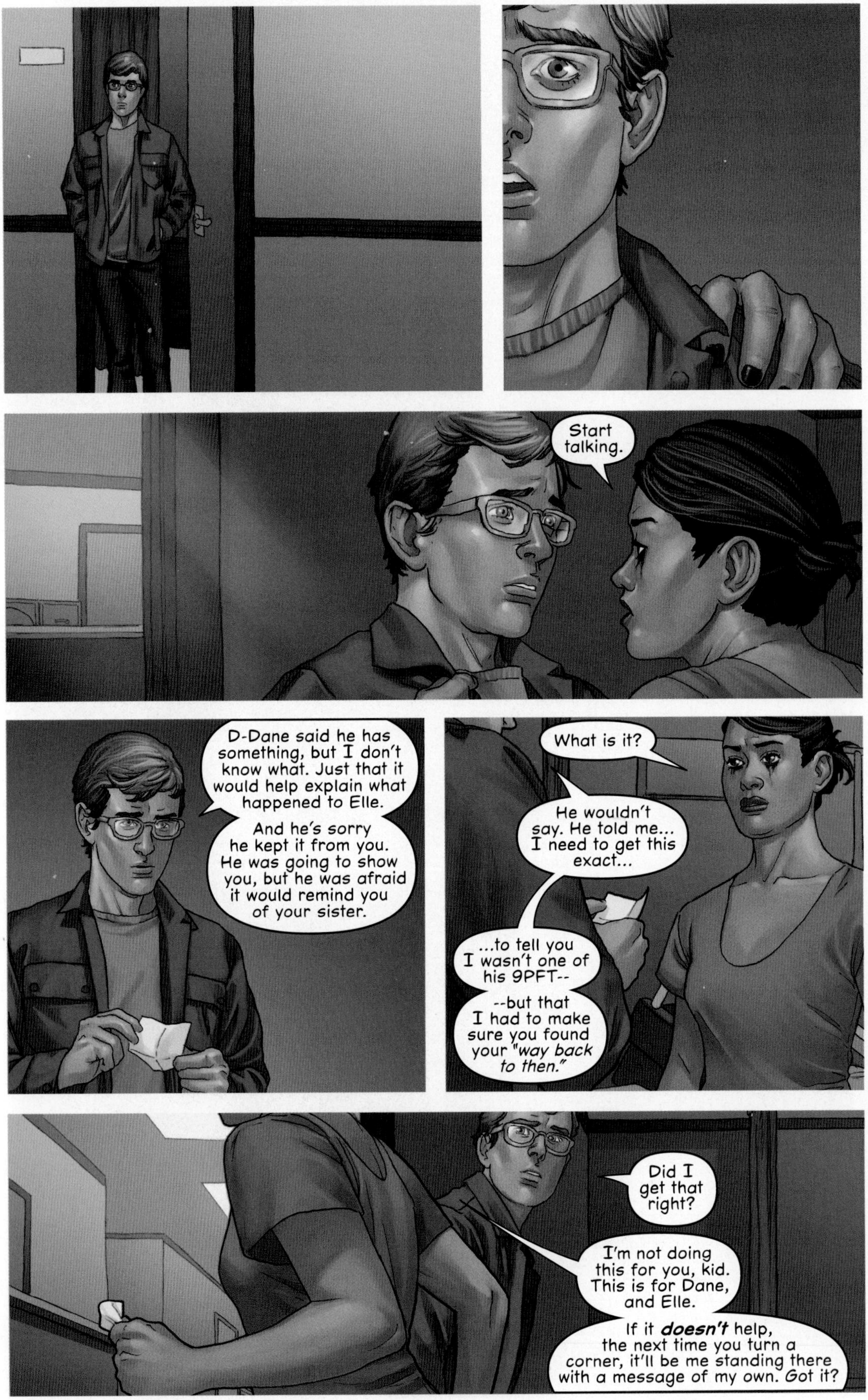
Start talking.
D-Dane said he has something, but I don't know what. Just that it would help explain what happened to Elle.
And he's sorry he kept it from you. He was going to show you, but he was afraid it would remind you of your sister.
What is it?
He wouldn't say. He told me... I need to get this exact...
...to tell you I wasn't one of his 9PFT--
--but that I had to make sure you found your *"way back to then."*
Did I get that right?
I'm not doing this for you, kid. This is for Dane, and Elle.
If it ***doesn't*** help, the next time you turn a corner, it'll be me standing there with a message of my own. Got it?

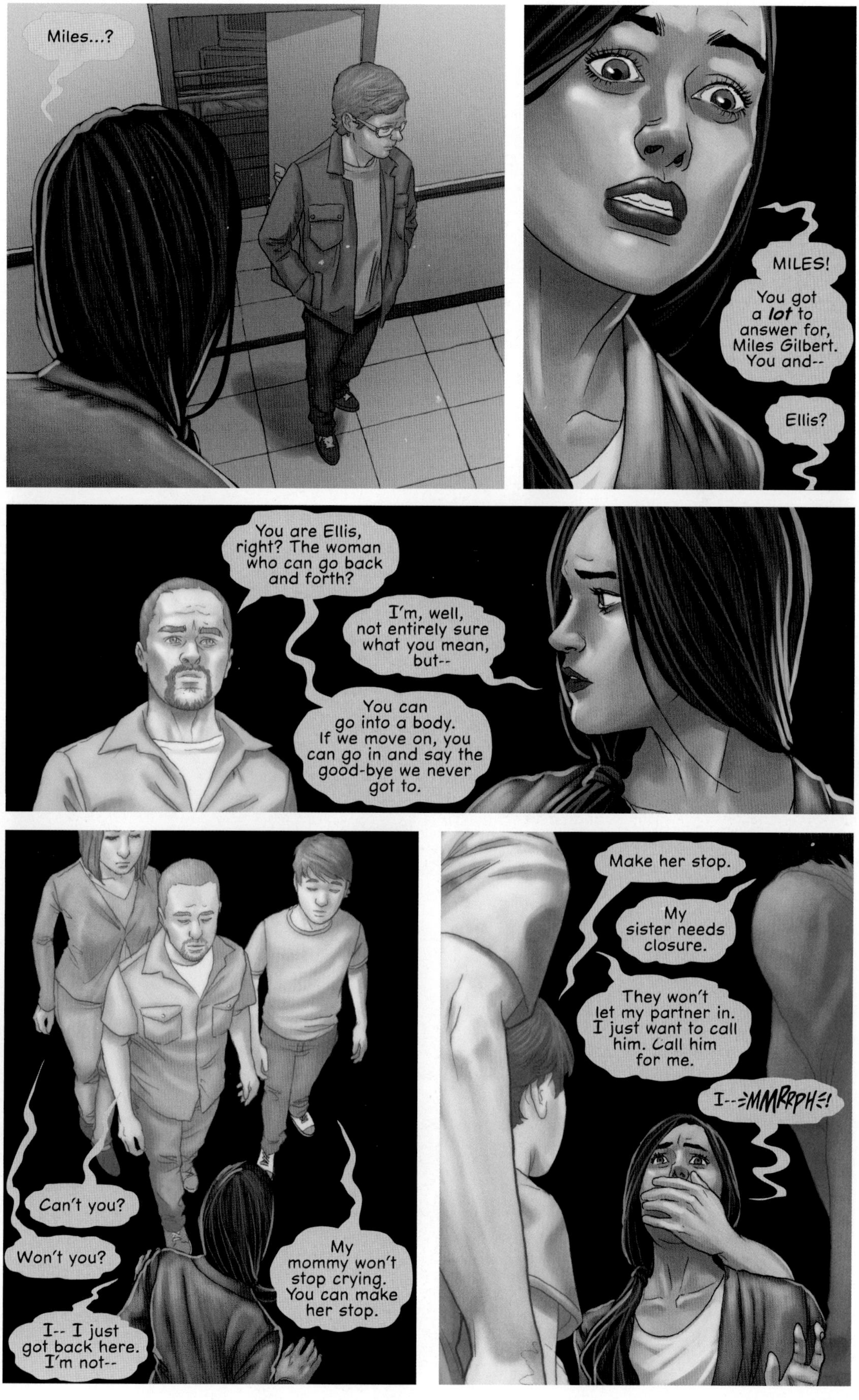
Miles...?
MILES!
You got a *lot* to answer for, Miles Gilbert. You and--
Ellis?
You are Ellis, right? The woman who can go back and forth?
I'm, well, not entirely sure what you mean, but--
You can go into a body. If we move on, you can go in and say the good-bye we never got to.
Can't you?
Won't you?
My mommy won't stop crying. You can make her stop.
I-- I just got back here. I'm not--
Make her stop.
My sister needs closure.
They won't let my partner in. I just want to call him. Call him for me.
I-- MMRRPH--!

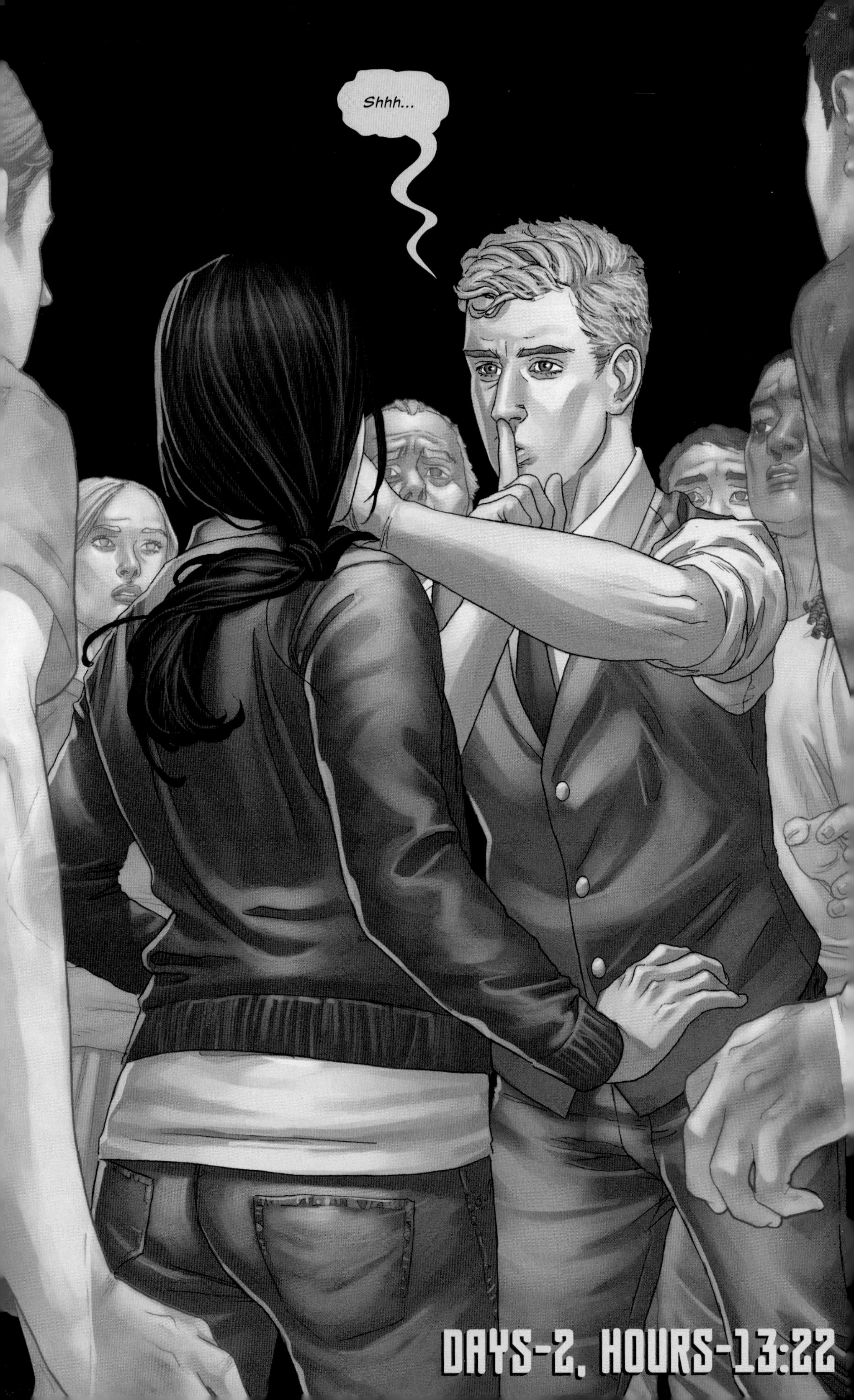
Shhh...
DAYS-2, HOURS-13:22

"Before aligning the mind, body and soul ... first one has to straighten their mind out."

— Stephen Richards

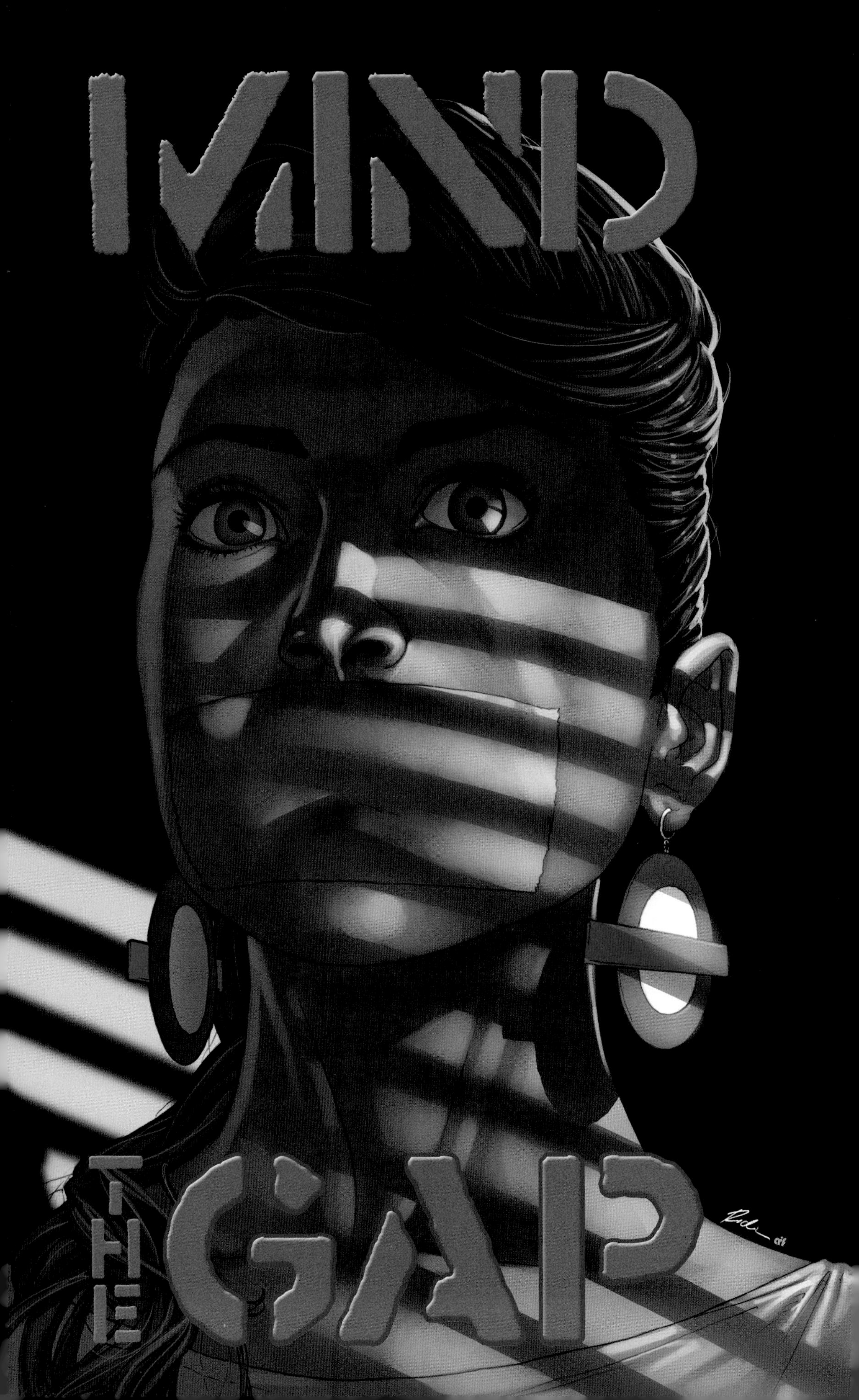
MIND
THE GAP

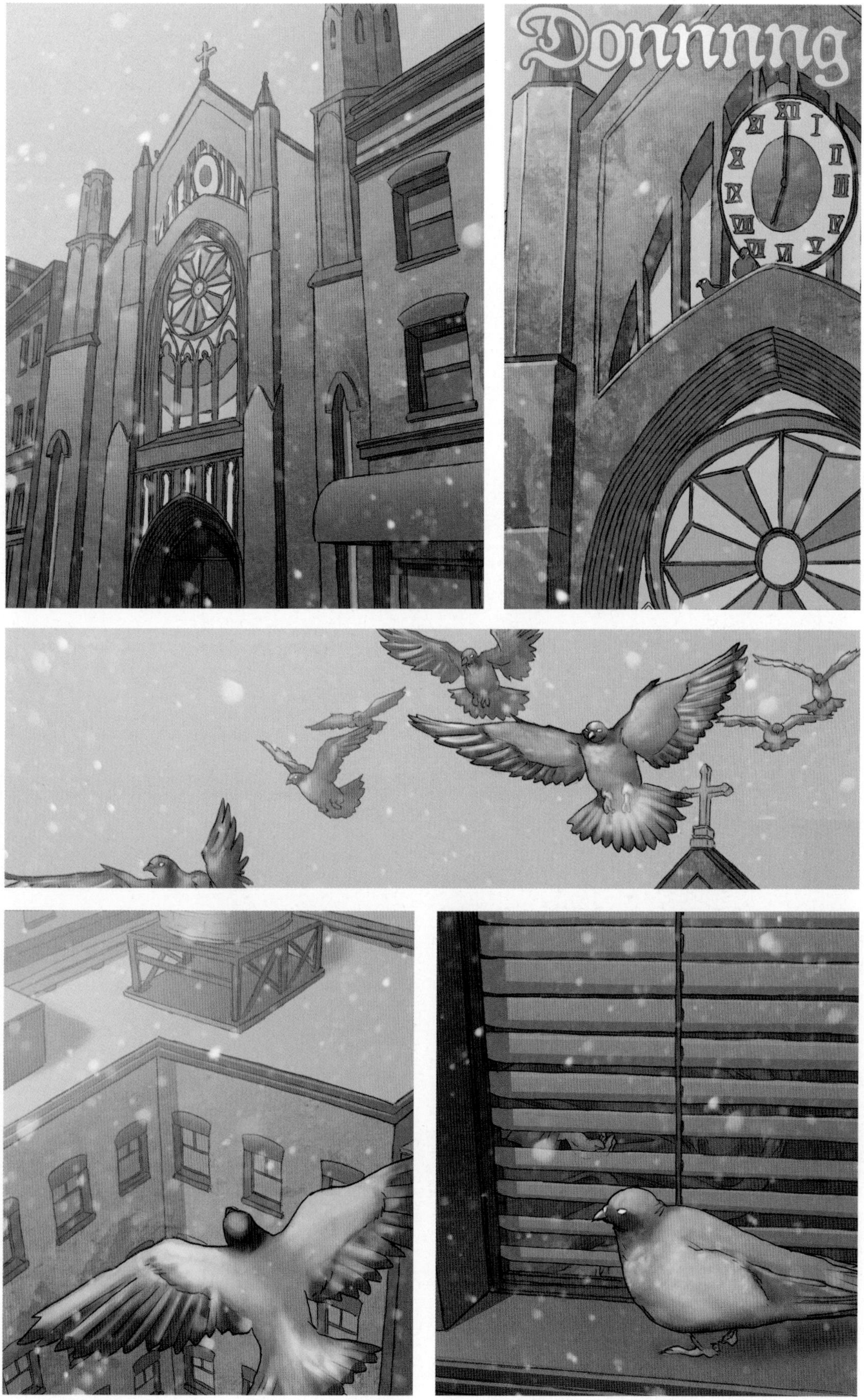
Donnnng

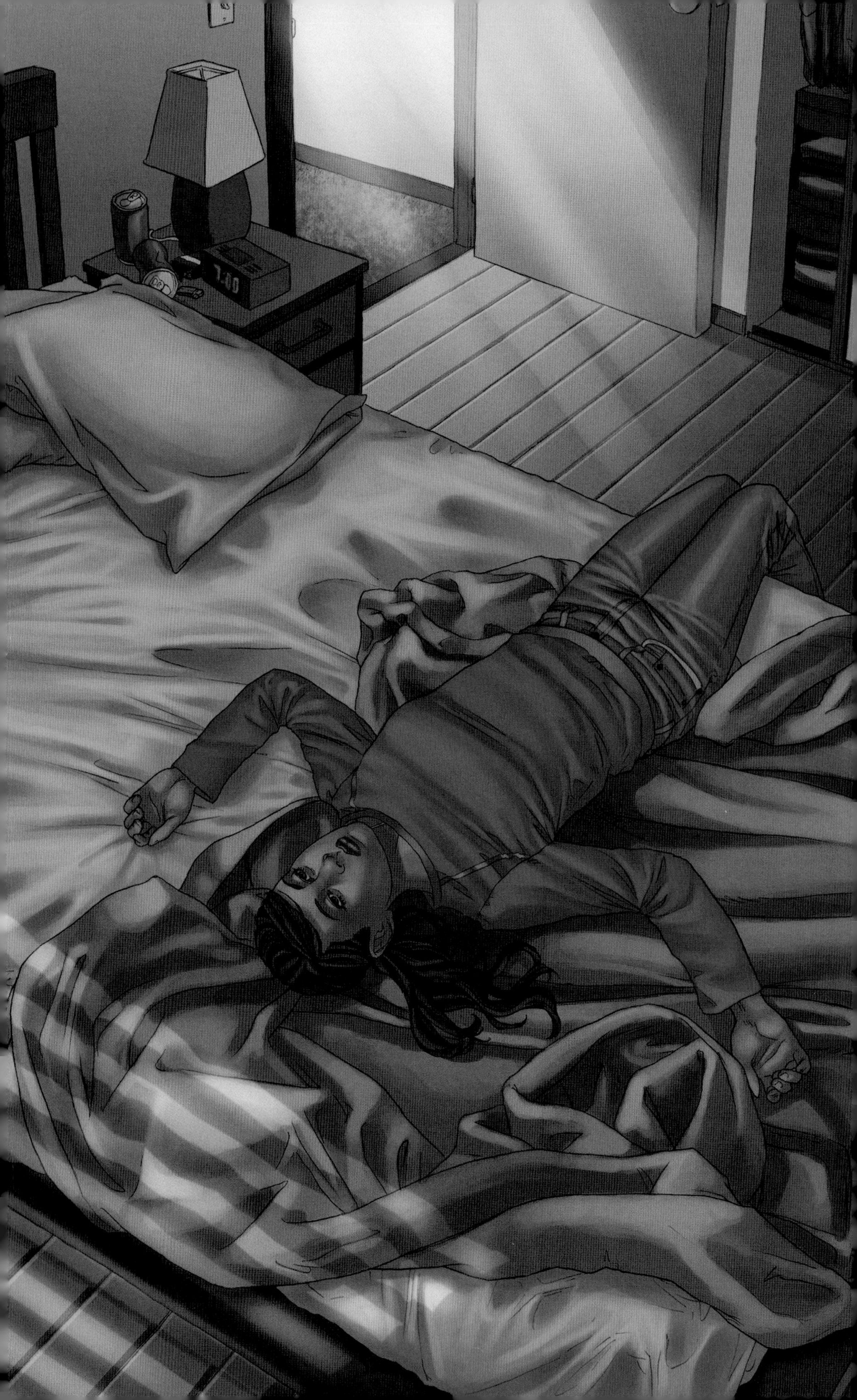
7:00

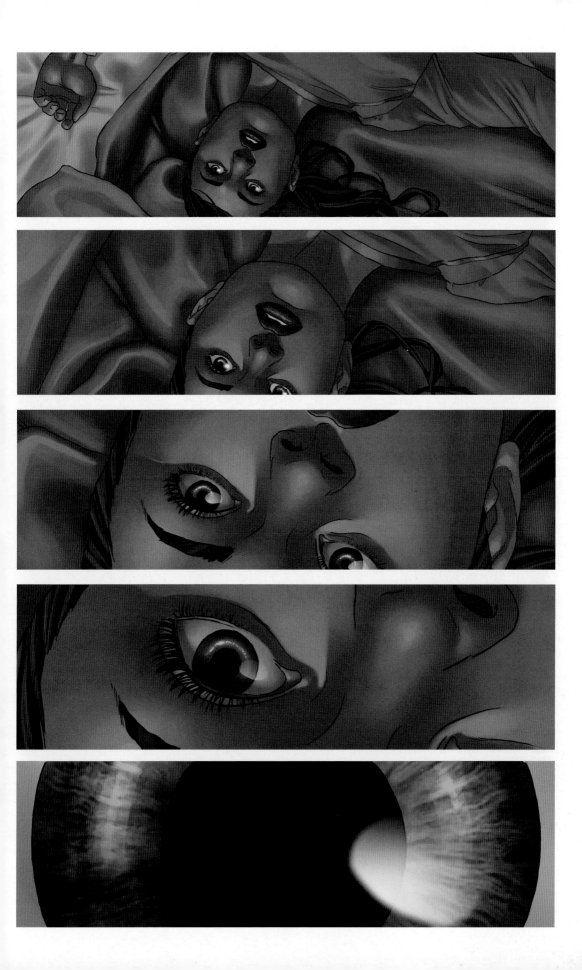

WISH YOU WERE HERE
PART 4
_"SPEECHLESS"

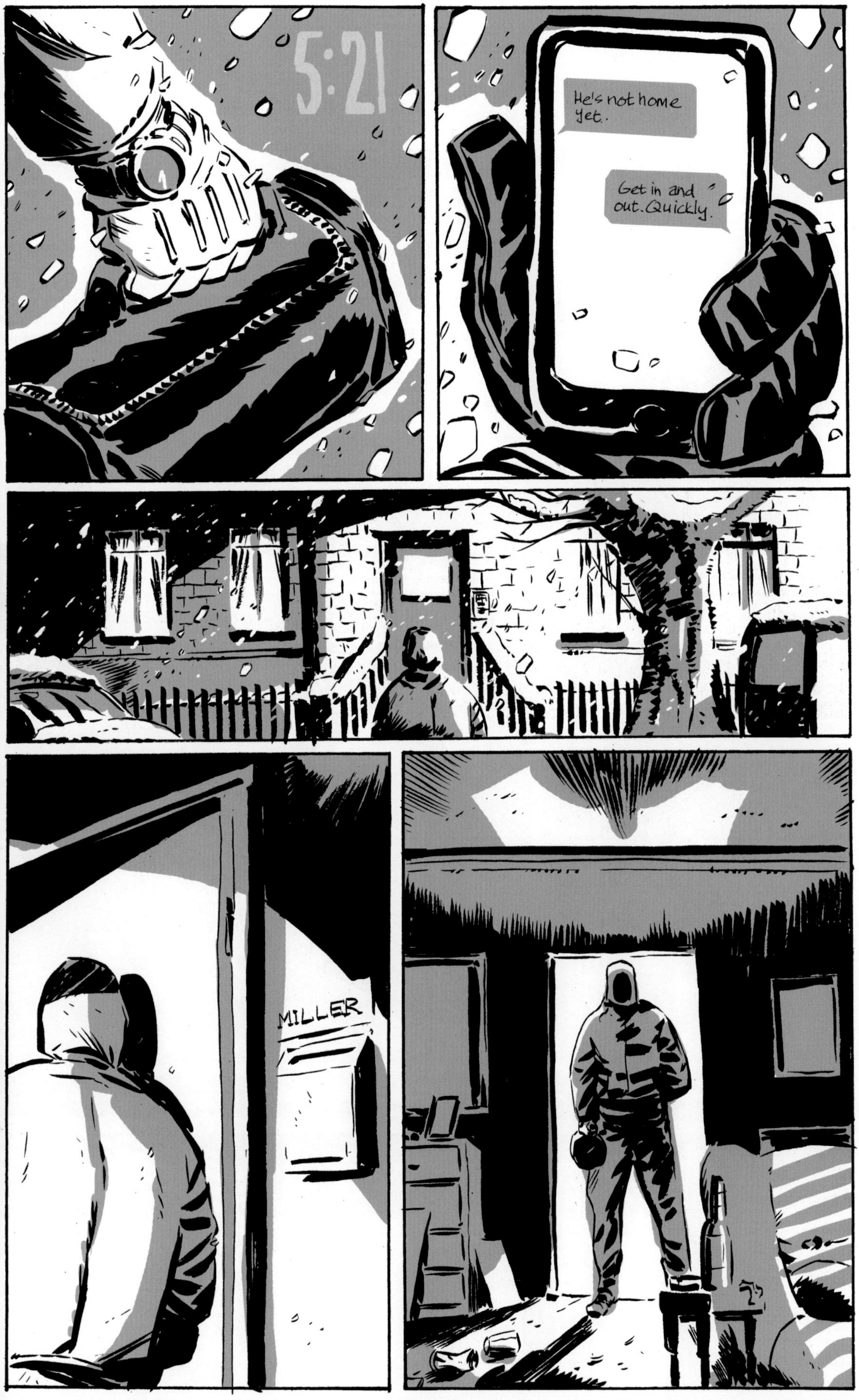
5:21
He's not home yet.
Get in and out. Quickly.
MILLER

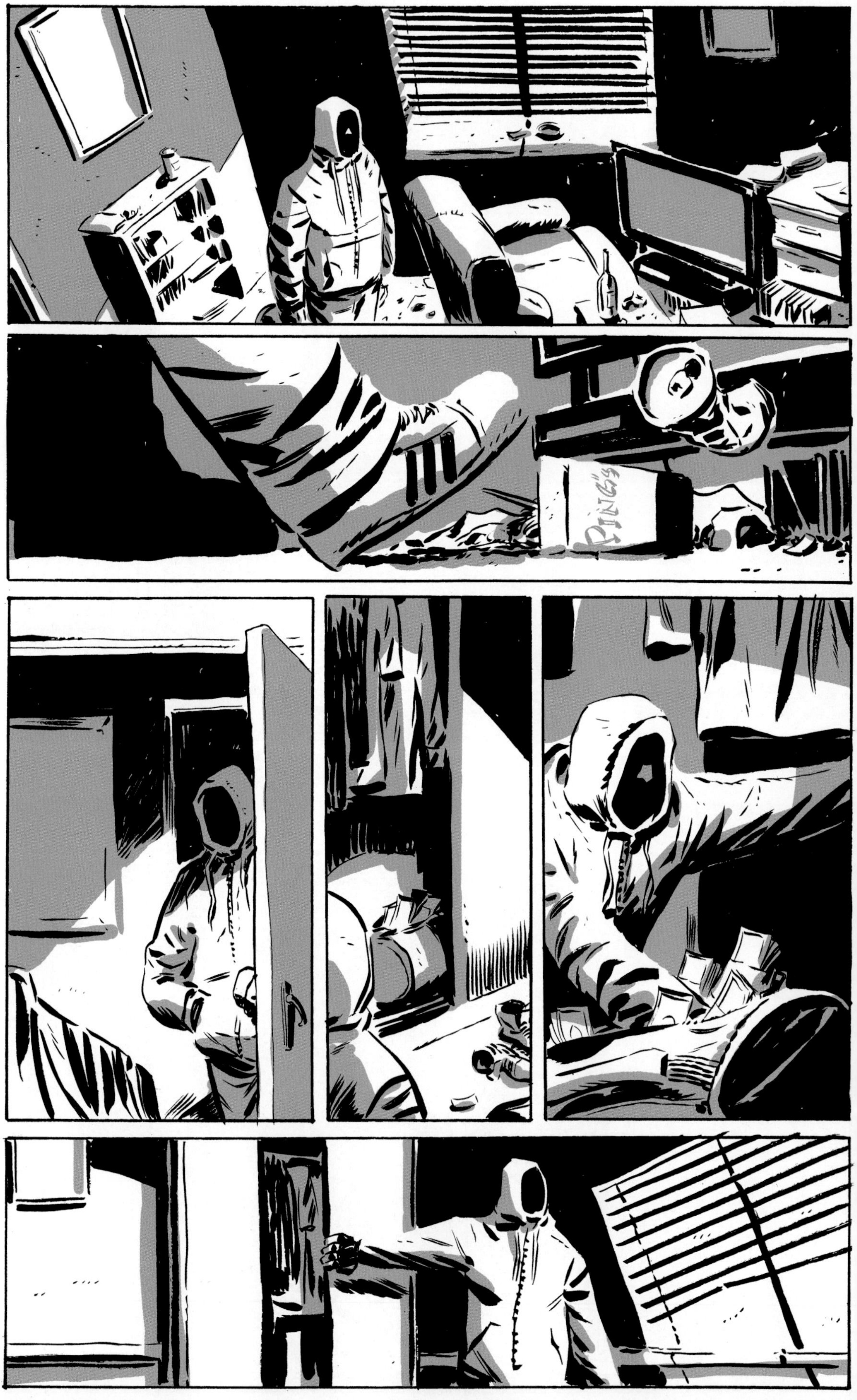

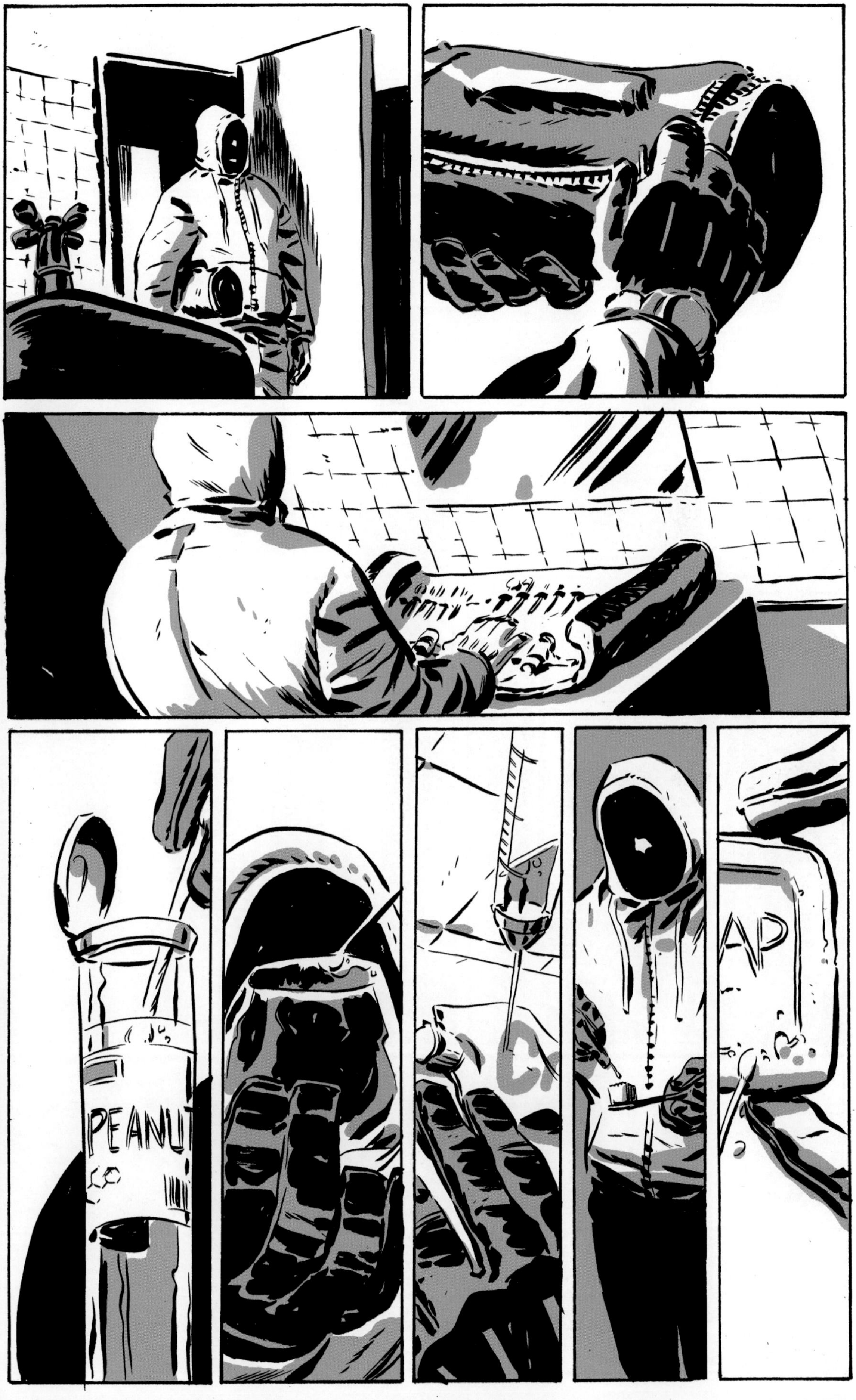
PEANUT
AP

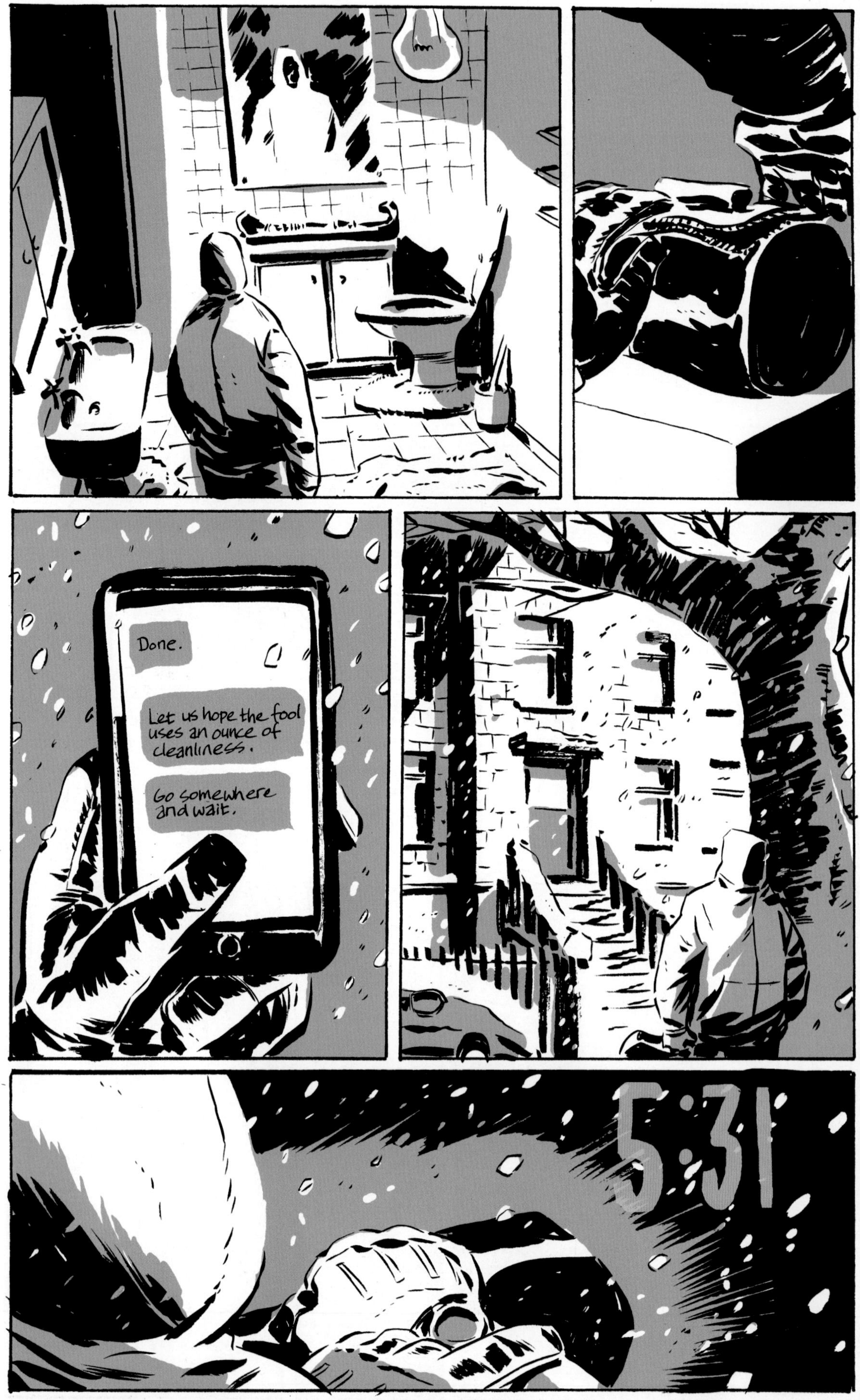
Done.
Let us hope the fool uses an ounce of cleanliness.
Go somewhere and wait.
5:31

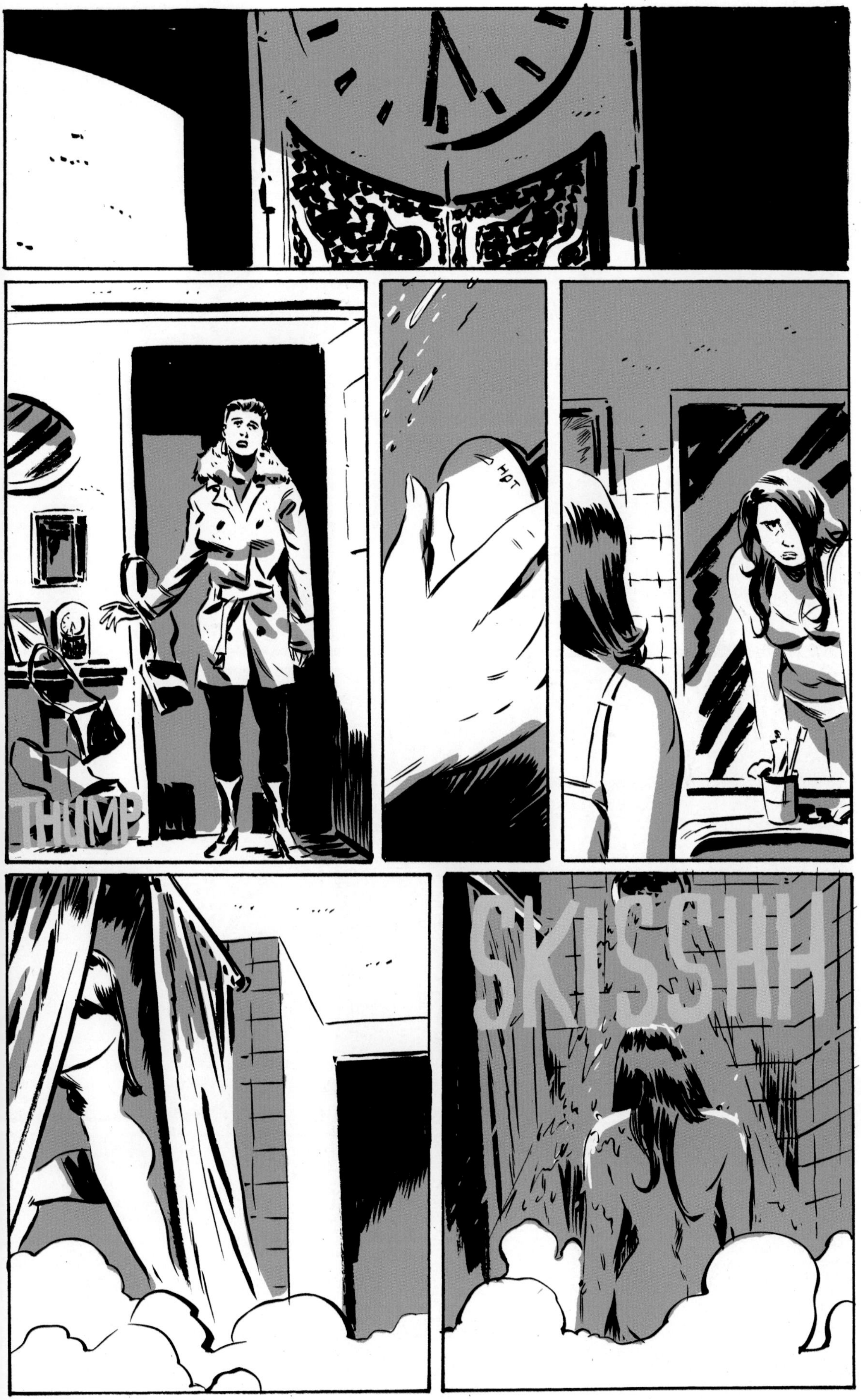
THUMP
HOT
SKISSHH

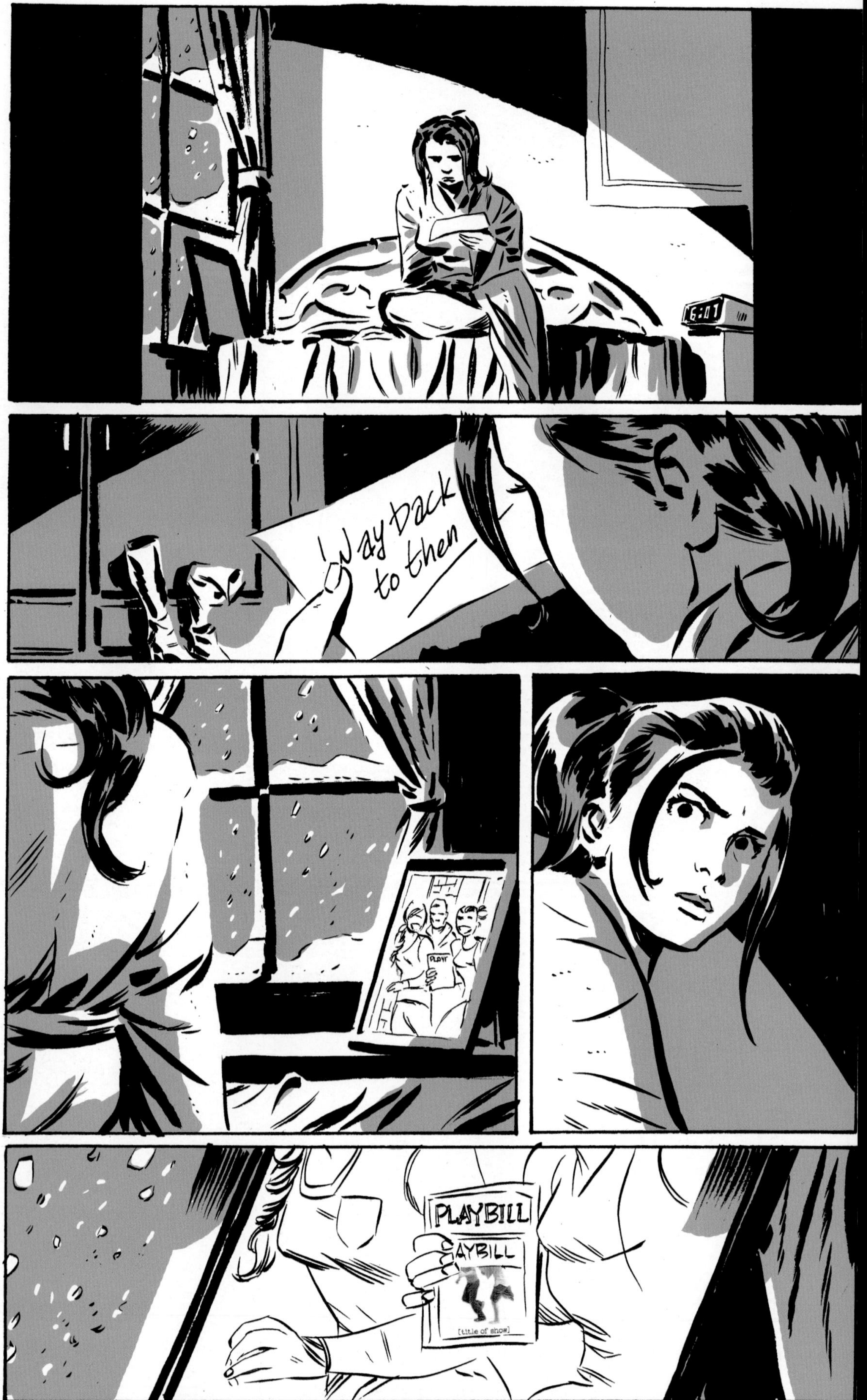
6:01
Way back to then
PLAYBILL
PLAYBILL
[title of show]

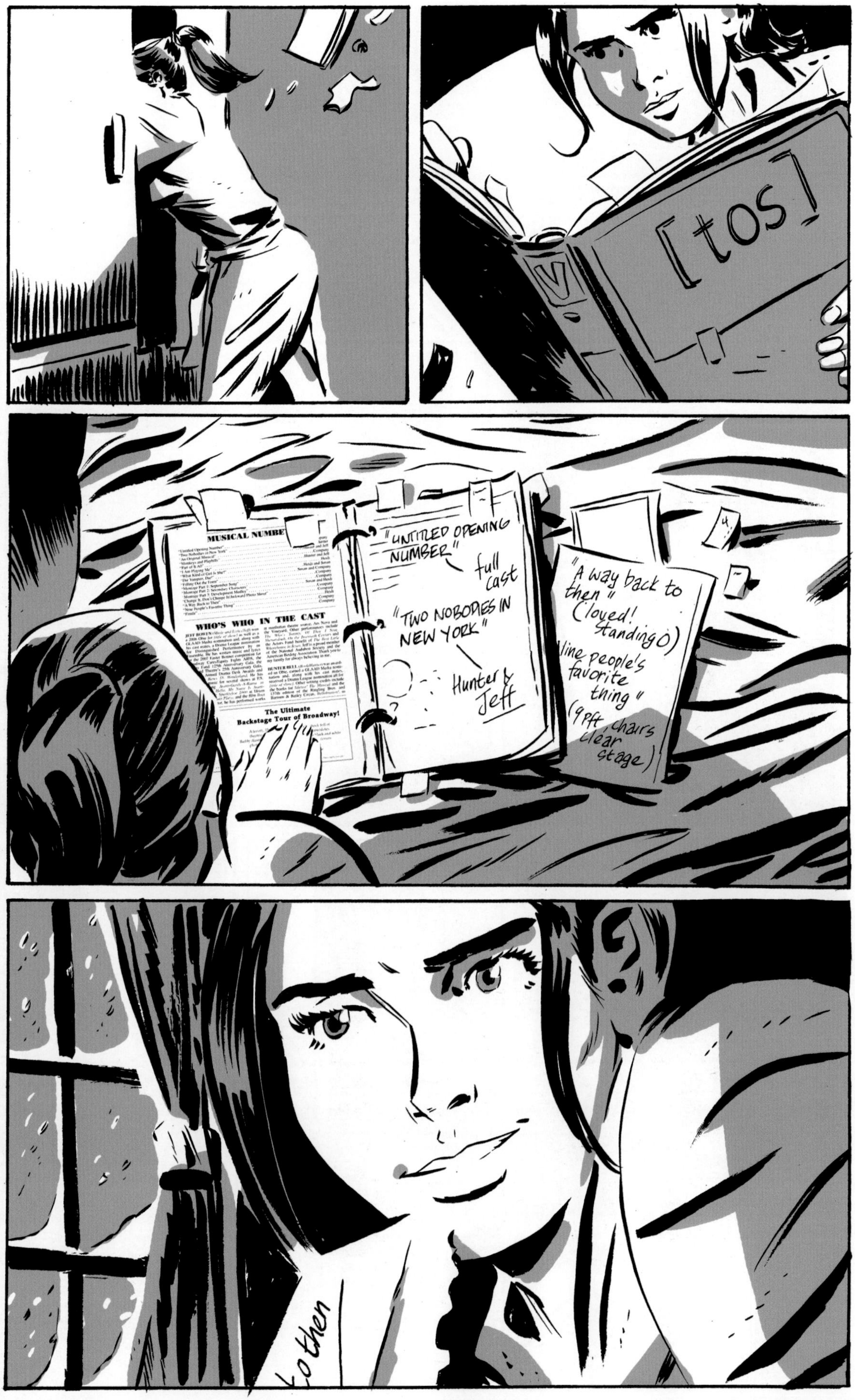

[tos]
MUSICAL NUMBE
WHO'S WHO IN THE CAST
The Ultimate Backstage Tour of Broadway!
"UNTITLED OPENING NUMBER" full cast
"TWO NOBODIES IN NEW YORK" Hunter & Jeff
"A way back to then" (loved! standing O)
"Nine people's favorite thing" (9 pft chairs clear stage)
to then

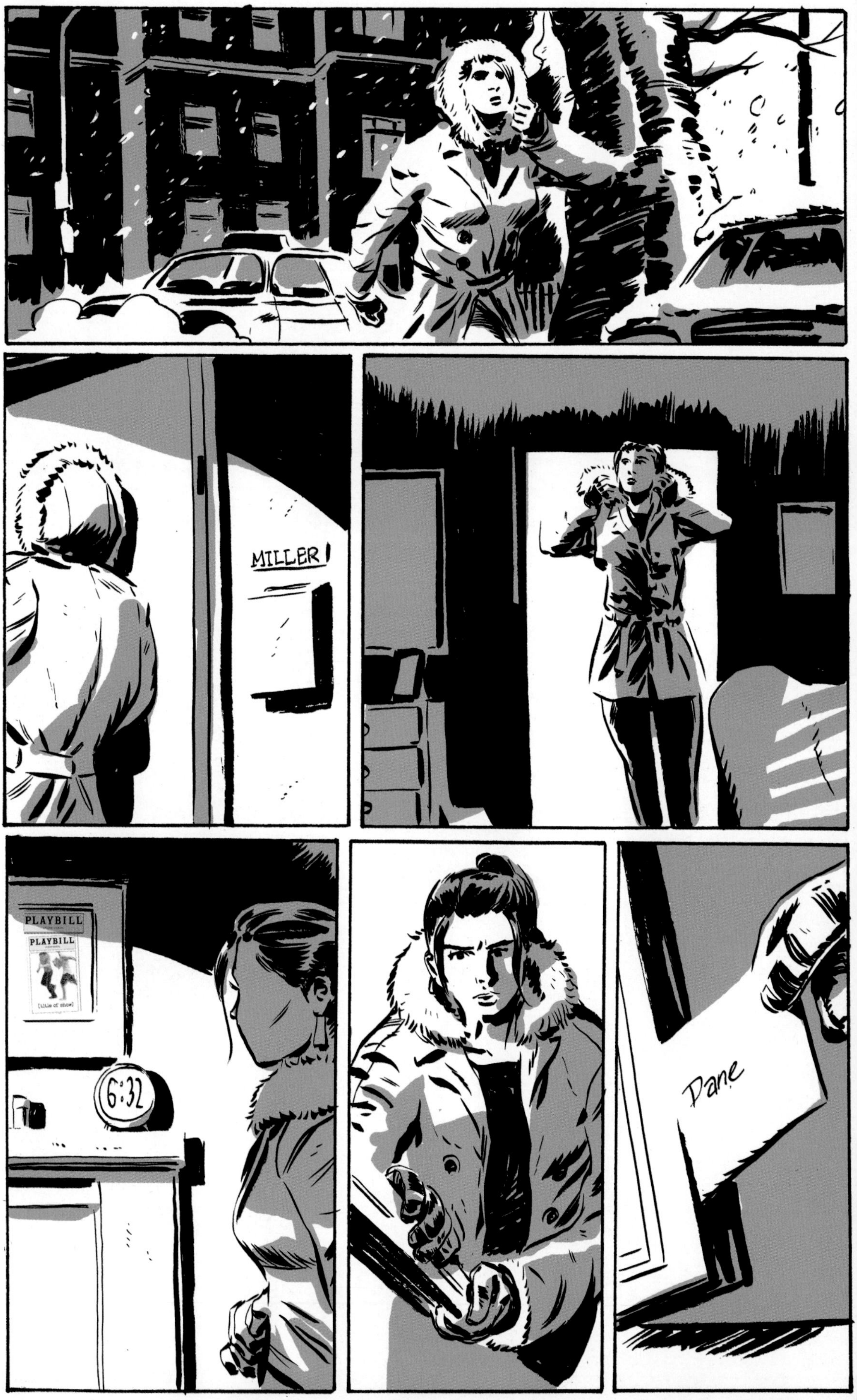
MILLER
PLAYBILL
PLAYBILL
[title of show]
6:32
Dane

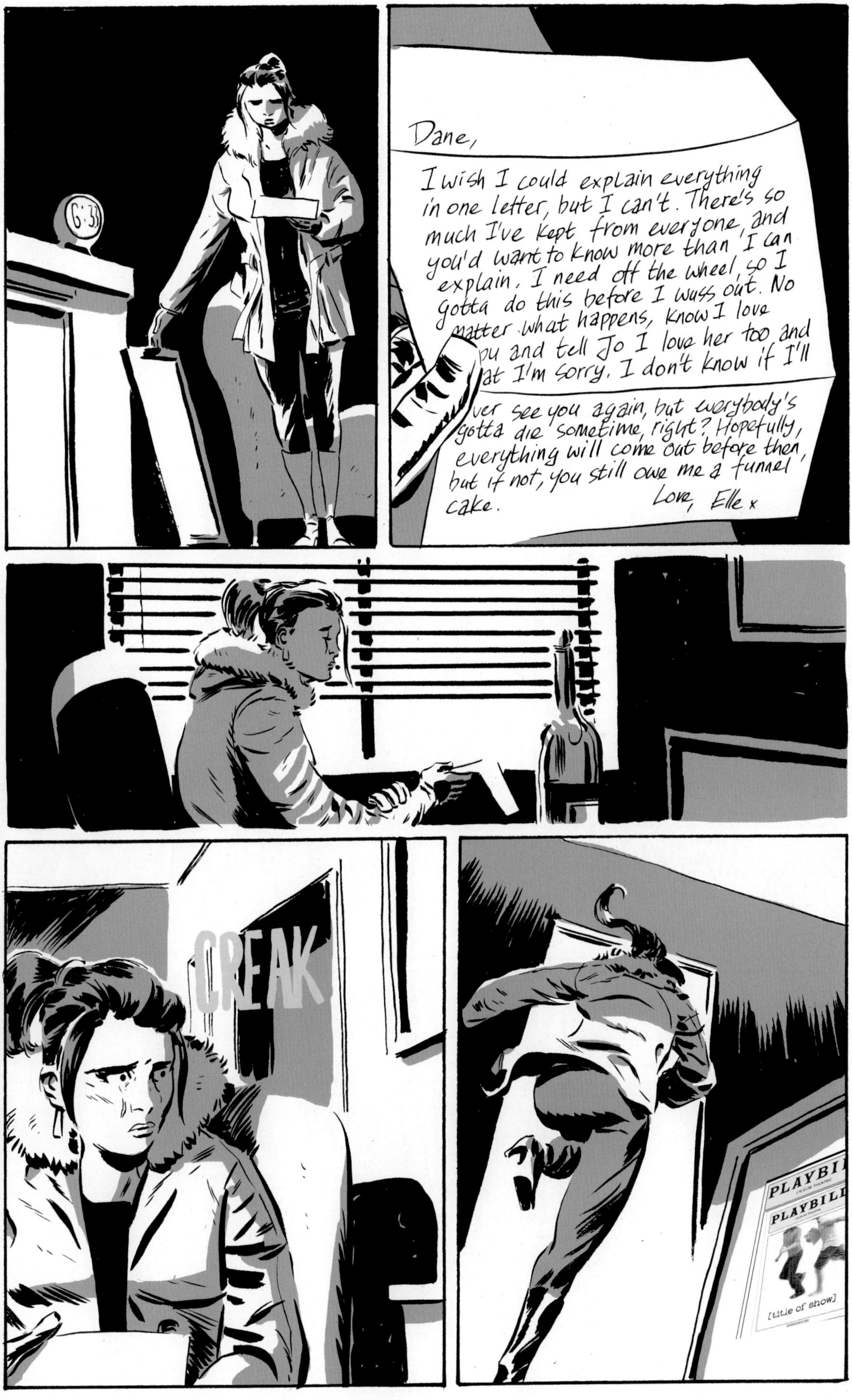

Dane,
I wish I could explain everything in one letter, but I can't. There's so much I've kept from everyone, and you'd want to know more than I can explain. I need off the wheel, so I gotta do this before I wuss out. No matter what happens, know I love ou and tell Jo I love her too and at I'm sorry. I don't know if I'll ver see you again, but everybody's gotta die sometime, right? Hopefully, everything will come out before then, but if not, you still owe me a funnel cake.
Love, Elle x
CREAK
PLAYBIL
PLAYBILL
[title of show]

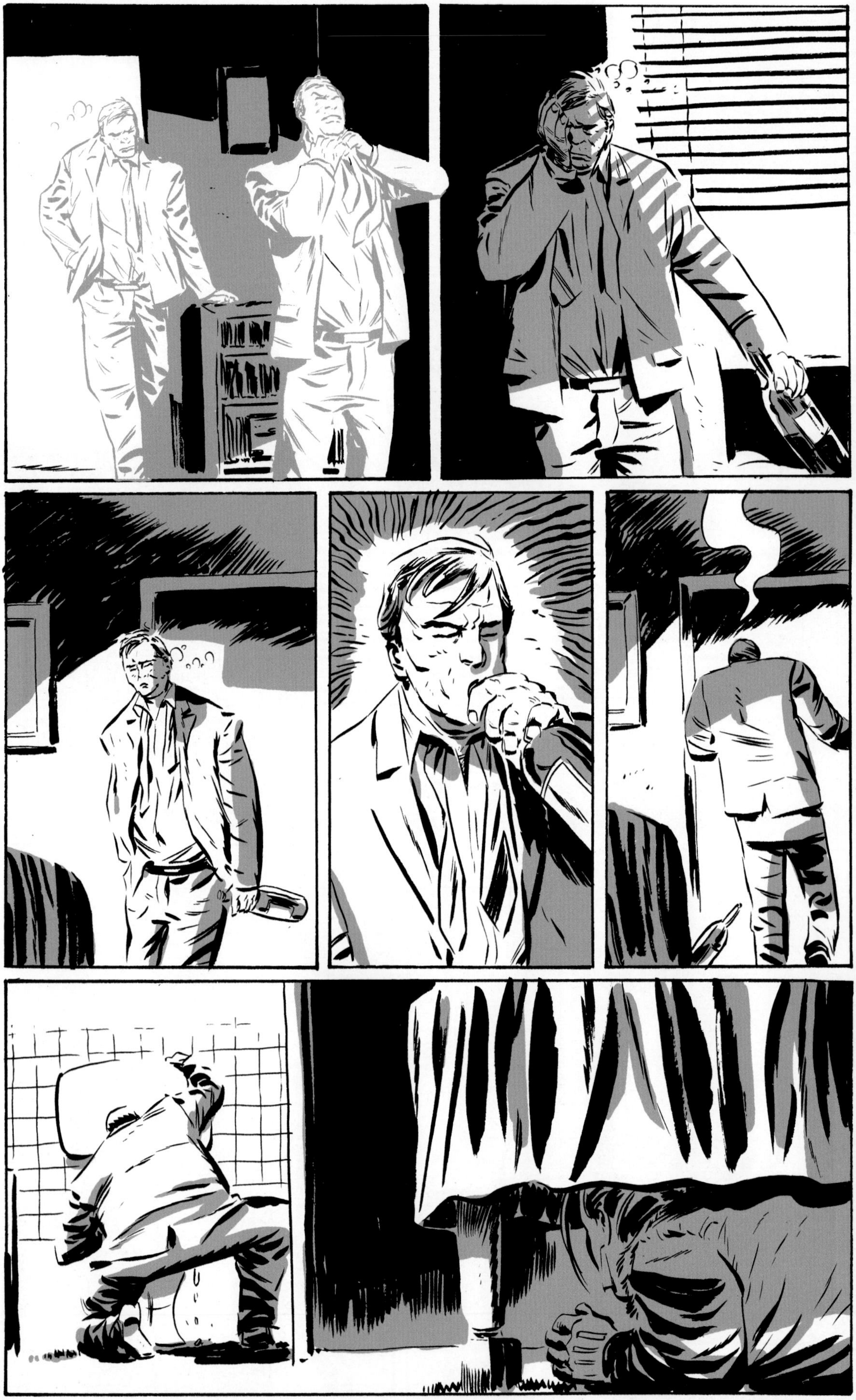

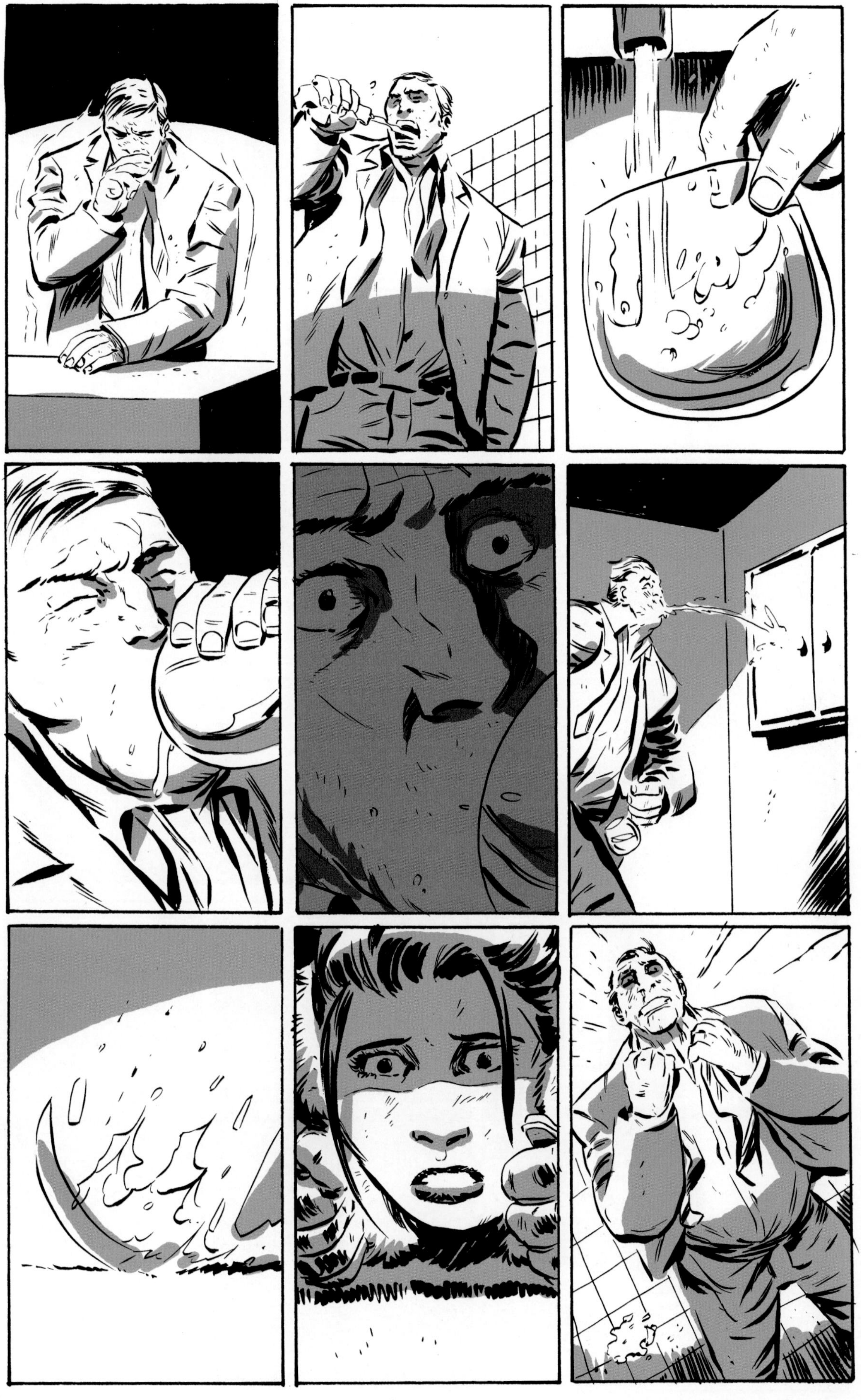

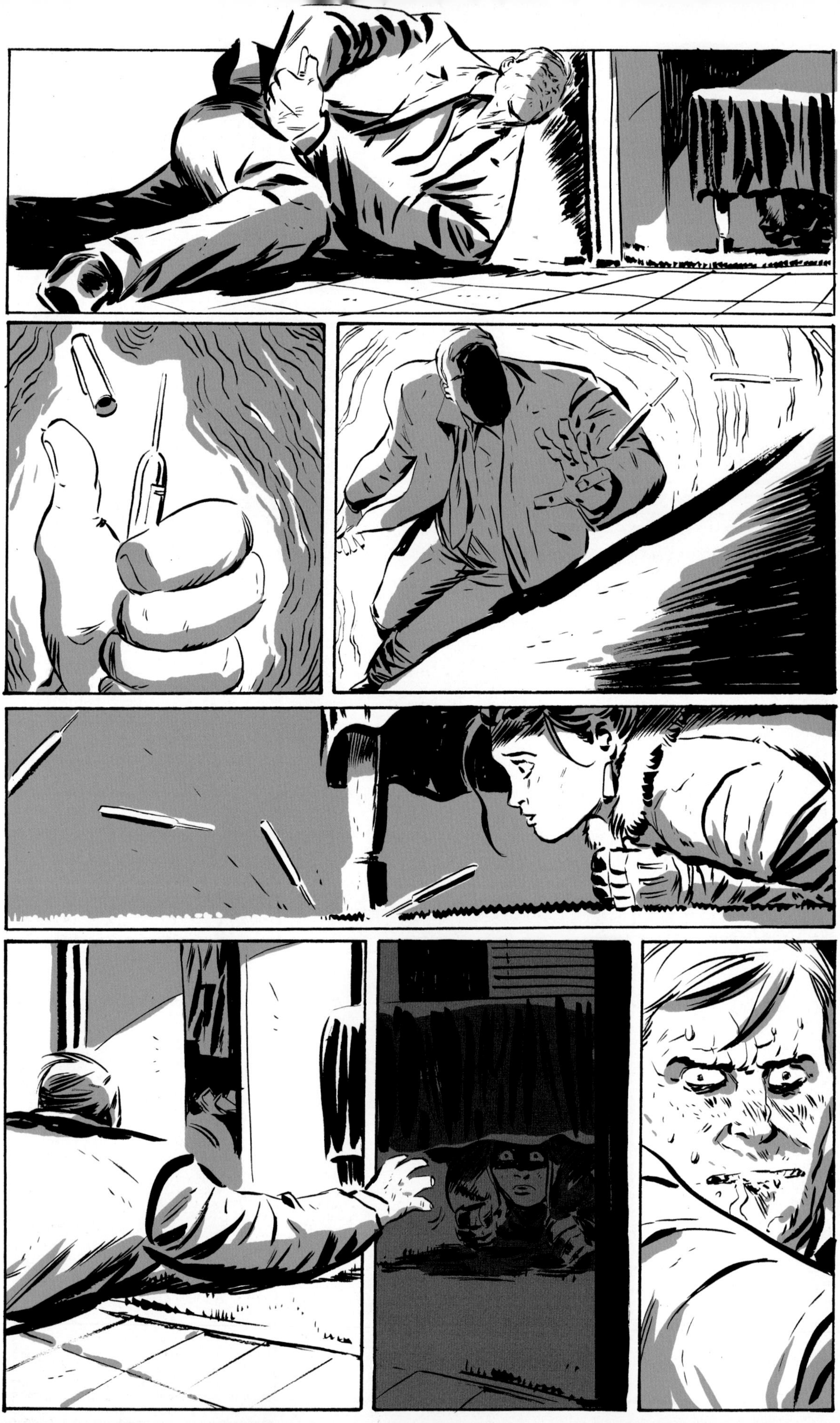

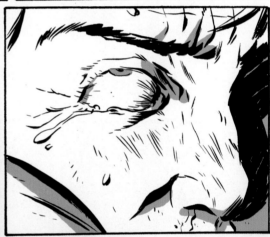

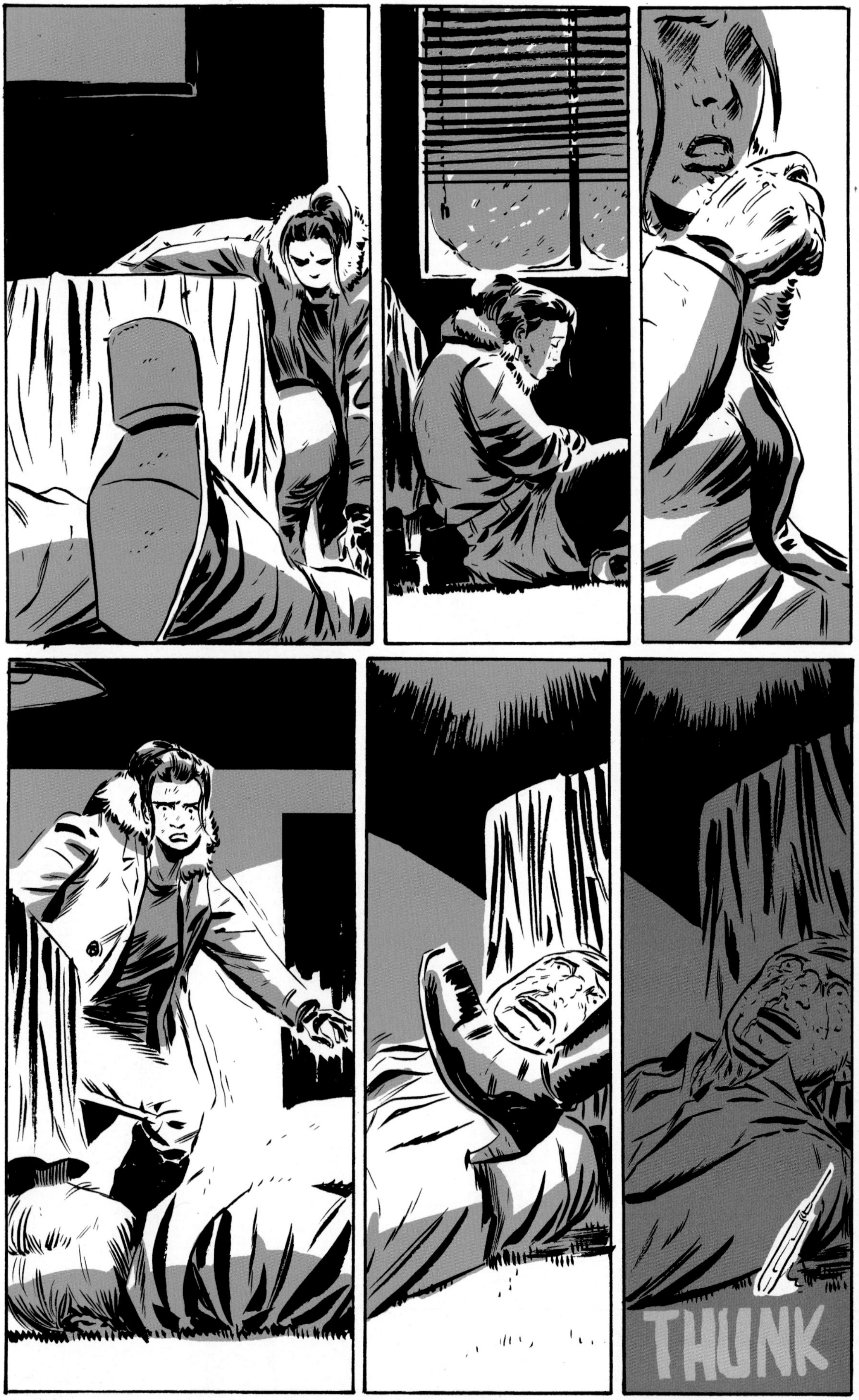
THUNK

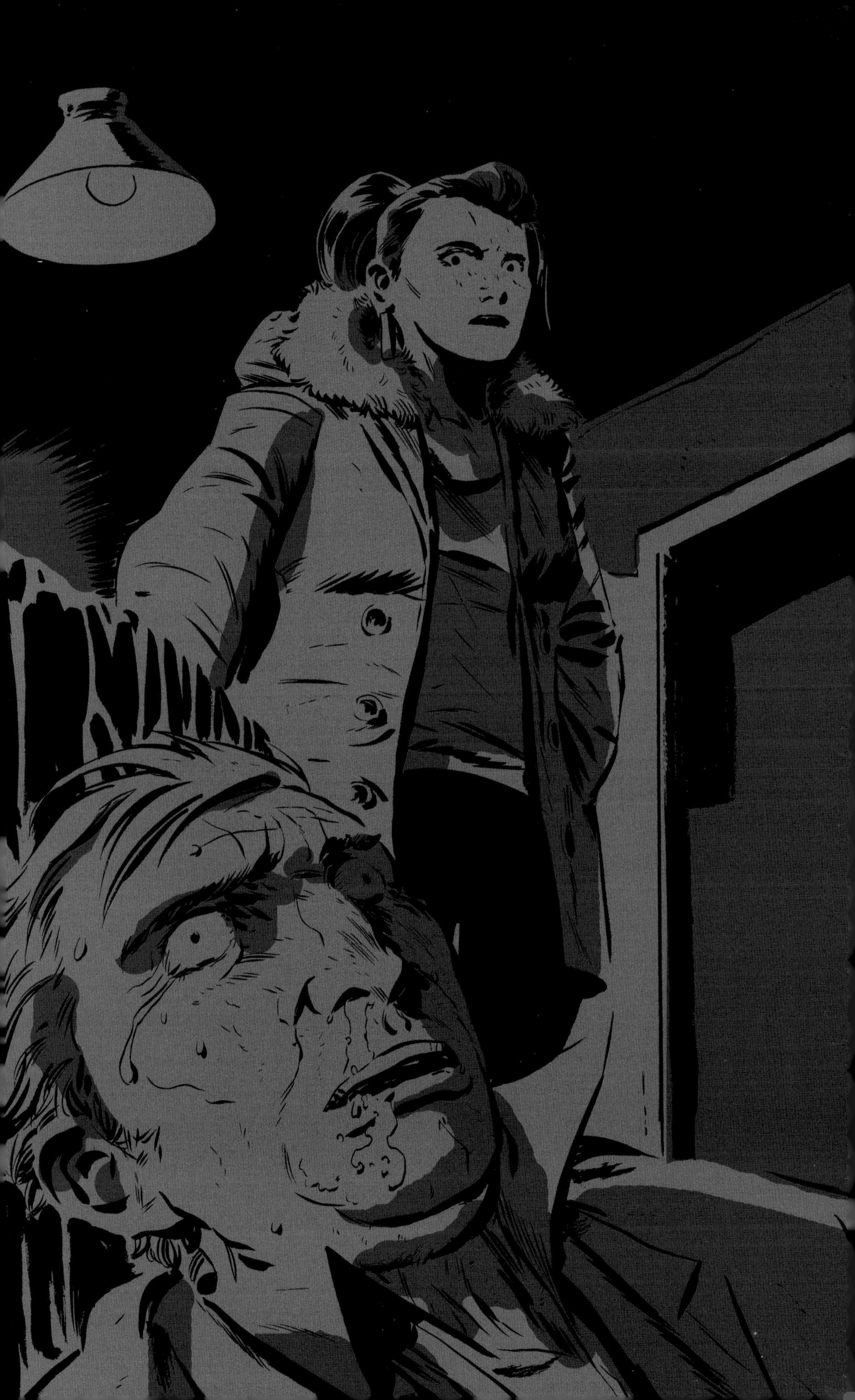

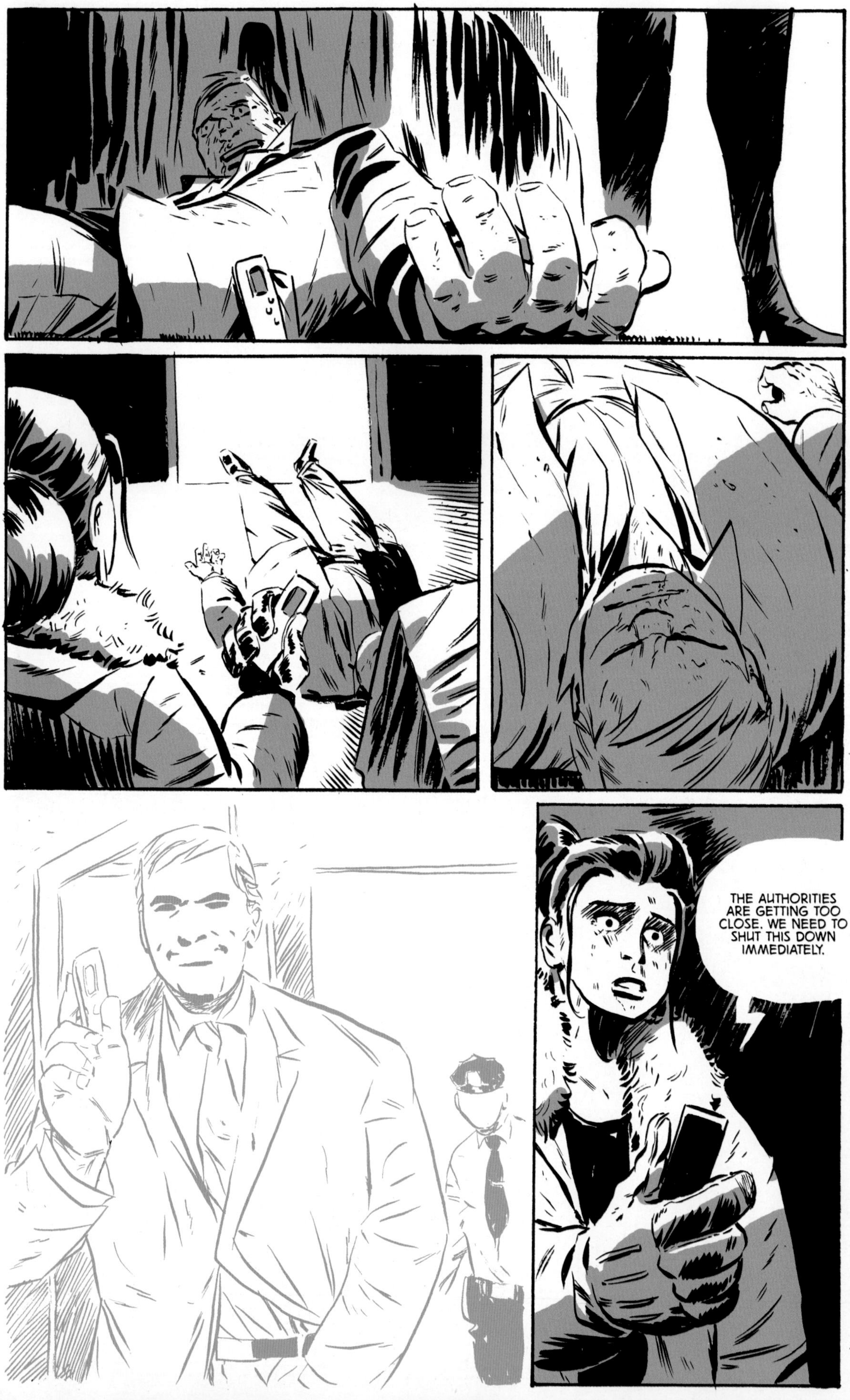
THE AUTHORITIES ARE GETTING TOO CLOSE. WE NEED TO SHUT THIS DOWN IMMEDIATELY.

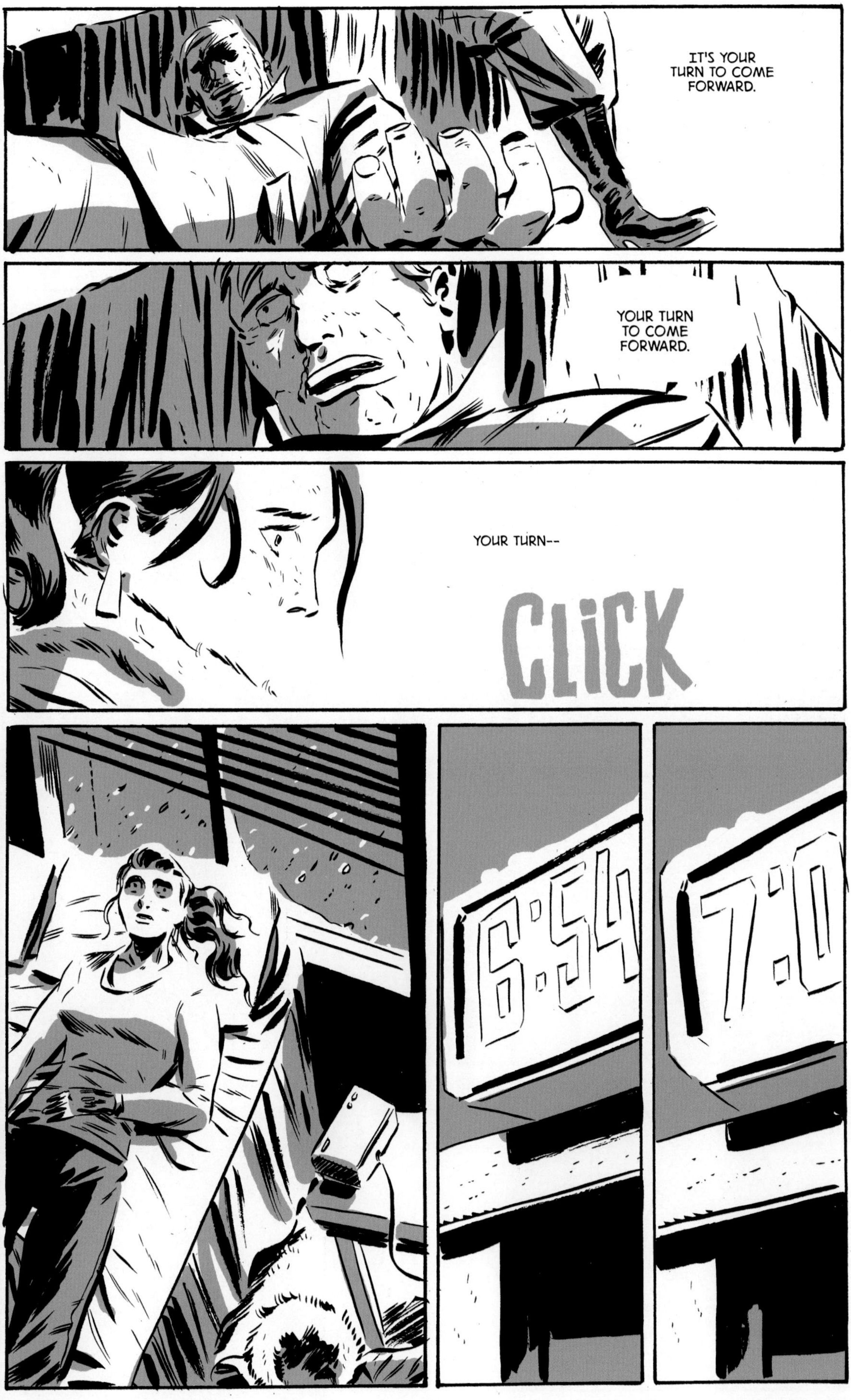
IT'S YOUR TURN TO COME FORWARD.
YOUR TURN TO COME FORWARD.
YOUR TURN--
CLICK
6:54

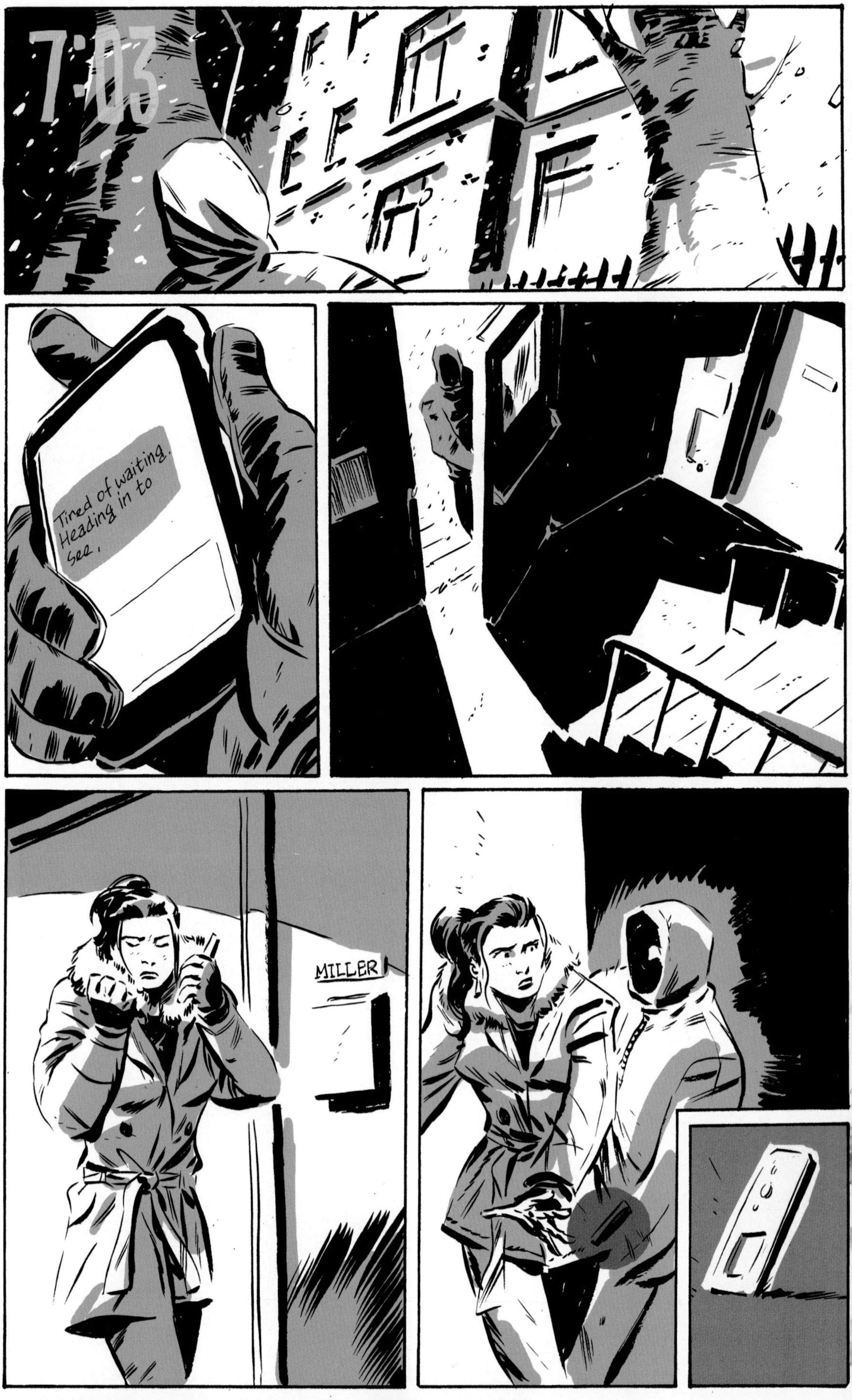
7:03
Tired of waiting. Heading in to see.
MILLER

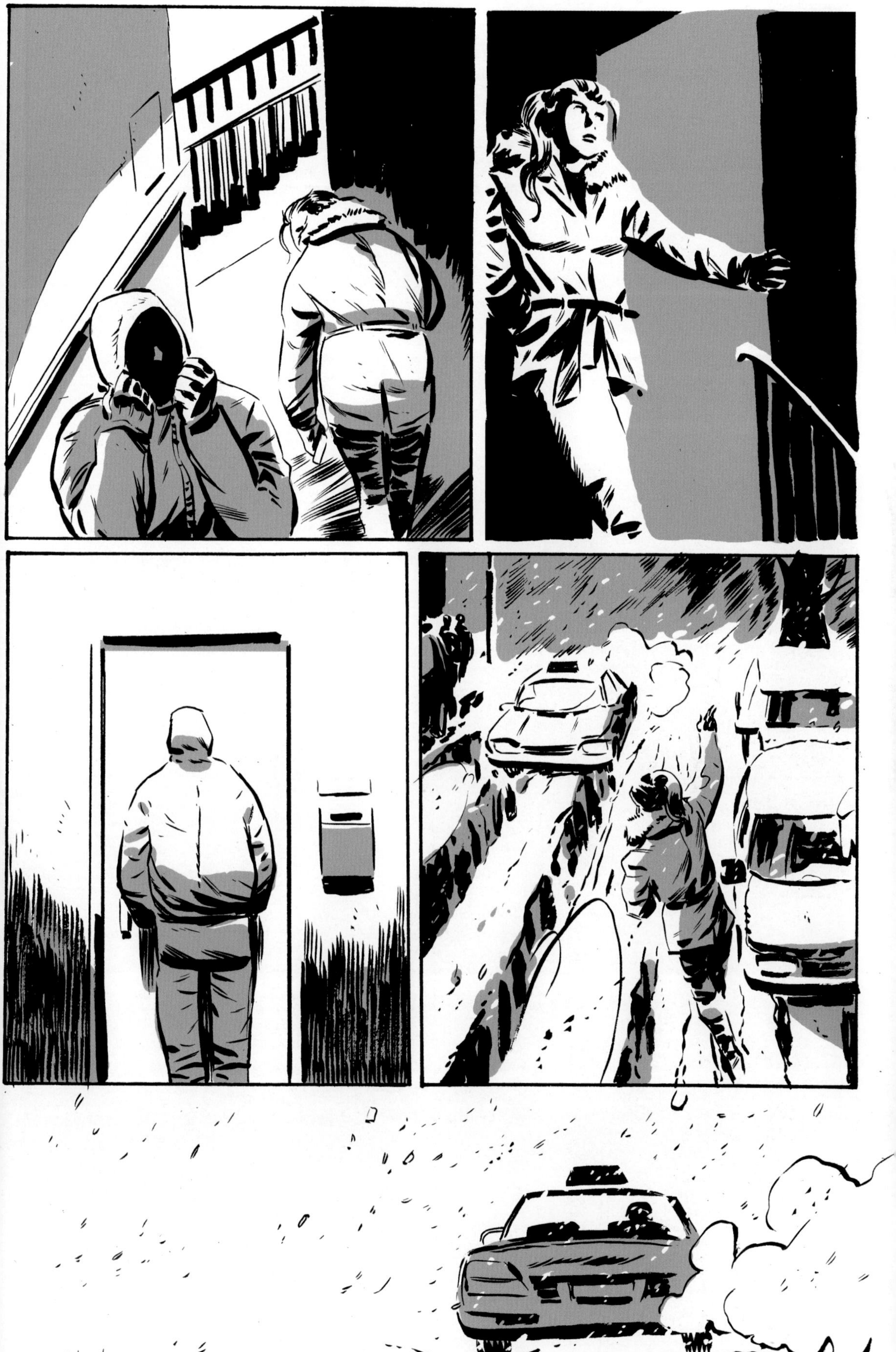

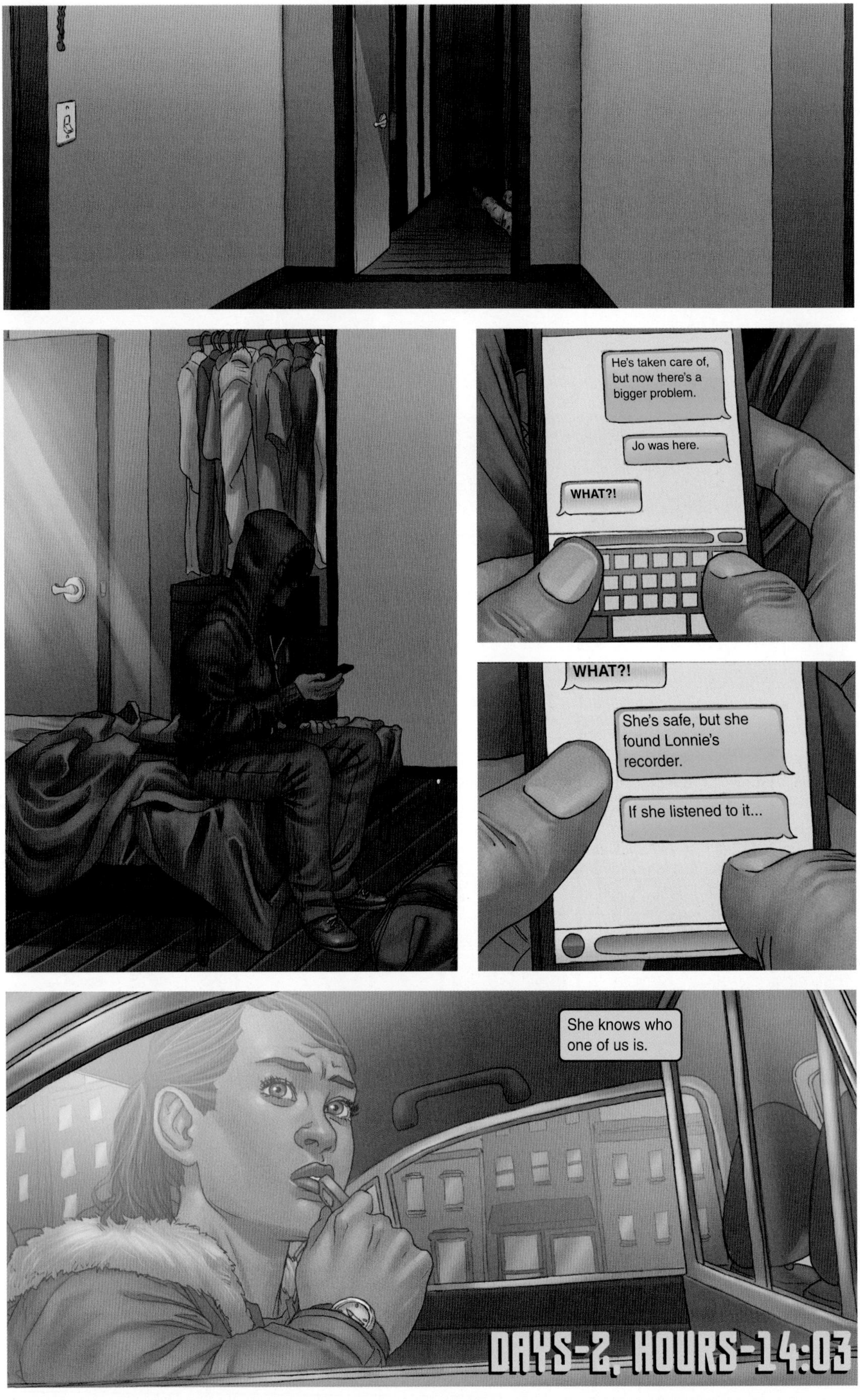
He's taken care of, but now there's a bigger problem.
Jo was here.
WHAT?!
WHAT?!
She's safe, but she found Lonnie's recorder.
If she listened to it...
She knows who one of us is.
DAYS-2, HOURS-14:03

"When we take revenge against another, we lose some of our innocence."

- Patrice Redd Vecchione,
"Revenge and Forgiveness."

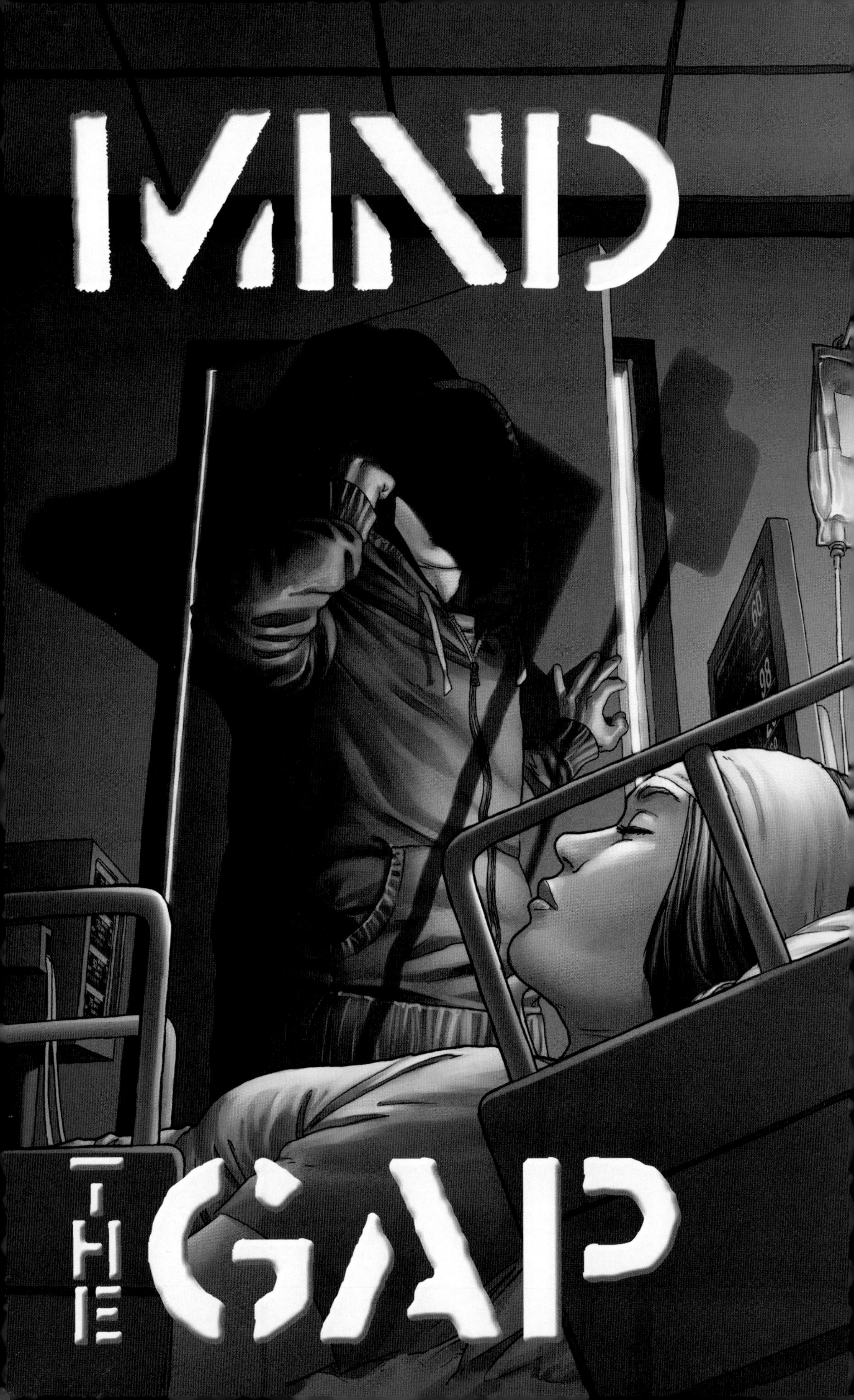
MIND
THE GAP

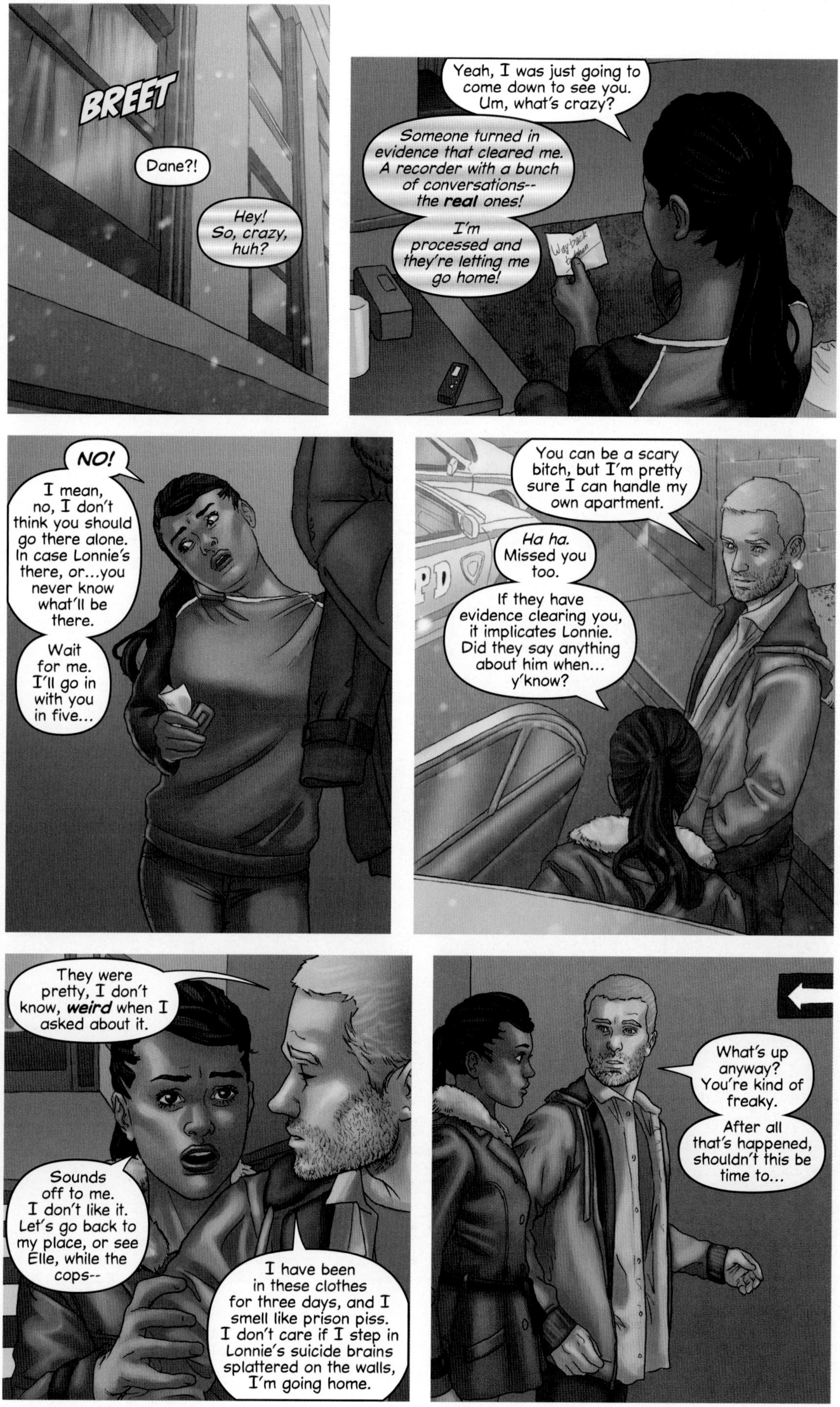
BREET
Dane?!
Hey! So, crazy, huh?
Yeah, I was just going to come down to see you. Um, what's crazy?
Someone turned in evidence that cleared me. A recorder with a bunch of conversations-- the **real** ones!
I'm processed and they're letting me go home!
NO!
I mean, no, I don't think you should go there alone. In case Lonnie's there, or...you never know what'll be there.
Wait for me. I'll go in with you in five...
You can be a scary bitch, but I'm pretty sure I can handle my own apartment.
Ha ha. Missed you too.
If they have evidence clearing you, it implicates Lonnie. Did they say anything about him when... y'know?
They were pretty, I don't know, **weird** when I asked about it.
Sounds off to me. I don't like it. Let's go back to my place, or see Elle, while the cops--
I have been in these clothes for three days, and I smell like prison piss. I don't care if I step in Lonnie's suicide brains splattered on the walls, I'm going home.
What's up anyway? You're kind of freaky.
After all that's happened, shouldn't this be time to...

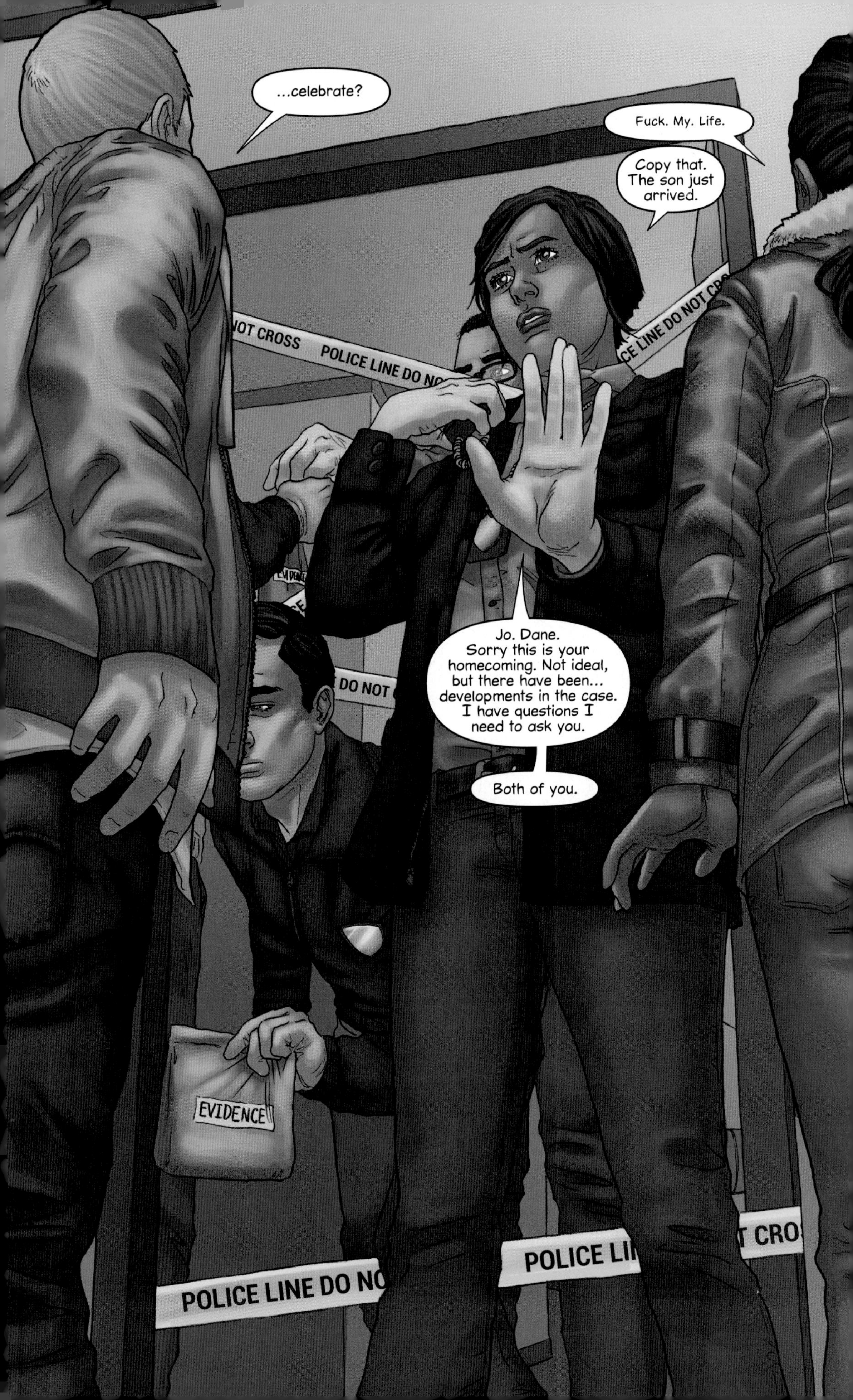
...celebrate?
Fuck. My. Life.
Copy that. The son just arrived.
NOT CROSS
POLICE LINE DO NO
CE LINE DO NOT CR
DO NOT
Jo. Dane. Sorry this is your homecoming. Not ideal, but there have been... developments in the case. I have questions I need to ask you.
Both of you.
EVIDENCE
POLICE LINE DO NO
POLICE LI
T CROS

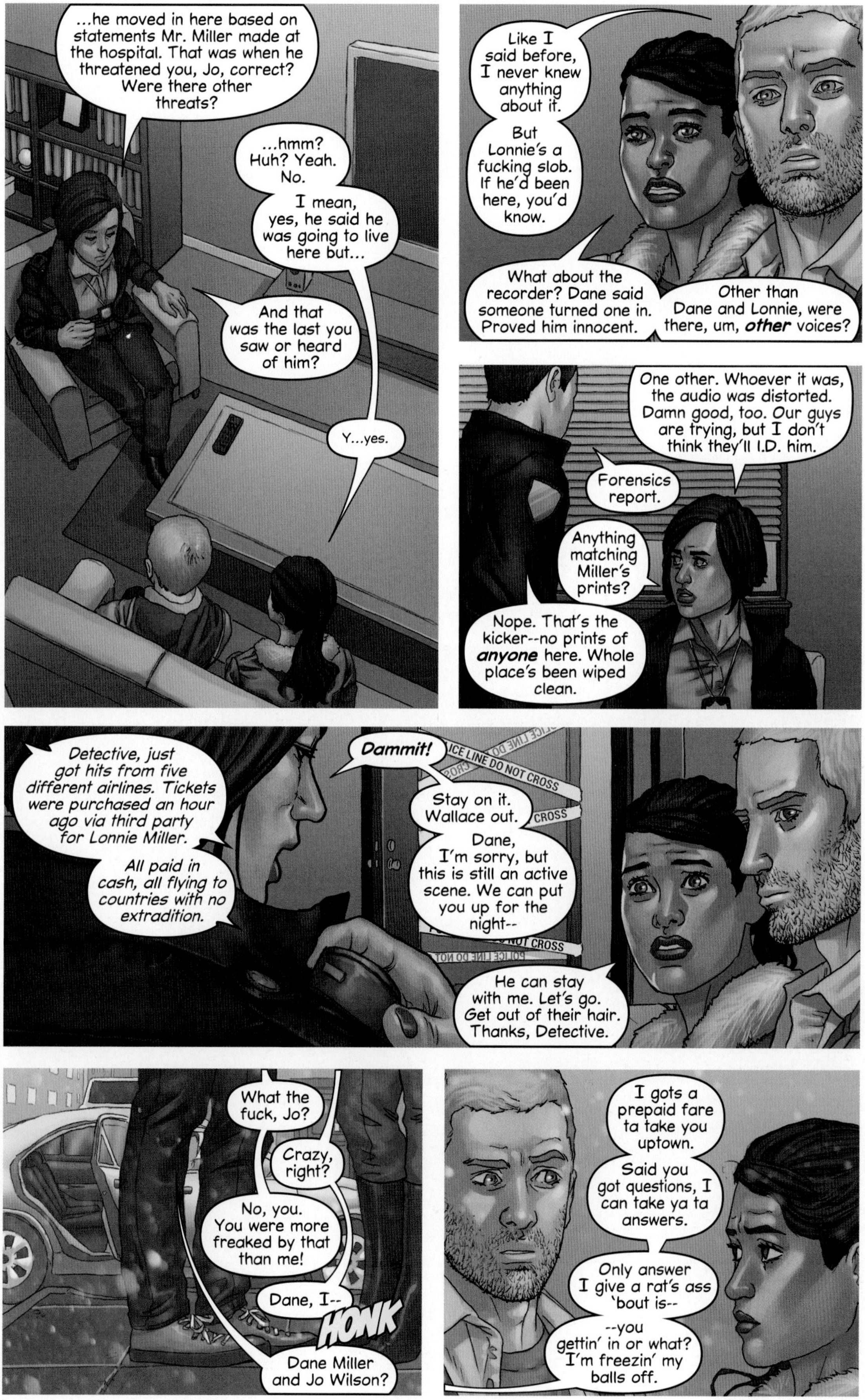
...he moved in here based on statements Mr. Miller made at the hospital. That was when he threatened you, Jo, correct? Were there other threats?
...hmm? Huh? Yeah. No.
I mean, yes, he said he was going to live here but...
And that was the last you saw or heard of him?
Y...yes.
Like I said before, I never knew anything about it.
But Lonnie's a fucking slob. If he'd been here, you'd know.
What about the recorder? Dane said someone turned one in. Proved him innocent.
Other than Dane and Lonnie, were there, um, *other* voices?
One other. Whoever it was, the audio was distorted. Damn good, too. Our guys are trying, but I don't think they'll I.D. him.
Forensics report.
Anything matching Miller's prints?
Nope. That's the kicker--no prints of *anyone* here. Whole place's been wiped clean.
Detective, just got hits from five different airlines. Tickets were purchased an hour ago via third party for Lonnie Miller.
All paid in cash, all flying to countries with no extradition.
Dammit!
POLICE LINE DO NOT CROSS
Stay on it. Wallace out.
Dane, I'm sorry, but this is still an active scene. We can put you up for the night--
He can stay with me. Let's go. Get out of their hair. Thanks, Detective.
What the fuck, Jo?
Crazy, right?
No, you. You were more freaked by that than me!
Dane, I--
HONK
Dane Miller and Jo Wilson?
I gots a prepaid fare ta take you uptown.
Said you got questions, I can take ya ta answers.
Only answer I give a rat's ass 'bout is--
--you gettin' in or what? I'm freezin' my balls off.

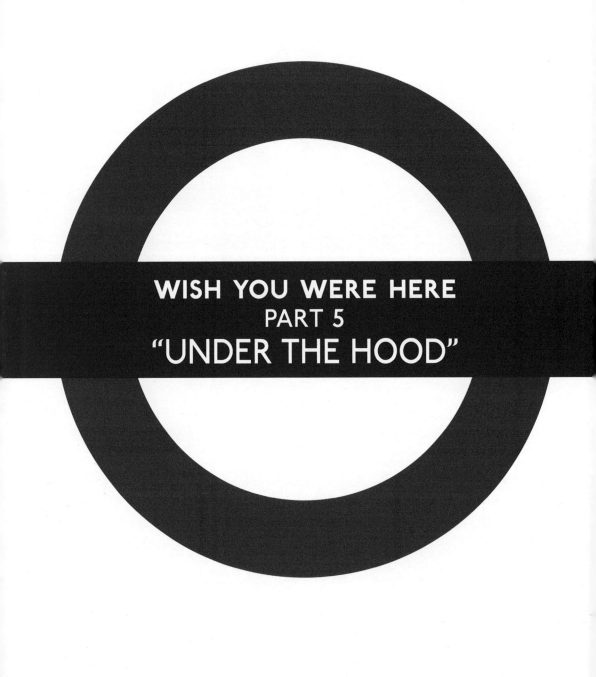

WISH YOU WERE HERE
PART 5
"UNDER THE HOOD"

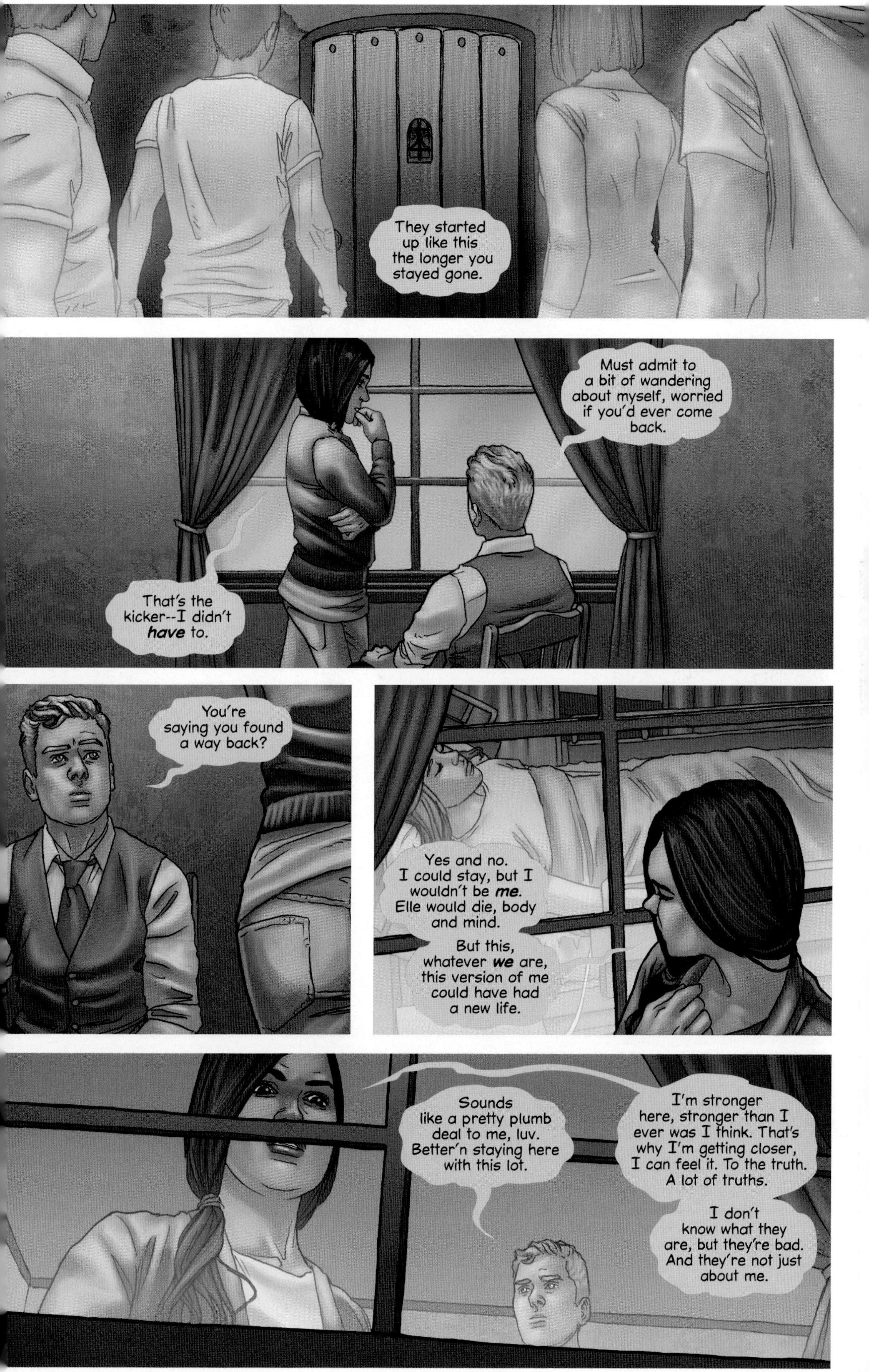
They started up like this the longer you stayed gone.
Must admit to a bit of wandering about myself, worried if you'd ever come back.
That's the kicker--I didn't *have* to.
You're saying you found a way back?
Yes and no. I could stay, but I wouldn't be *me*. Elle would die, body and mind.
But this, whatever *we* are, this version of me could have had a new life.
Sounds like a pretty plumb deal to me, luv. Better'n staying here with this lot.
I'm stronger here, stronger than I ever was I think. That's why I'm getting closer, I can feel it. To the truth. A lot of truths.
I don't know what they are, but they're bad. And they're not just about me.

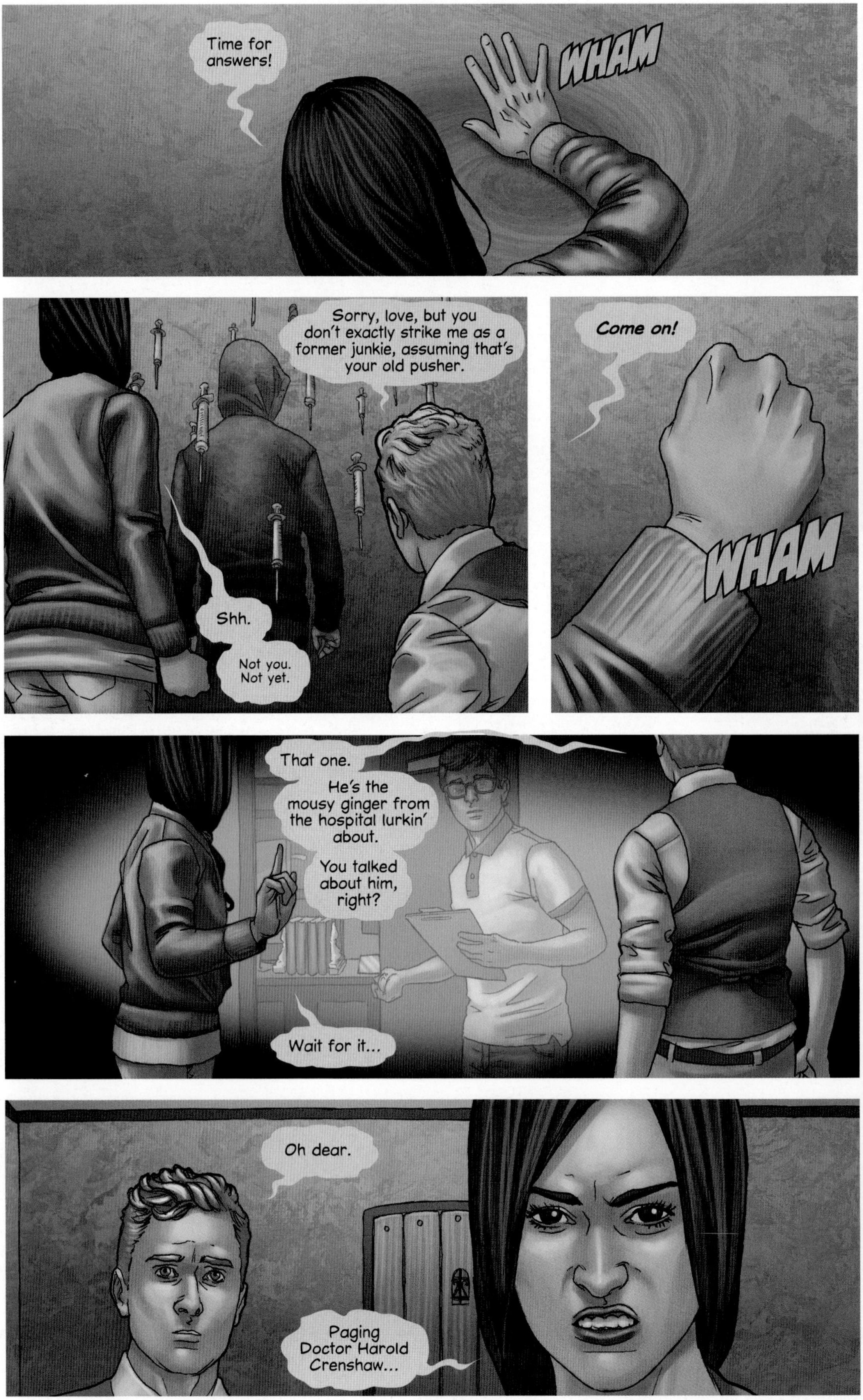
Time for answers!
WHAM
Sorry, love, but you don't exactly strike me as a former junkie, assuming that's your old pusher.
Shh.
Not you. Not yet.
Come on!
WHAM
That one.
He's the mousy ginger from the hospital lurkin' about.
You talked about him, right?
Wait for it...
Oh dear.
Paging Doctor Harold Crenshaw...

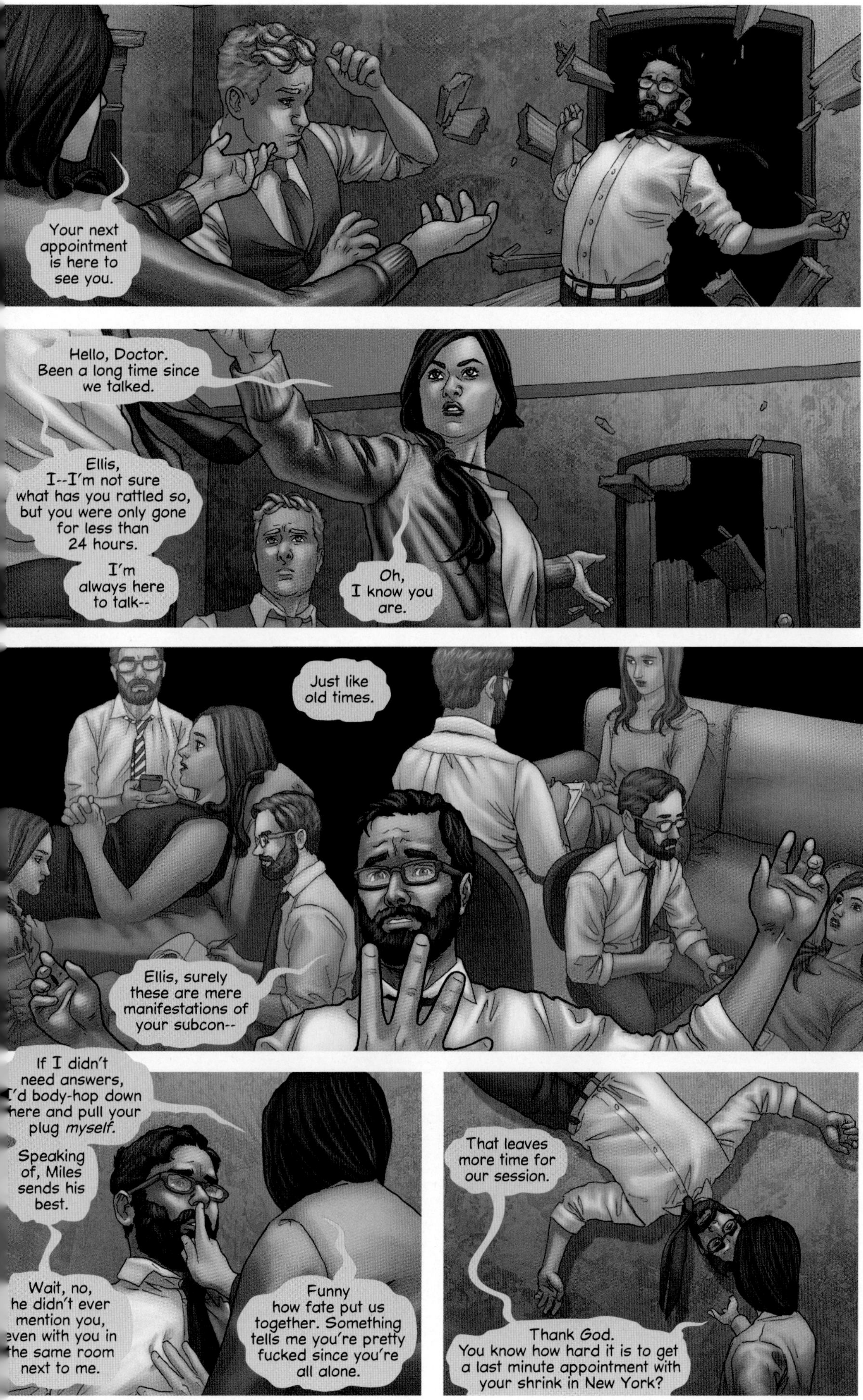

Your next appointment is here to see you.
Hello, Doctor. Been a long time since we talked.
Ellis, I--I'm not sure what has you rattled so, but you were only gone for less than 24 hours.
I'm always here to talk--
Oh, I know you are.
Just like old times.
Ellis, surely these are mere manifestations of your subcon--
If I didn't need answers, I'd body-hop down here and pull your plug *myself*.
Speaking of, Miles sends his best.
Wait, no, he didn't ever mention you, even with you in the same room next to me.
Funny how fate put us together. Something tells me you're pretty fucked since you're all alone.
That leaves more time for our session.
Thank God. You know how hard it is to get a last minute appointment with your shrink in New York?

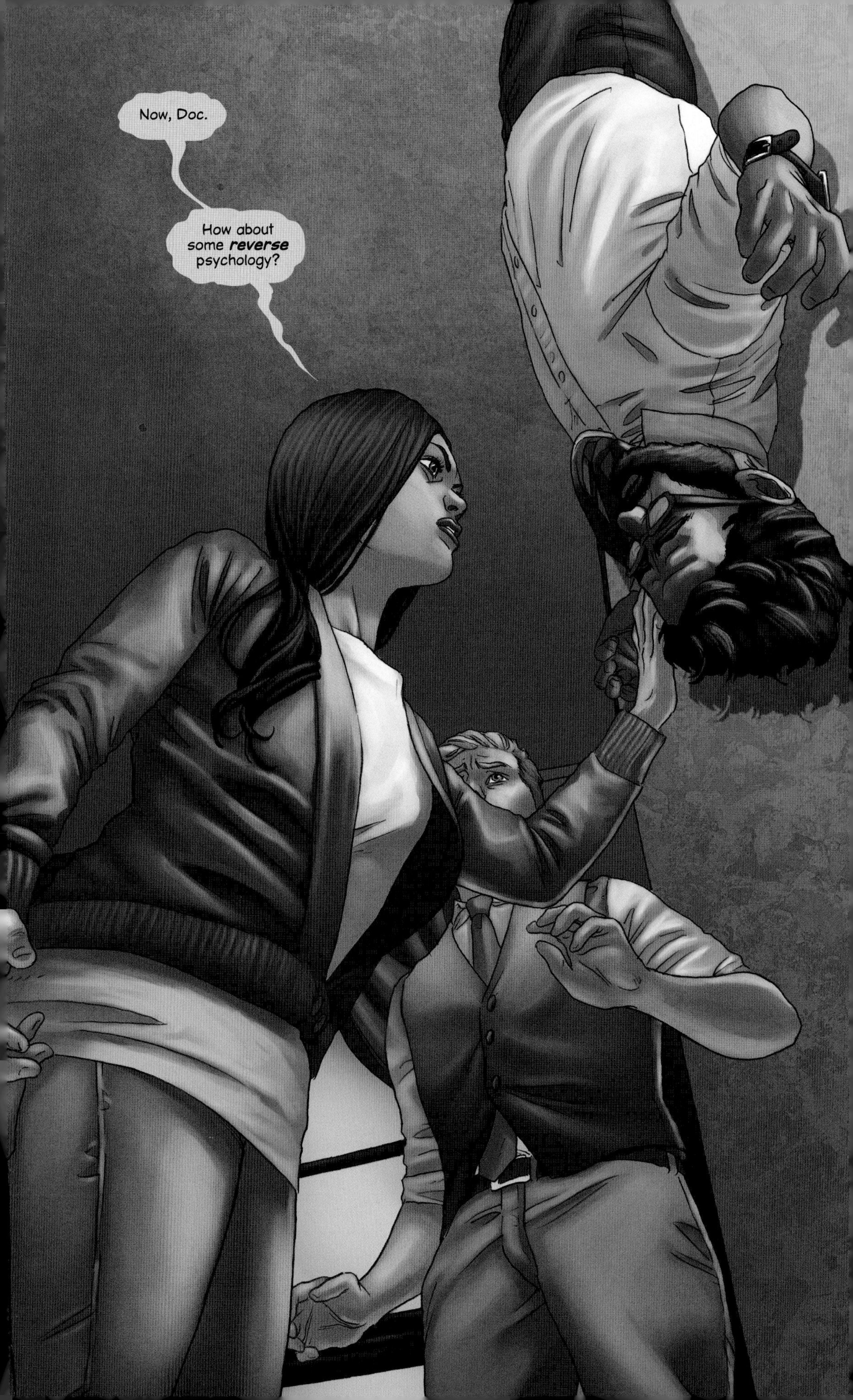
Now, Doc.
How about some *reverse* psychology?

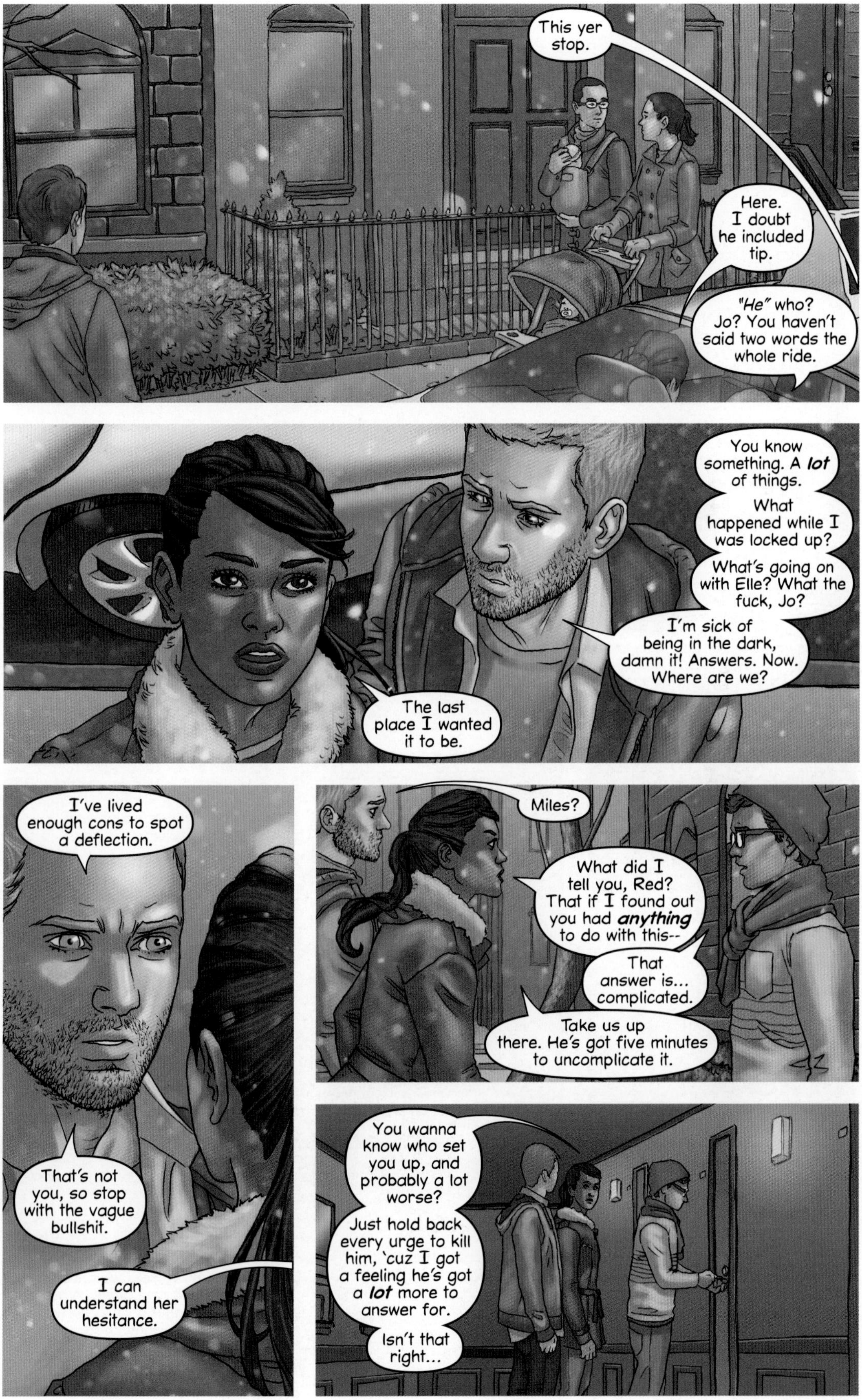
This yer stop.
Here. I doubt he included tip.
"He" who? Jo? You haven't said two words the whole ride.
You know something. A *lot* of things.
What happened while I was locked up?
What's going on with Elle? What the fuck, Jo?
I'm sick of being in the dark, damn it! Answers. Now. Where are we?
The last place I wanted it to be.
I've lived enough cons to spot a deflection.
That's not you, so stop with the vague bullshit.
I can understand her hesitance.
Miles?
What did I tell you, Red? That if I found out you had ***anything*** to do with this--
That answer is... complicated.
Take us up there. He's got five minutes to uncomplicate it.
You wanna know who set you up, and probably a lot worse?
Just hold back every urge to kill him, 'cuz I got a feeling he's got a *lot* more to answer for.
Isn't that right...

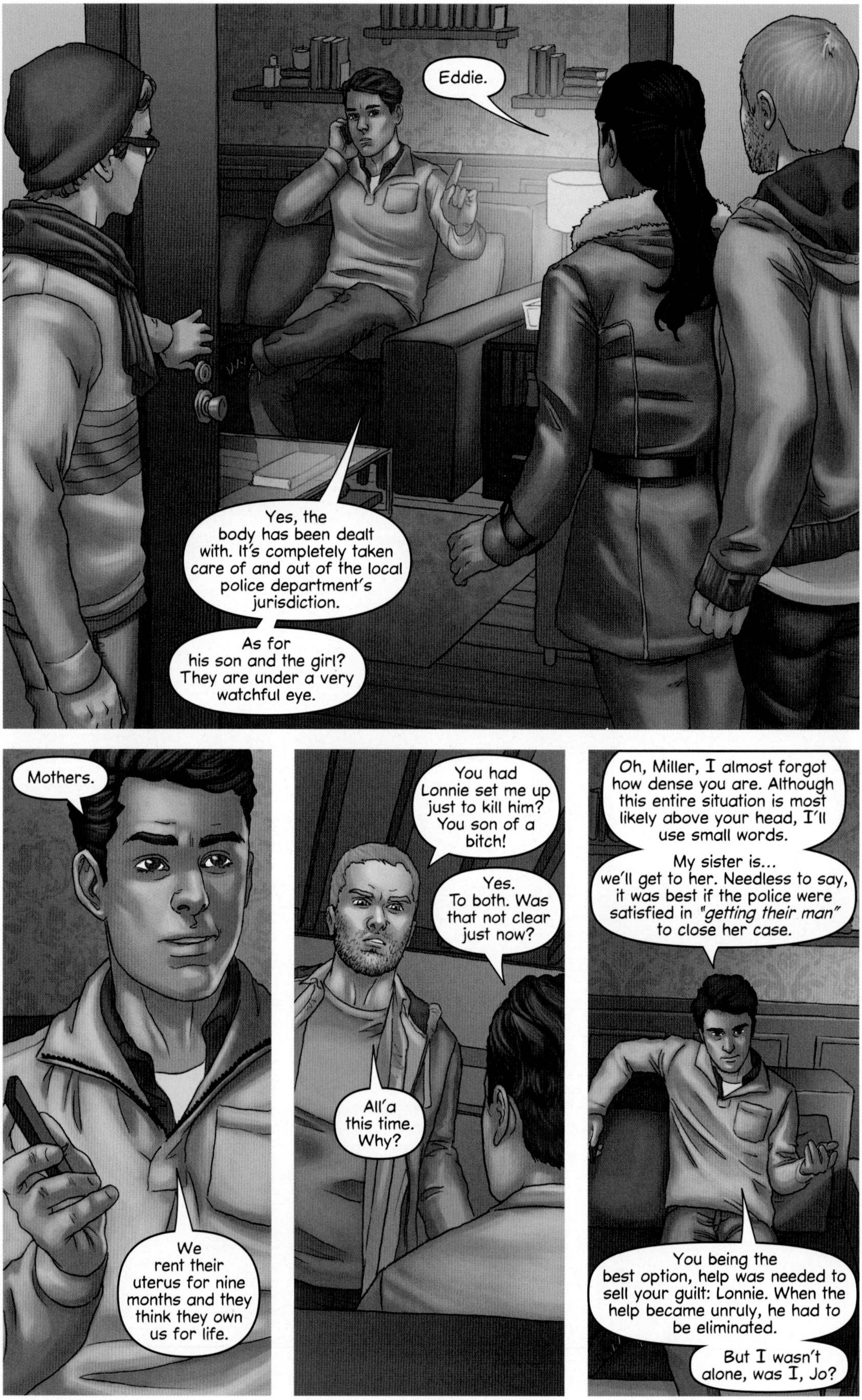
Eddie.
Yes, the body has been dealt with. It's completely taken care of and out of the local police department's jurisdiction.
As for his son and the girl? They are under a very watchful eye.
Mothers.
We rent their uterus for nine months and they think they own us for life.
You had Lonnie set me up just to kill him? You son of a bitch!
Yes. To both. Was that not clear just now?
All'a this time. Why?
Oh, Miller, I almost forgot how dense you are. Although this entire situation is most likely above your head, I'll use small words.
My sister is... we'll get to her. Needless to say, it was best if the police were satisfied in *"getting their man"* to close her case.
You being the best option, help was needed to sell your guilt: Lonnie. When the help became unruly, he had to be eliminated.
But I wasn't alone, was I, Jo?

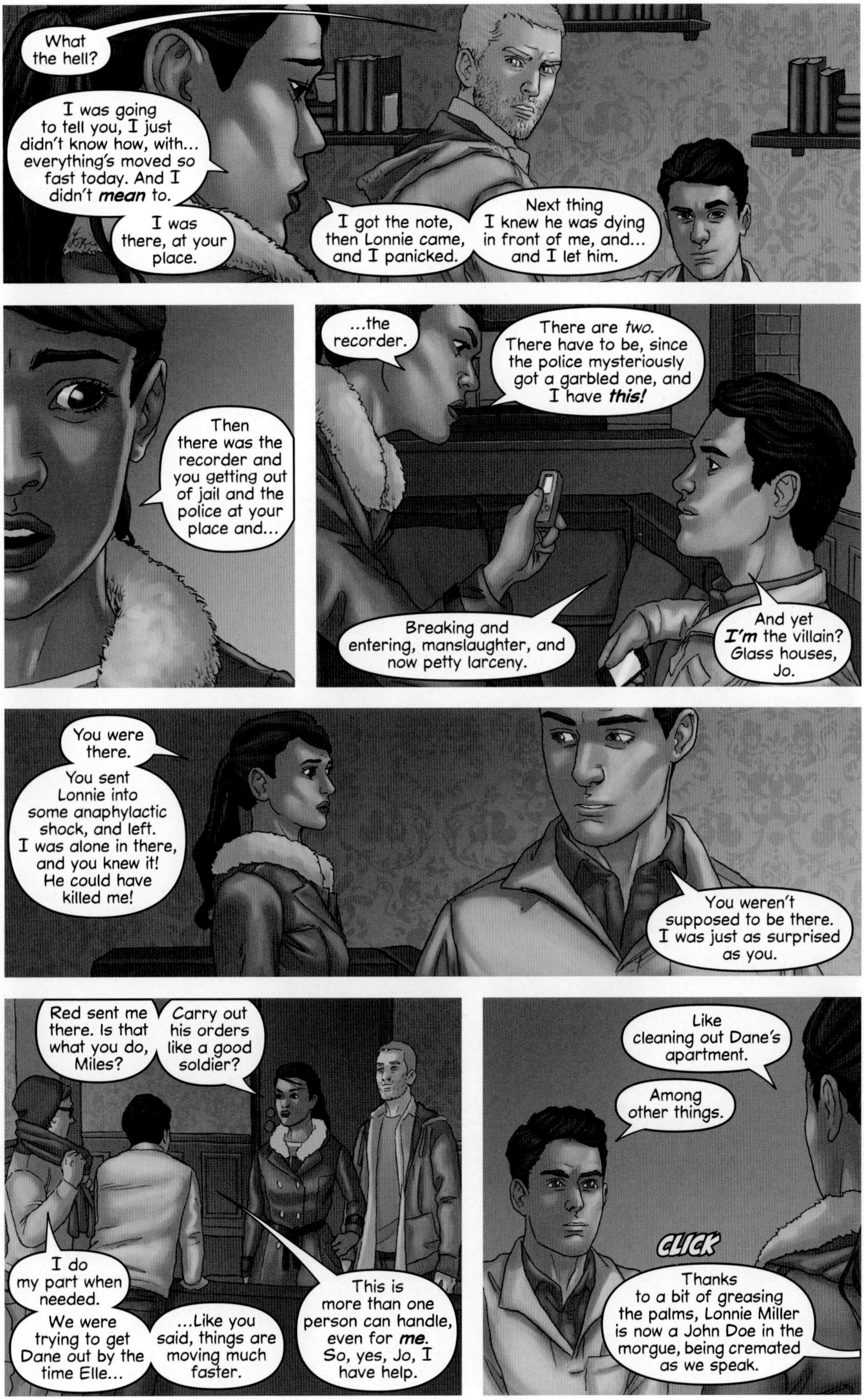
What the hell?
I was going to tell you, I just didn't know how, with... everything's moved so fast today. And I didn't *mean* to.
I was there, at your place.
I got the note, then Lonnie came, and I panicked.
Next thing I knew he was dying in front of me, and... and I let him.
Then there was the recorder and you getting out of jail and the police at your place and...
...the recorder.
There are *two.* There have to be, since the police mysteriously got a garbled one, and I have ***this!***
Breaking and entering, manslaughter, and now petty larceny.
And yet ***I'm*** the villain? Glass houses, Jo.
You were there.
You sent Lonnie into some anaphylactic shock, and left. I was alone in there, and you knew it! He could have killed me!
You weren't supposed to be there. I was just as surprised as you.
Red sent me there. Is that what you do, Miles?
Carry out his orders like a good soldier?
I do my part when needed.
We were trying to get Dane out by the time Elle...
...Like you said, things are moving much faster.
This is more than one person can handle, even for ***me.*** So, yes, Jo, I have help.
Like cleaning out Dane's apartment.
Among other things.
CLICK
Thanks to a bit of greasing the palms, Lonnie Miller is now a John Doe in the morgue, being cremated as we speak.

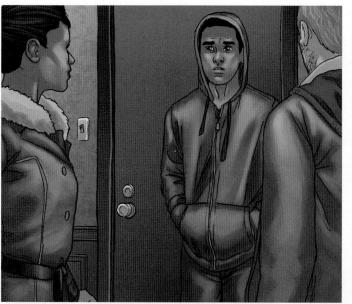

THIS you don't text me about?!

This isn't what it looks like, Dane.

So you didn't come here to tell my dad's killer you just made the body go away? Cover his tracks?

Okay, that part is what it looks like. But Jo, I--

Save it. Your *"let me explain"* eyes, in your fucking scrubs and that damn hoodie. I can't even...

...hoodie...

Elle said, her last words before she-- before Katie died--she said something about being attacked by someone in a hoodie. That's what put her in the coma.

It was one of you. Which of you fuckers tried to kill Elle?

As usual, Jo, you only know part of the story, filling in the rest with your imagination. My sister's condition...

I was with her on the 50th Street platform, but I assure you, she was not attacked.

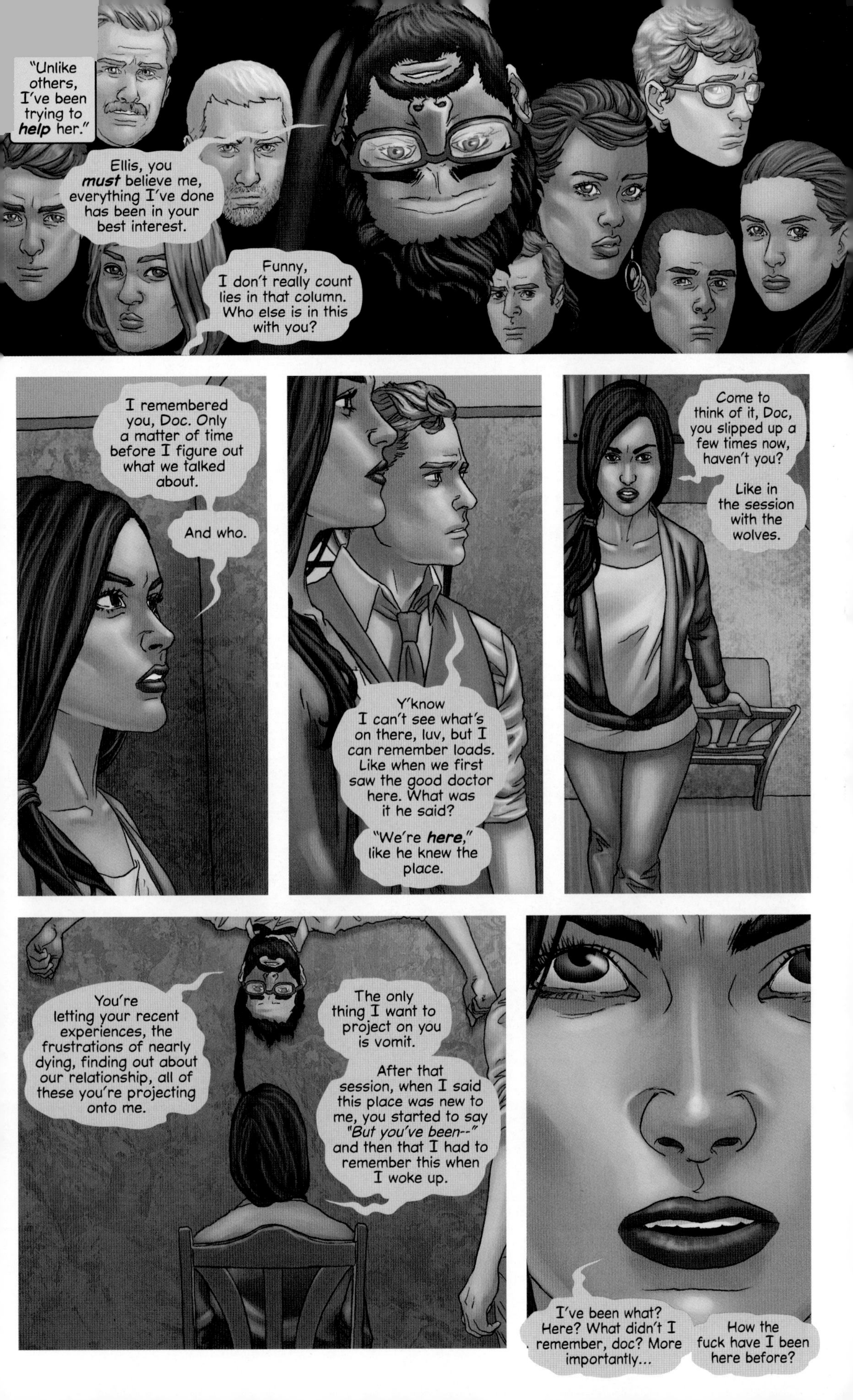
"Unlike others, I've been trying to *help* her."
Ellis, you *must* believe me, everything I've done has been in your best interest.
Funny, I don't really count lies in that column. Who else is in this with you?
I remembered you, Doc. Only a matter of time before I figure out what we talked about.
And who.
Y'know I can't see what's on there, luv, but I can remember loads. Like when we first saw the good doctor here. What was it he said?
"We're *here*," like he knew the place.
Come to think of it, Doc, you slipped up a few times now, haven't you?
Like in the session with the wolves.
You're letting your recent experiences, the frustrations of nearly dying, finding out about our relationship, all of these you're projecting onto me.
The only thing I want to project on you is vomit.
After that session, when I said this place was new to me, you started to say *"But you've been--"* and then that I had to remember this when I woke up.
I've been what? Here? What didn't I remember, doc? More importantly...
How the fuck have I been here before?

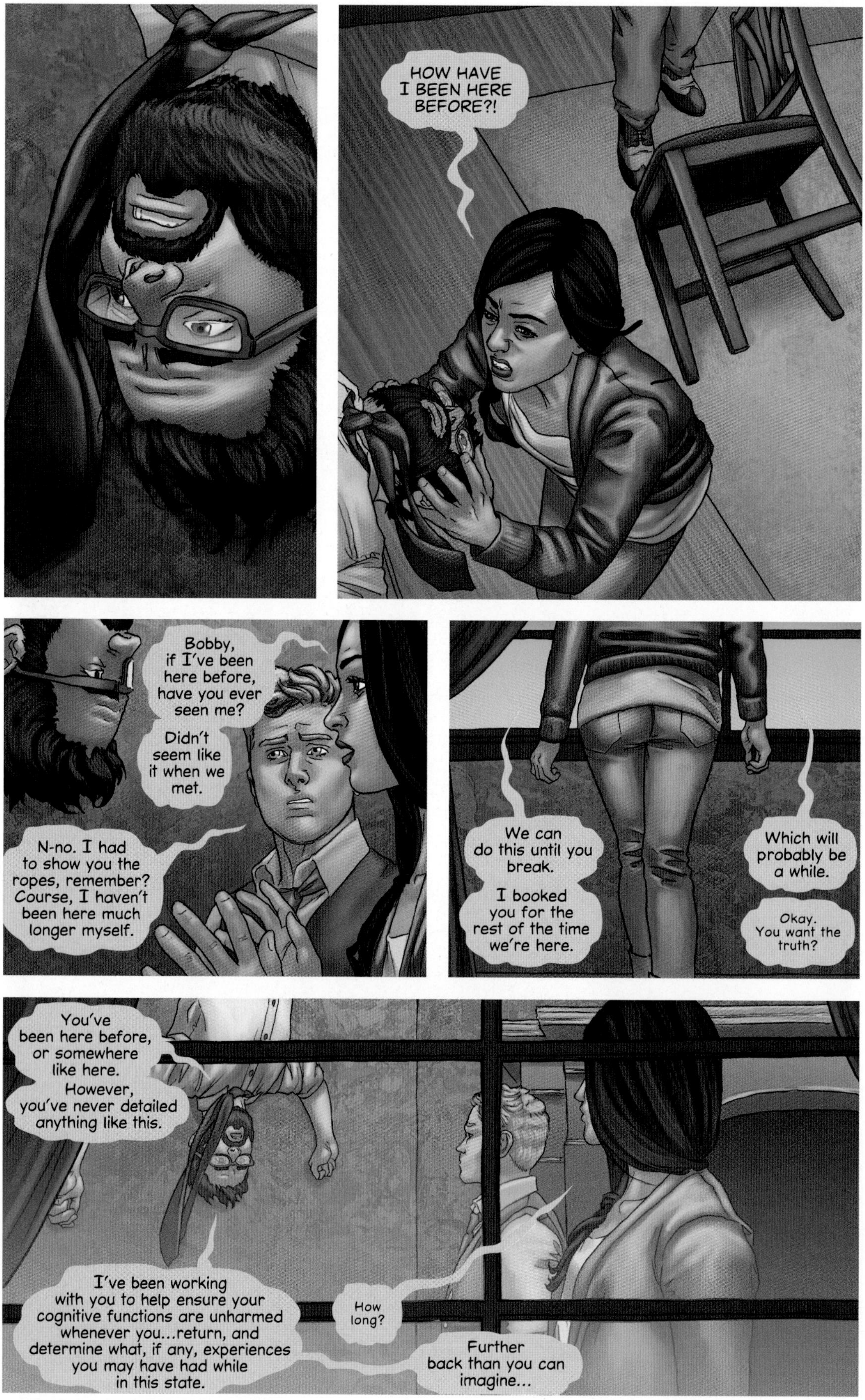

HOW HAVE I BEEN HERE BEFORE?!
Bobby, if I've been here before, have you ever seen me?
Didn't seem like it when we met.
N-no. I had to show you the ropes, remember? Course, I haven't been here much longer myself.
We can do this until you break.
I booked you for the rest of the time we're here.
Which will probably be a while.
Okay. You want the truth?
You've been here before, or somewhere like here.
However, you've never detailed anything like this.
I've been working with you to help ensure your cognitive functions are unharmed whenever you...return, and determine what, if any, experiences you may have had while in this state.
How long?
Further back than you can imagine...

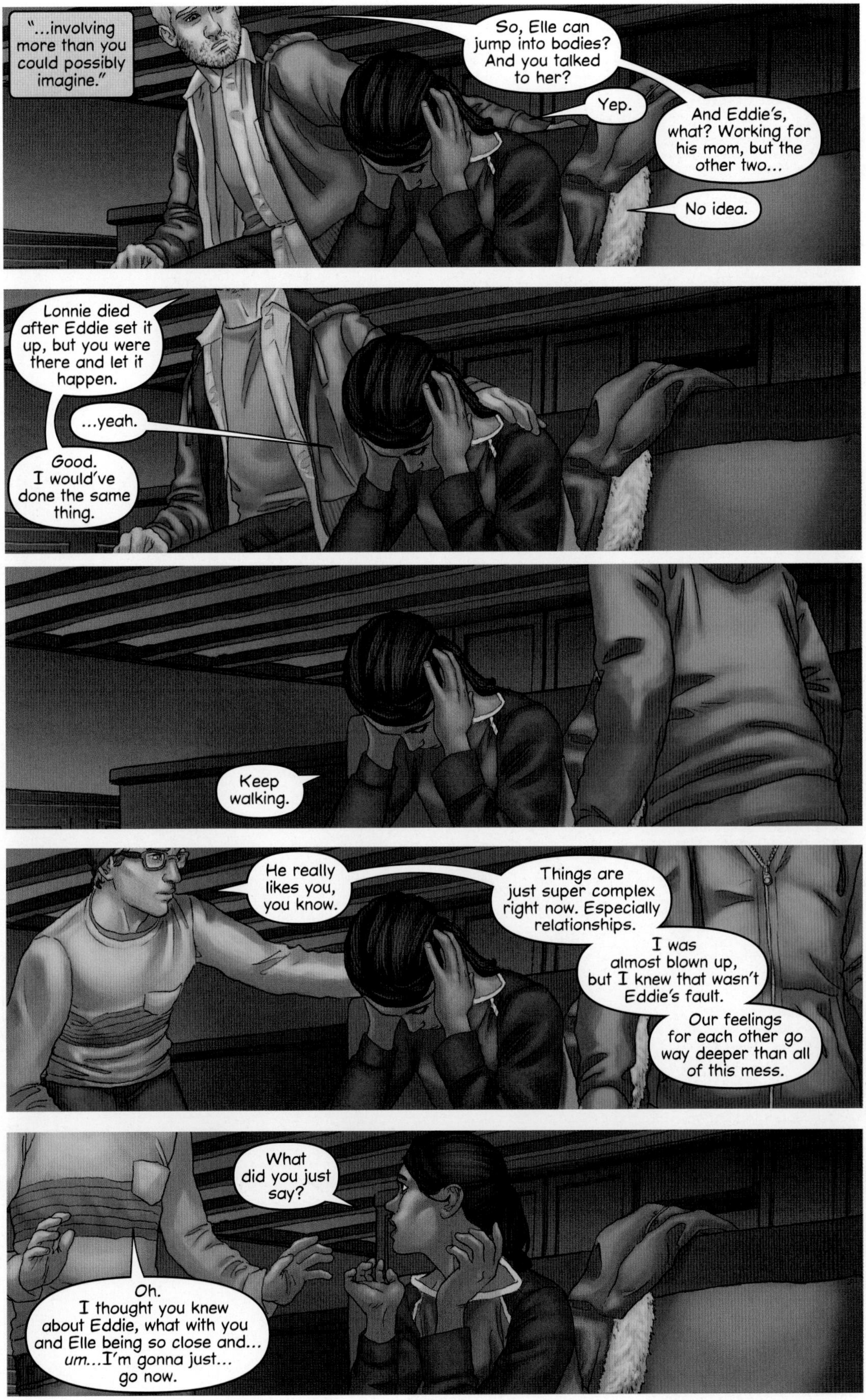
"...involving more than you could possibly imagine."
So, Elle can jump into bodies? And you talked to her?
Yep.
And Eddie's, what? Working for his mom, but the other two...
No idea.
Lonnie died after Eddie set it up, but you were there and let it happen.
...yeah.
Good. I would've done the same thing.
Keep walking.
He really likes you, you know.
Things are just super complex right now. Especially relationships.
I was almost blown up, but I knew that wasn't Eddie's fault.
Our feelings for each other go way deeper than all of this mess.
What did you just say?
Oh. I thought you knew about Eddie, what with you and Elle being so close and... *um*...I'm gonna just... go now.

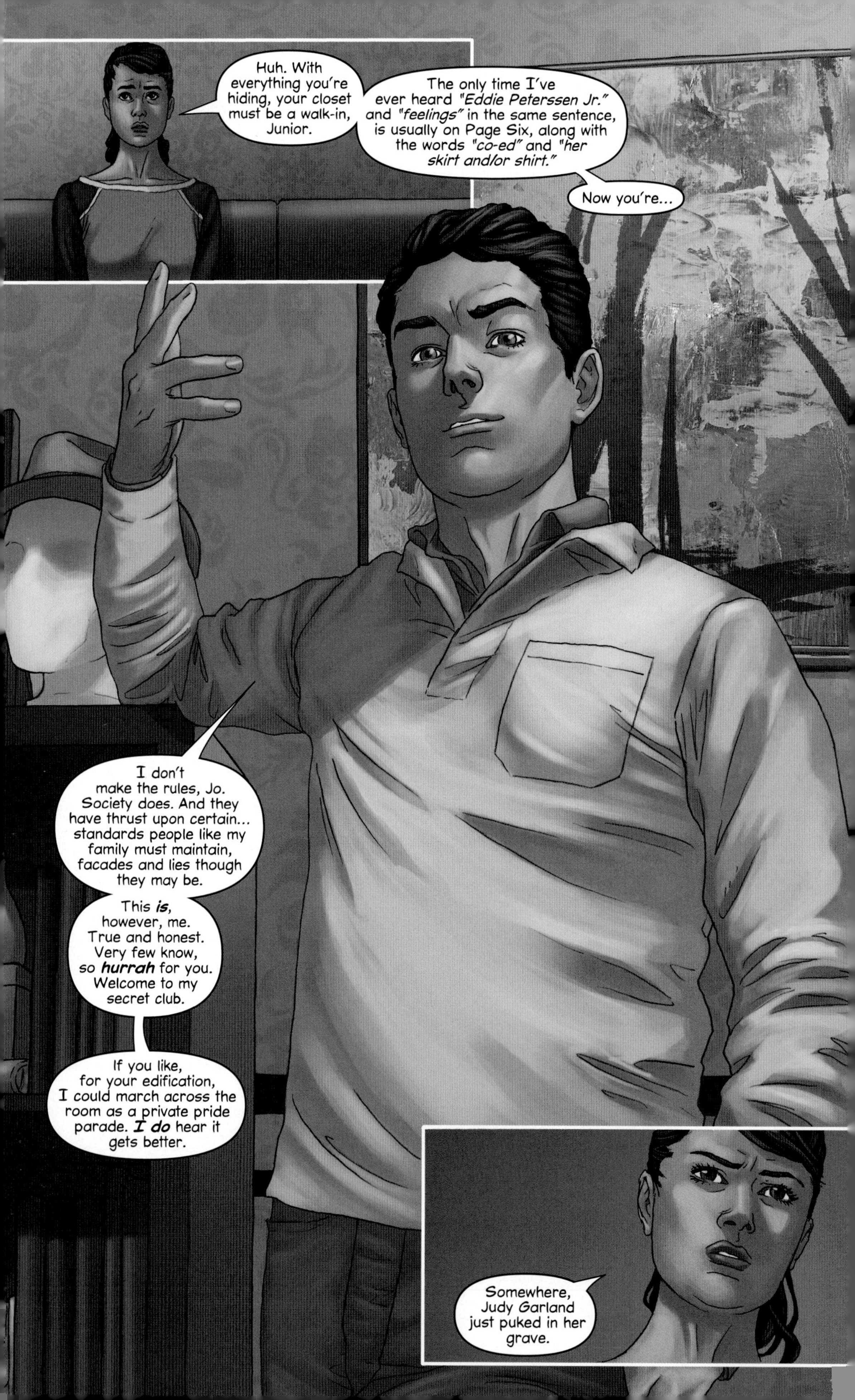

Huh. With everything you're hiding, your closet must be a walk-in, Junior.
The only time I've ever heard *"Eddie Peterssen Jr."* and *"feelings"* in the same sentence, is usually on Page Six, along with the words *"co-ed"* and *"her skirt and/or shirt."*
Now you're...
I don't make the rules, Jo. Society does. And they have thrust upon certain... standards people like my family must maintain, facades and lies though they may be.
This ***is***, however, me. True and honest. Very few know, so ***hurrah*** for you. Welcome to my secret club.
If you like, for your edification, I could march across the room as a private pride parade. ***I do*** hear it gets better.
Somewhere, Judy Garland just puked in her grave.

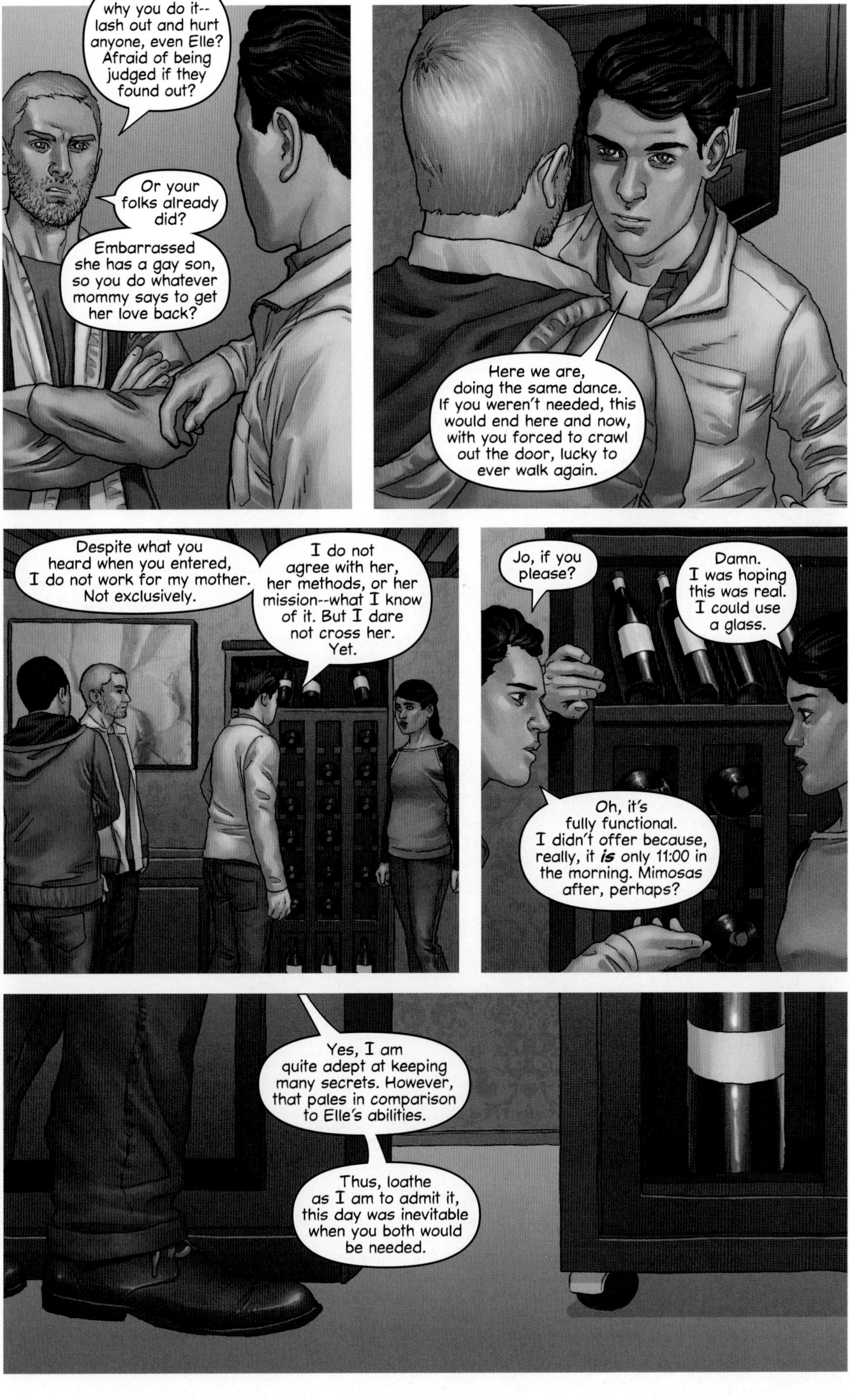
So that's why you do it--lash out and hurt anyone, even Elle? Afraid of being judged if they found out?
Or your folks already did?
Embarrassed she has a gay son, so you do whatever mommy says to get her love back?
Here we are, doing the same dance. If you weren't needed, this would end here and now, with you forced to crawl out the door, lucky to ever walk again.
Despite what you heard when you entered, I do not work for my mother. Not exclusively.
I do not agree with her, her methods, or her mission--what I know of it. But I dare not cross her. Yet.
Jo, if you please?
Damn. I was hoping this was real. I could use a glass.
Oh, it's fully functional. I didn't offer because, really, it *is* only 11:00 in the morning. Mimosas after, perhaps?
Yes, I am quite adept at keeping many secrets. However, that pales in comparison to Elle's abilities.
Thus, loathe as I am to admit it, this day was inevitable when you both would be needed.

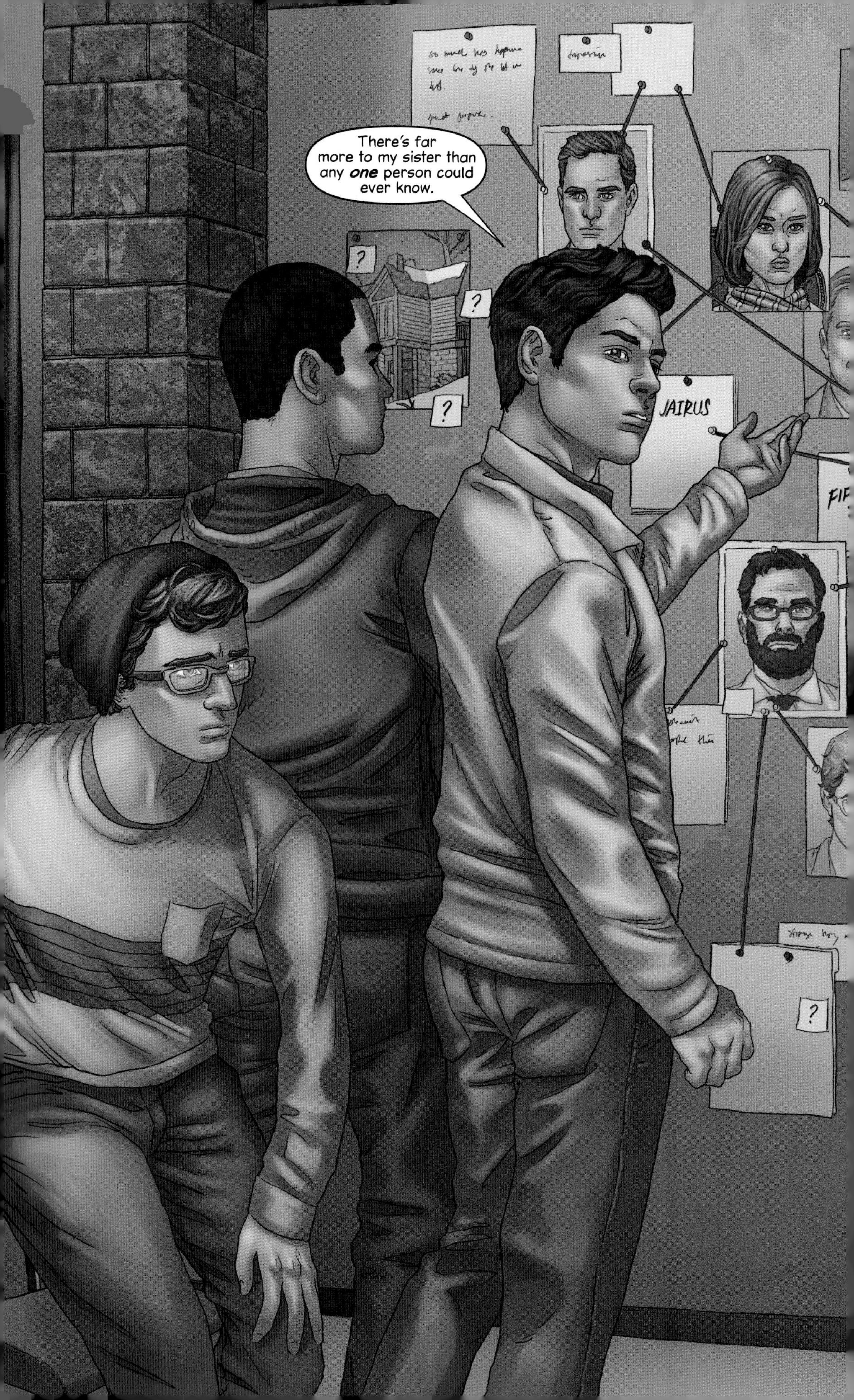
There's far more to my sister than any ***one*** person could ever know.
JAIRUS

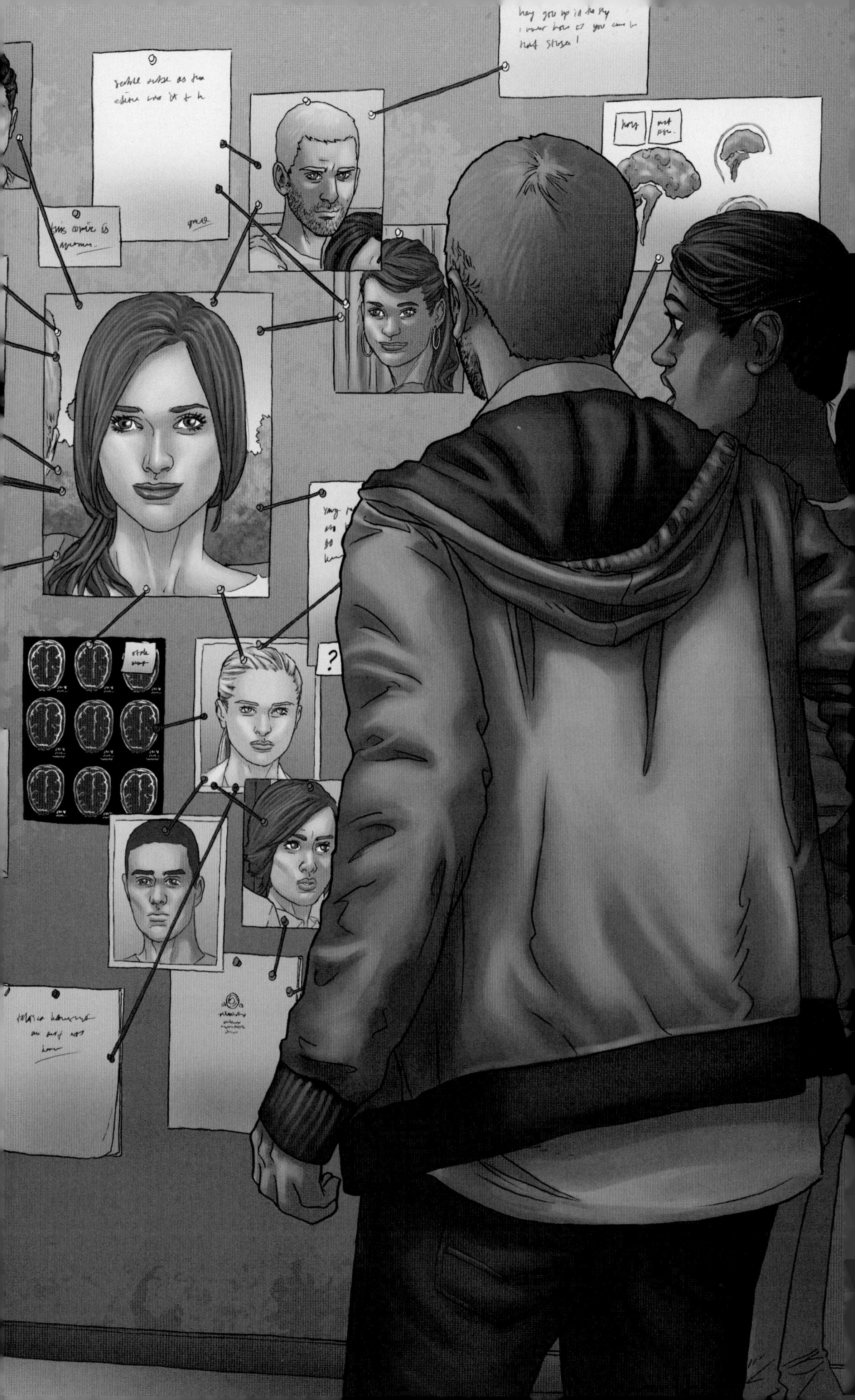

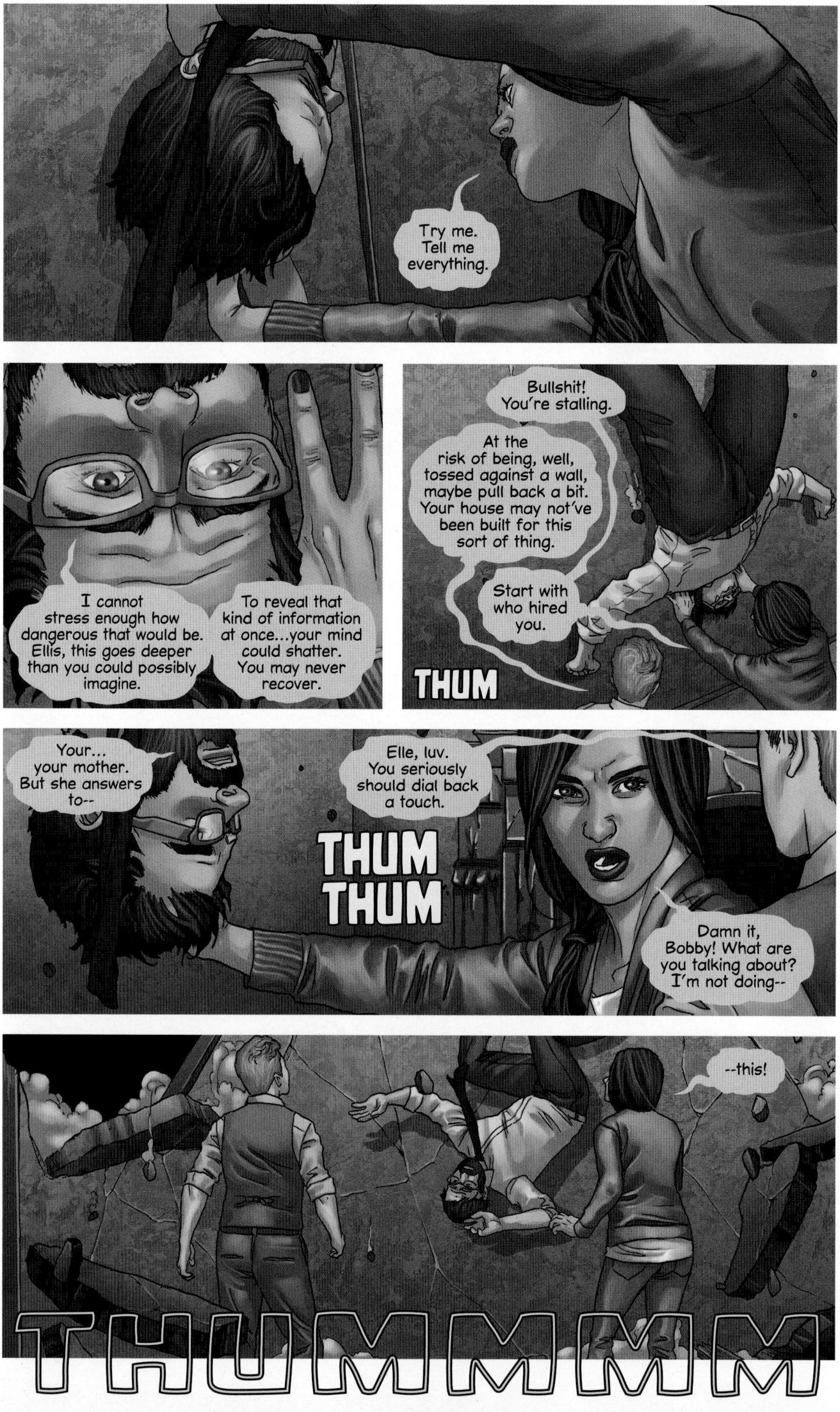
Try me. Tell me everything.
I cannot stress enough how dangerous that would be. Ellis, this goes deeper than you could possibly imagine.
To reveal that kind of information at once...your mind could shatter. You may never recover.
Bullshit! You're stalling.
At the risk of being, well, tossed against a wall, maybe pull back a bit. Your house may not've been built for this sort of thing.
Start with who hired you.
THUM
Your... your mother. But she answers to--
Elle, luv. You seriously should dial back a touch.
THUM THUM
Damn it, Bobby! What are you talking about? I'm not doing--
--this!
THUMMMMM

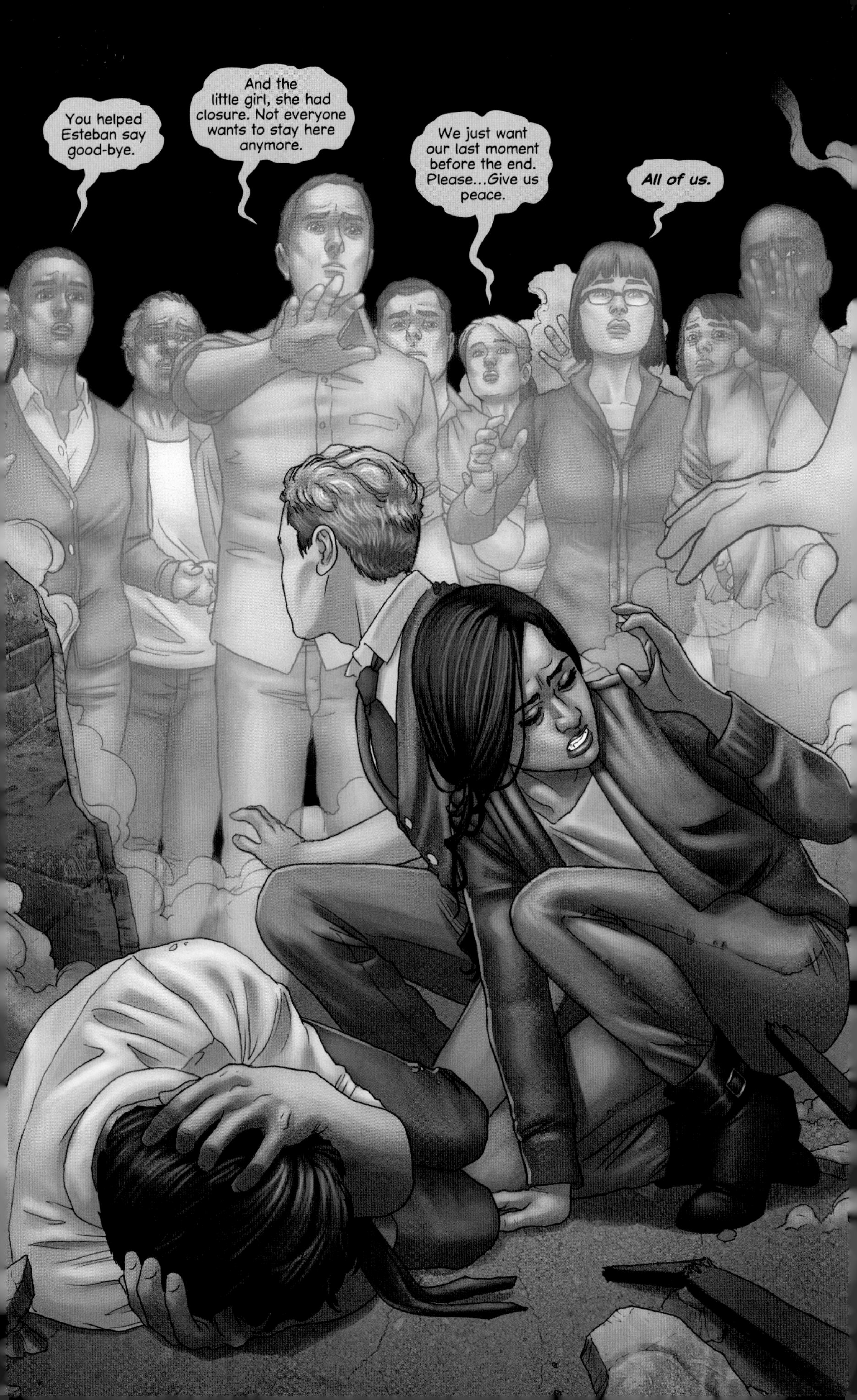
You helped Esteban say good-bye.
And the little girl, she had closure. Not everyone wants to stay here anymore.
We just want our last moment before the end. Please...Give us peace.
All of us.

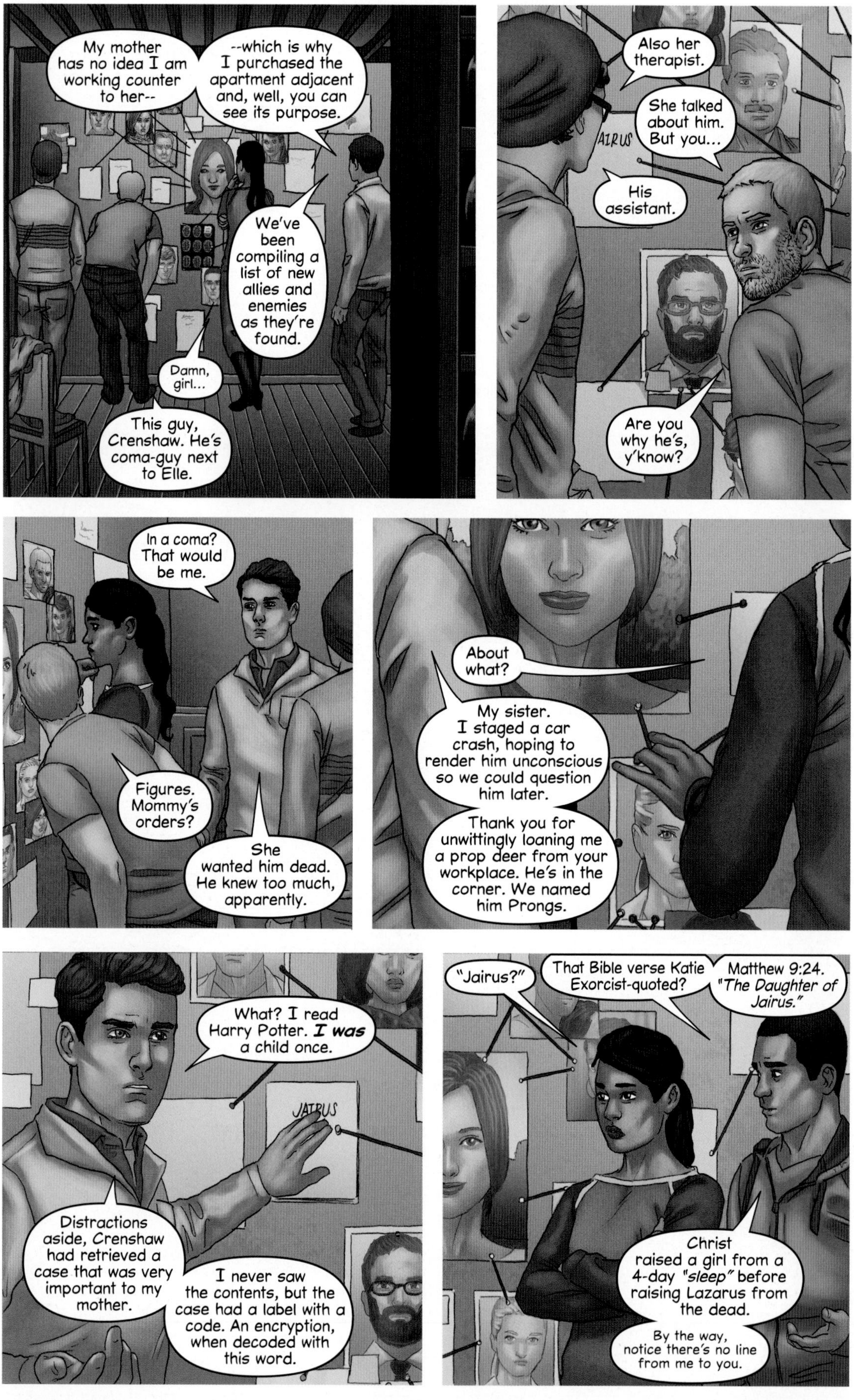
My mother has no idea I am working counter to her--
--which is why I purchased the apartment adjacent and, well, you can see its purpose.
We've been compiling a list of new allies and enemies as they're found.
Damn, girl...
This guy, Crenshaw. He's coma-guy next to Elle.
Also her therapist.
She talked about him. But you...
His assistant.
Are you why he's, y'know?
In a coma? That would be me.
Figures. Mommy's orders?
She wanted him dead. He knew too much, apparently.
About what?
My sister. I staged a car crash, hoping to render him unconscious so we could question him later.
Thank you for unwittingly loaning me a prop deer from your workplace. He's in the corner. We named him Prongs.
What? I read Harry Potter. **I was** a child once.
JAIRUS
Distractions aside, Crenshaw had retrieved a case that was very important to my mother.
I never saw the contents, but the case had a label with a code. An encryption, when decoded with this word.
"Jairus?"
That Bible verse Katie Exorcist-quoted?
Matthew 9:24. *"The Daughter of Jairus."*
Christ raised a girl from a 4-day *"sleep"* before raising Lazarus from the dead.
By the way, notice there's no line from me to you.

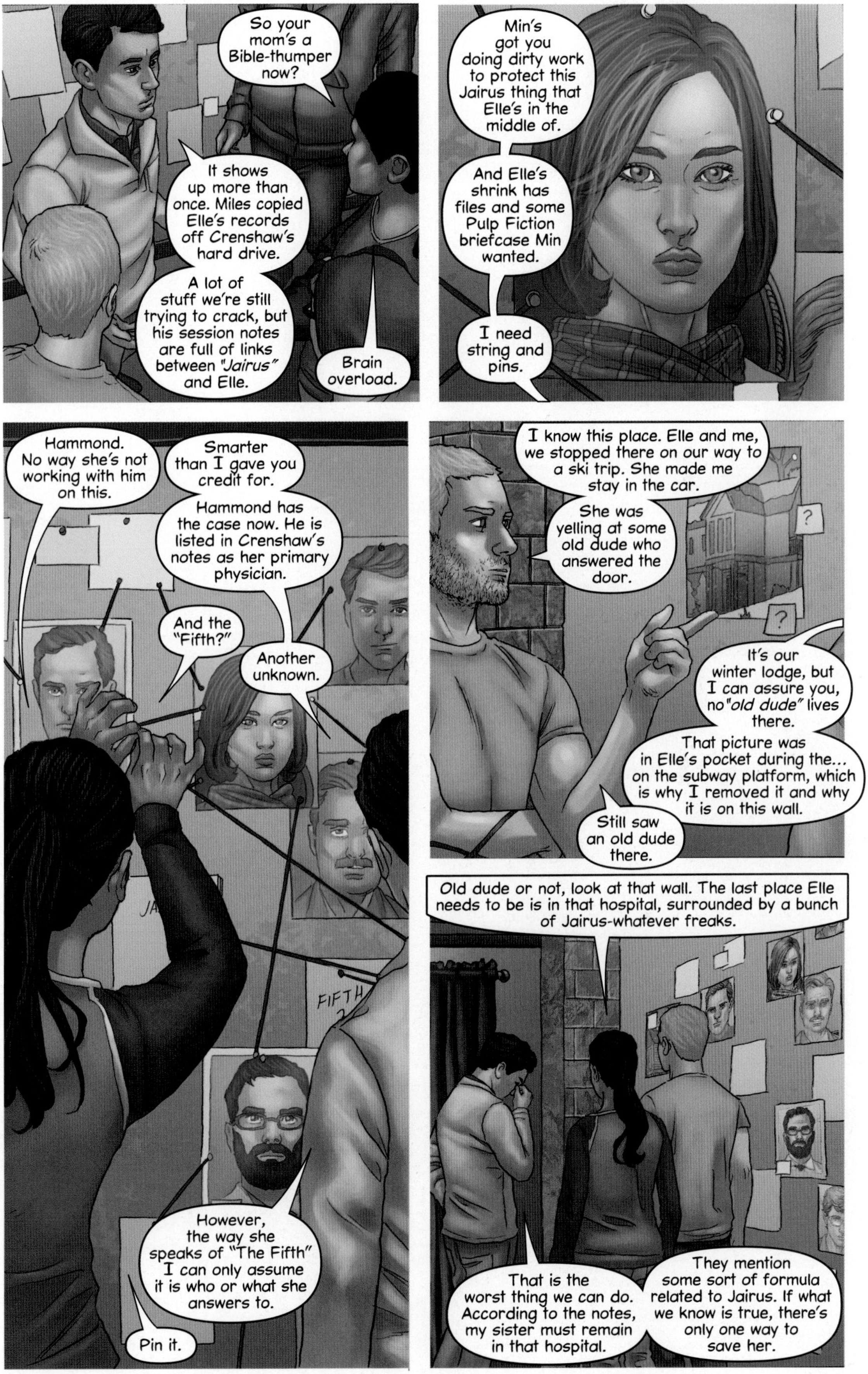
So your mom's a Bible-thumper now?
It shows up more than once. Miles copied Elle's records off Crenshaw's hard drive.
A lot of stuff we're still trying to crack, but his session notes are full of links between "Jairus" and Elle.
Brain overload.
Min's got you doing dirty work to protect this Jairus thing that Elle's in the middle of.
And Elle's shrink has files and some Pulp Fiction briefcase Min wanted.
I need string and pins.
Hammond. No way she's not working with him on this.
Smarter than I gave you credit for.
Hammond has the case now. He is listed in Crenshaw's notes as her primary physician.
And the "Fifth?"
Another unknown.
FIFTH
However, the way she speaks of "The Fifth" I can only assume it is who or what she answers to.
Pin it.
I know this place. Elle and me, we stopped there on our way to a ski trip. She made me stay in the car.
She was yelling at some old dude who answered the door.
?
?
It's our winter lodge, but I can assure you, no "old dude" lives there.
That picture was in Elle's pocket during the... on the subway platform, which is why I removed it and why it is on this wall.
Still saw an old dude there.
Old dude or not, look at that wall. The last place Elle needs to be is in that hospital, surrounded by a bunch of Jairus-whatever freaks.
That is the worst thing we can do. According to the notes, my sister must remain in that hospital.
They mention some sort of formula related to Jairus. If what we know is true, there's only one way to save her.

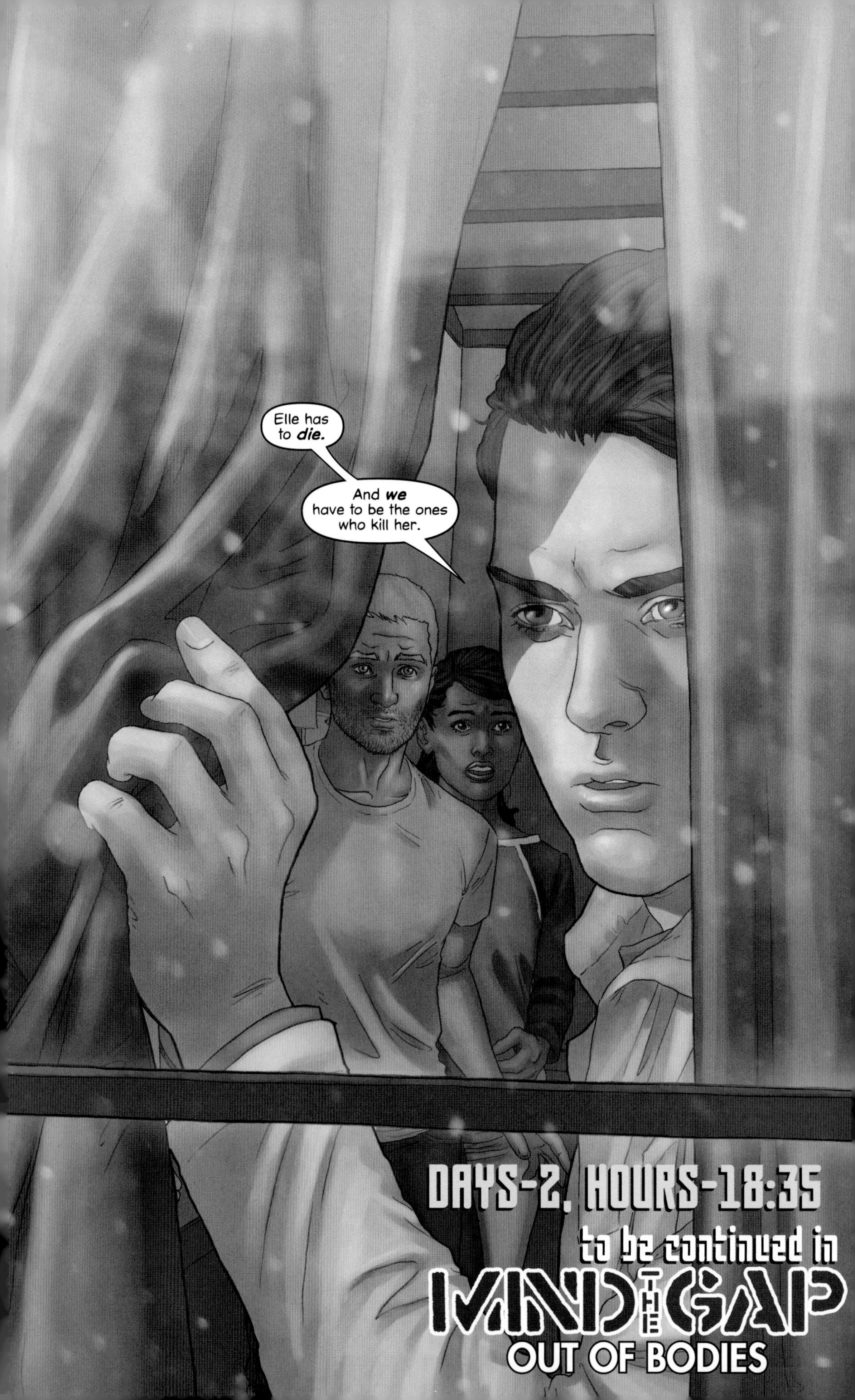
Elle has to *die.*
And *we* have to be the ones who kill her.
DAYS-2, HOURS-18:35
to be continued in
MIND THE GAP
OUT OF BODIES

"Truth is rarely pure and never simple."

-Oscar Wilde

FILLING IN THE GAP

9PFT?!

Ever since issue #1, page 1, where Jo says Elle's call woke her "from a pre-show nap," it's been established that the New York theater scene is an important part of Elle, Jo, and Dane's lives-being employed at the Vineyard Theater together-and as a set-piece that ties them, giving the trio a sort of "secret language" or short hand that many self-proclaimed theater-geeks, myself included, have. Since so much of that was very integral in this, and previous issues, I thought it's time to pull back the curtain, so to speak, and give special thanks and a spotlight to the REAL people and places that have allowed us in MIND THE GAP to include them in making this book a grounded, "living" work.

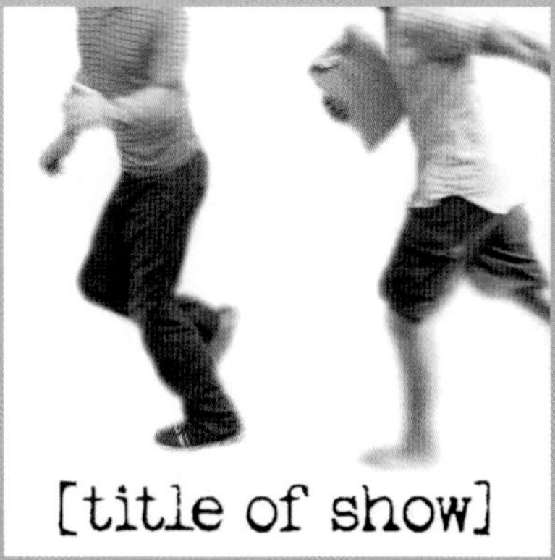
[title of show]

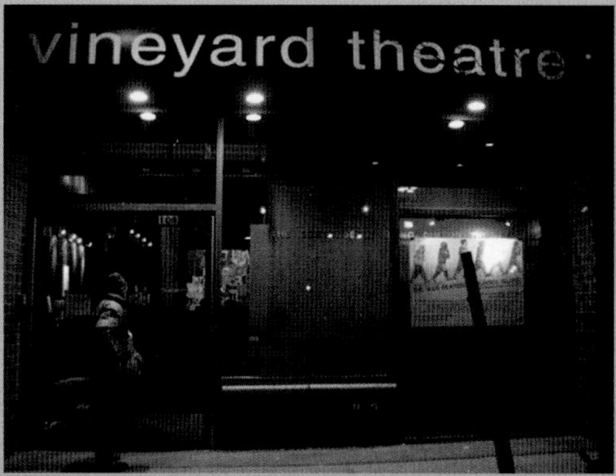
vineyard theatre

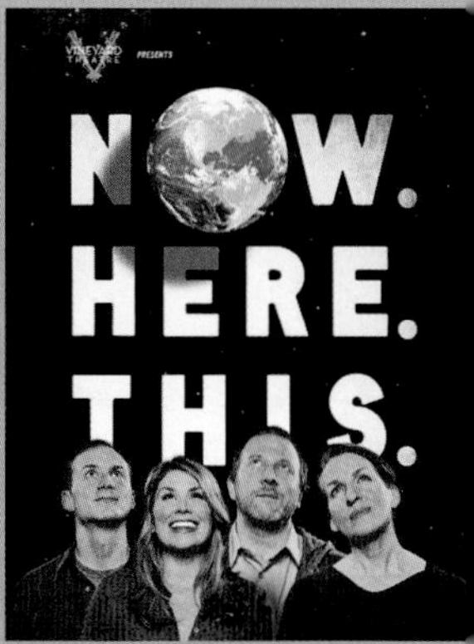
NOW.
HERE.
THIS.

"9pft" and "A Way Back To Then" both come from the Tony-nominated (Word, Hunter.) Broadway musical [title of show], or [tos], which you saw Jo digging through her production workbook. (In our world, Jo works in costume design, Dane is a set-tech, and Elle is a stage manager.) [tos] is a literal piece of living art that began as a musical about two friends wanting to write a musical about two friends wanting to write a musical (still with me?). It was submitted for a festival in NYC before eventually enjoying a long run at the Vineyard Theatre (more on them in a sec). The show starred the book writer, the composer & lyricist, as well as the two actresses who workshopped it all the way through until it made it to the Great White Way, the Broadway Theatre where I saw it for the first of many times (and began a great friendship with the cast), the Lyceum. Its lyrics and story evolved as its journey did, and the musical blew me away. The two songs mentioned in particular are personal inspirations. In fact, if you go to YouTube and look up "9pft" you might see a familiar face flash by holding up the word "Advice" with Hulk hands.

After that show closed, the four friends (along with their director and musician) eventually reunited for Now. Here. This., which is the show we currently have our characters also working on in MIND THE GAP. It is a wonderful show that I have only been able to hear, not see, as I was in LA while it ran in NYC at the Vineyard.

The Vineyard Theatre is an amazing venue that is currently celebrating its 30th anniversary. If you are ever in New York, I highly suggest seeing a show, ANY show there.
In closing, I'd like to personally thank my friends & fellow nerds for letting us play in your world, and you are all one of my 9. Thank you Jeff, Hunter, Susan, Heidi & the Vineyard!

To find out more, please visit the following:
http://www.vineyardtheatre.org/ @vineyardtheatre
http://www.titleofshow.com/ @titleofshow
http://nowherethis.com/

With the craziest of company, you're having a kick-ass time...

Answers & Ties

The Mystery Wall. Conspiracy Corner. Elle's Web-Head. It has many names, but this is actually the first thing I wrote down on index cards and sticky notes and scraps of paper before writing the script. It was the spine of my outline- the most important thing to me in this whole story: the Relationship Chart.

The script page describing this was intense but Rodin pulled it off as did the coloring crew. It's amazing to finally see it realized (much prettier than my version) on the page. But in true MIND THE GAP fashion, there are strings yet to be connected, question marks to be answered, and a few missing players on the wall.

This is your map, for those playing detective. Use it well. As Eddie Jr says, there's far more than any one person can ever know...

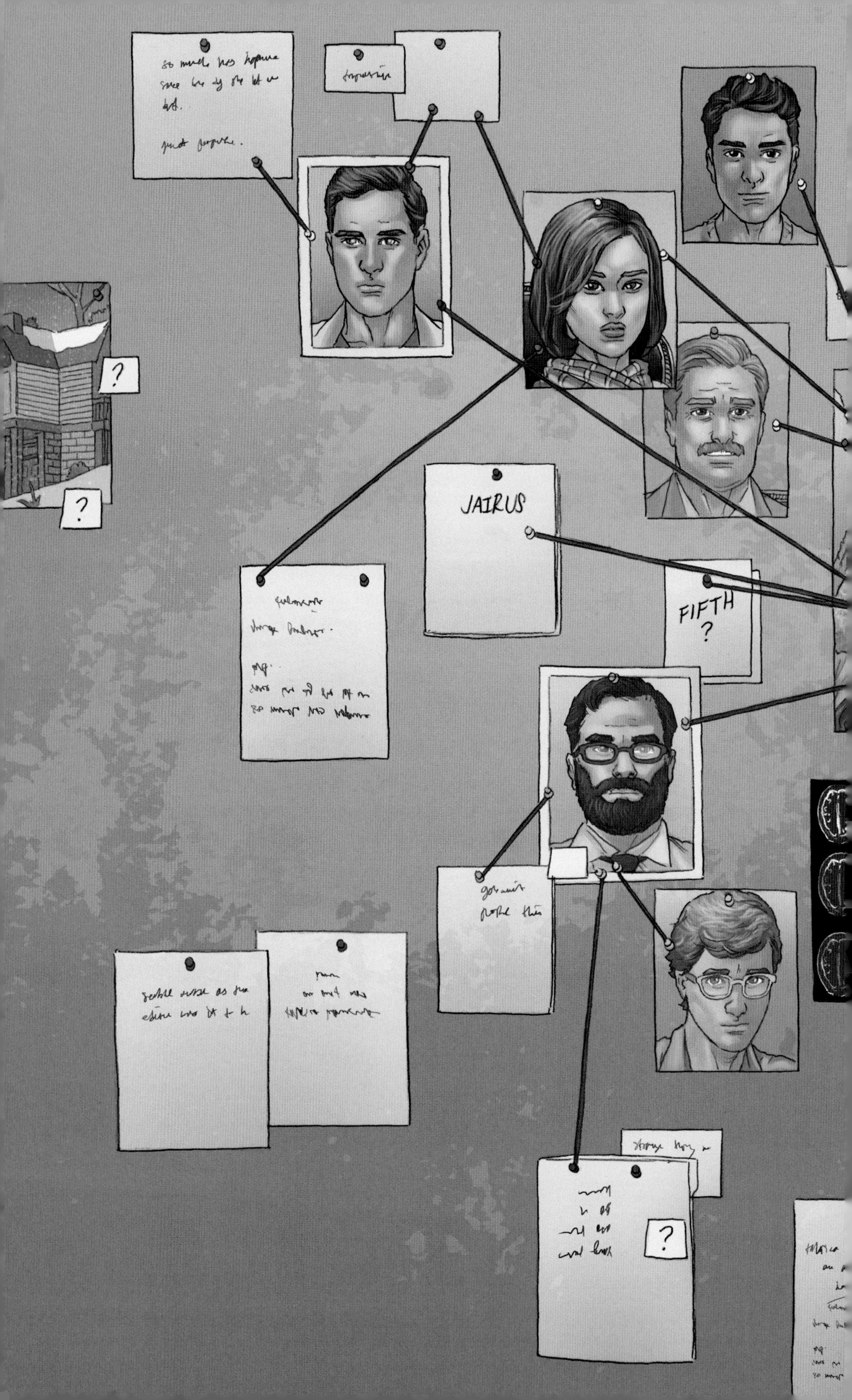
?
?
JAIRUS
FIFTH
?
?

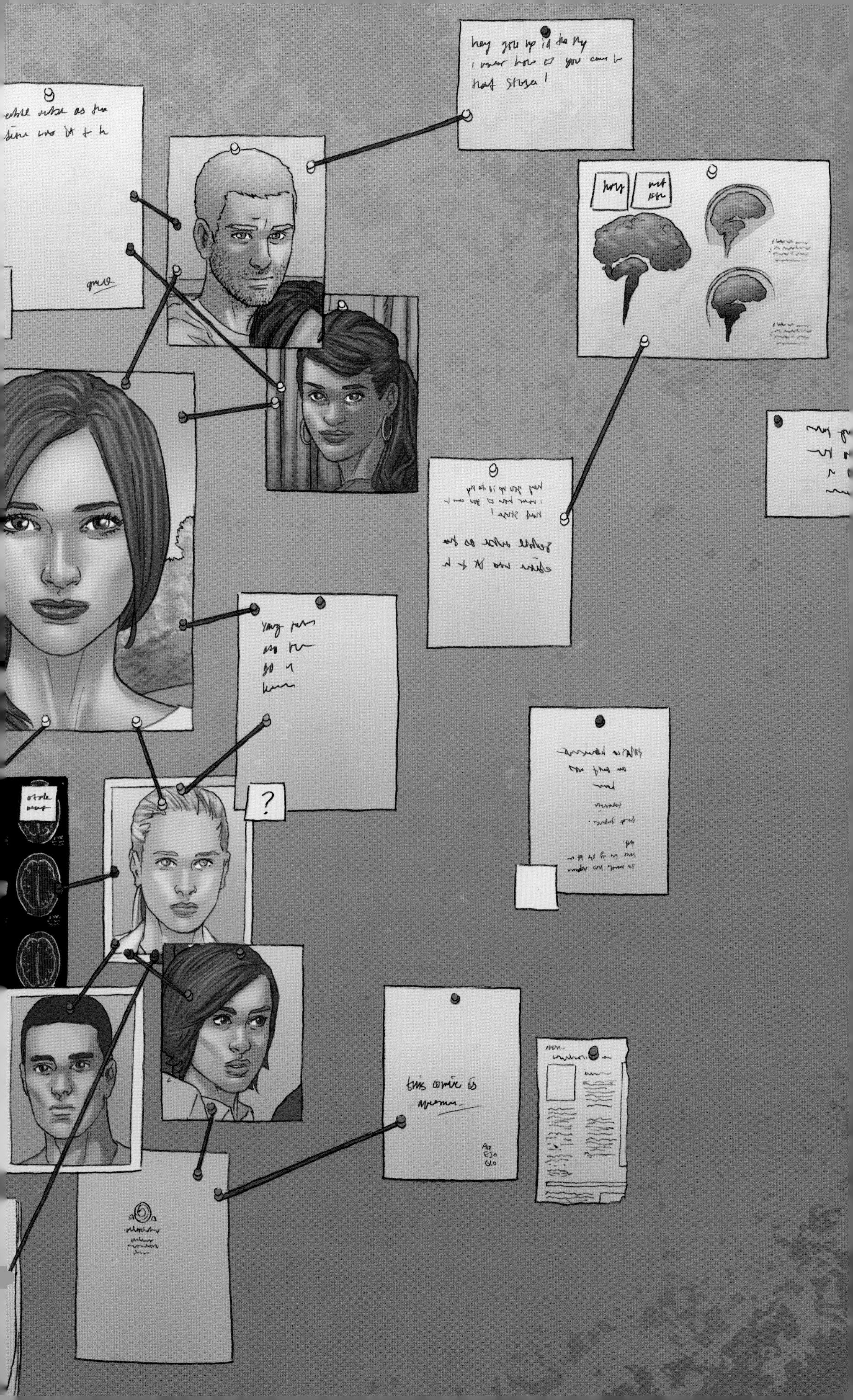
?
this comic is

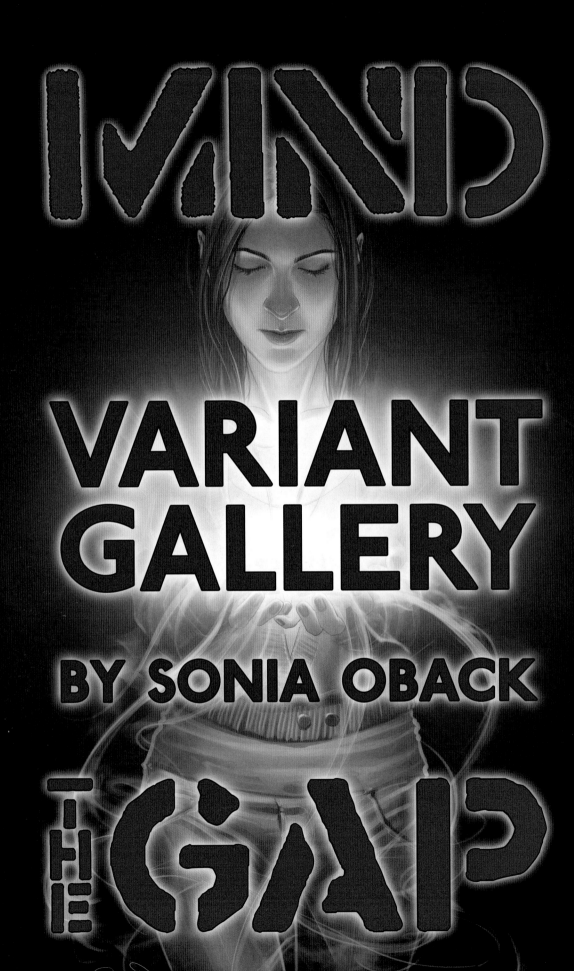

MIND

VARIANT GALLERY

BY SONIA OBACK

THE GAP

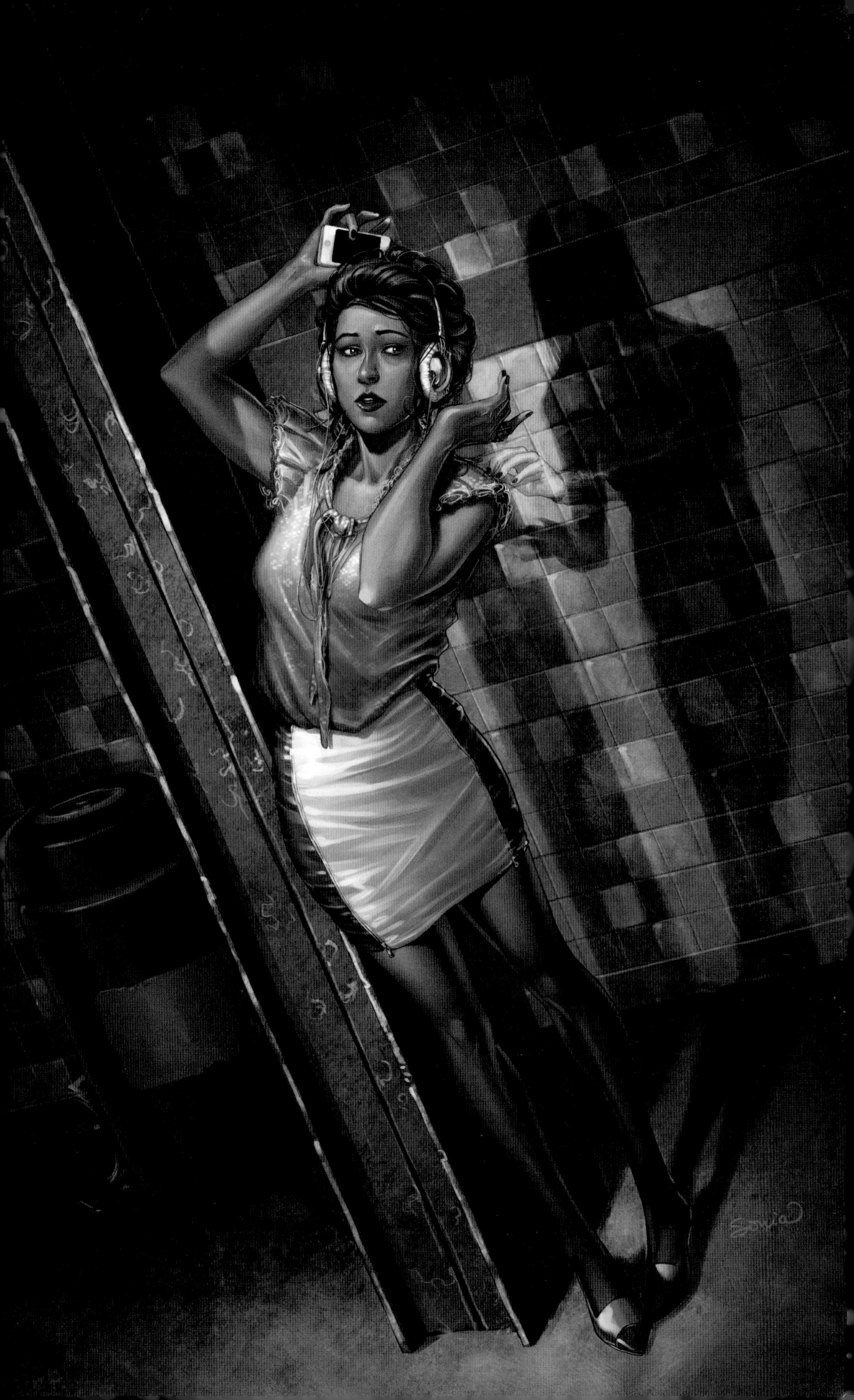

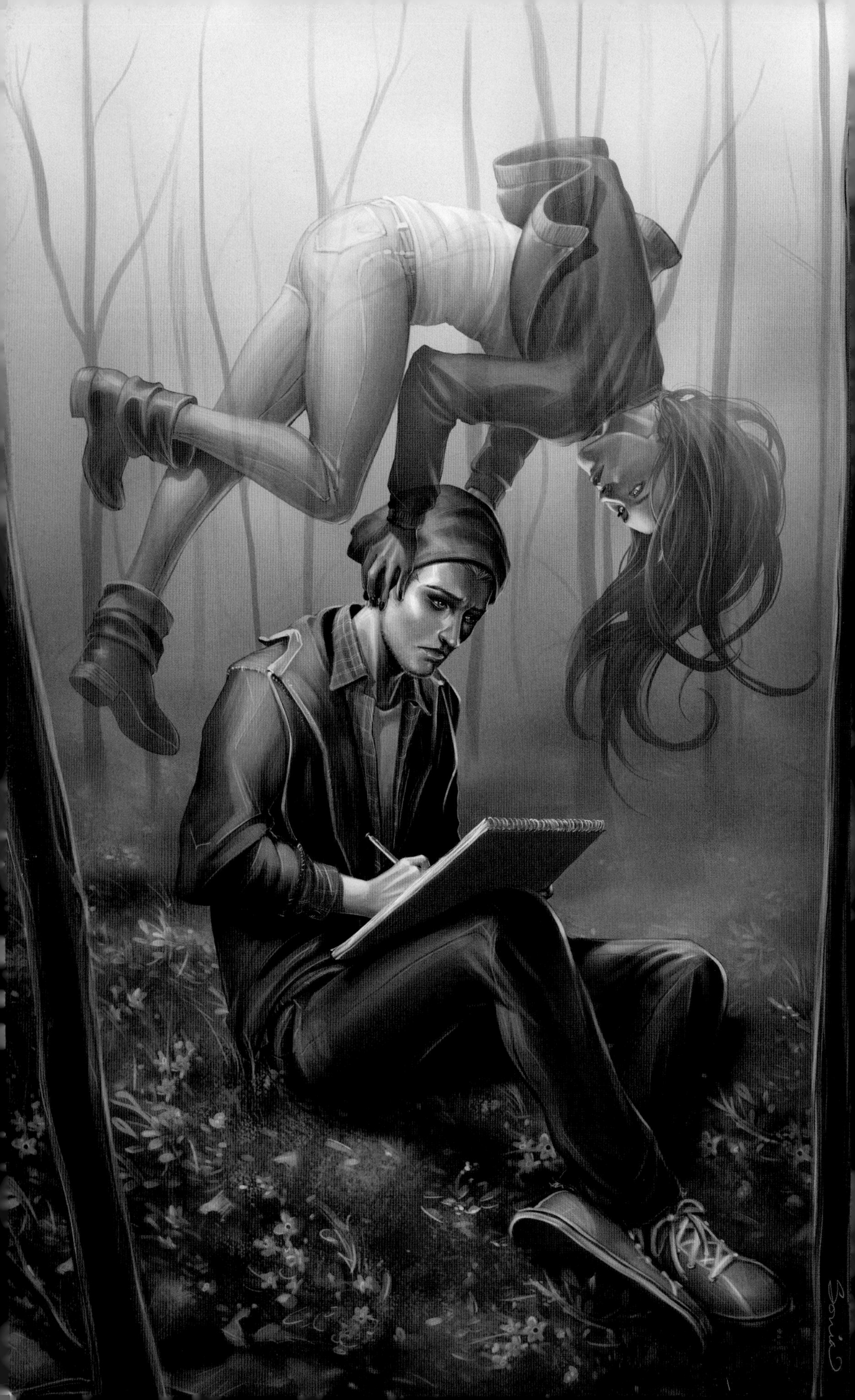

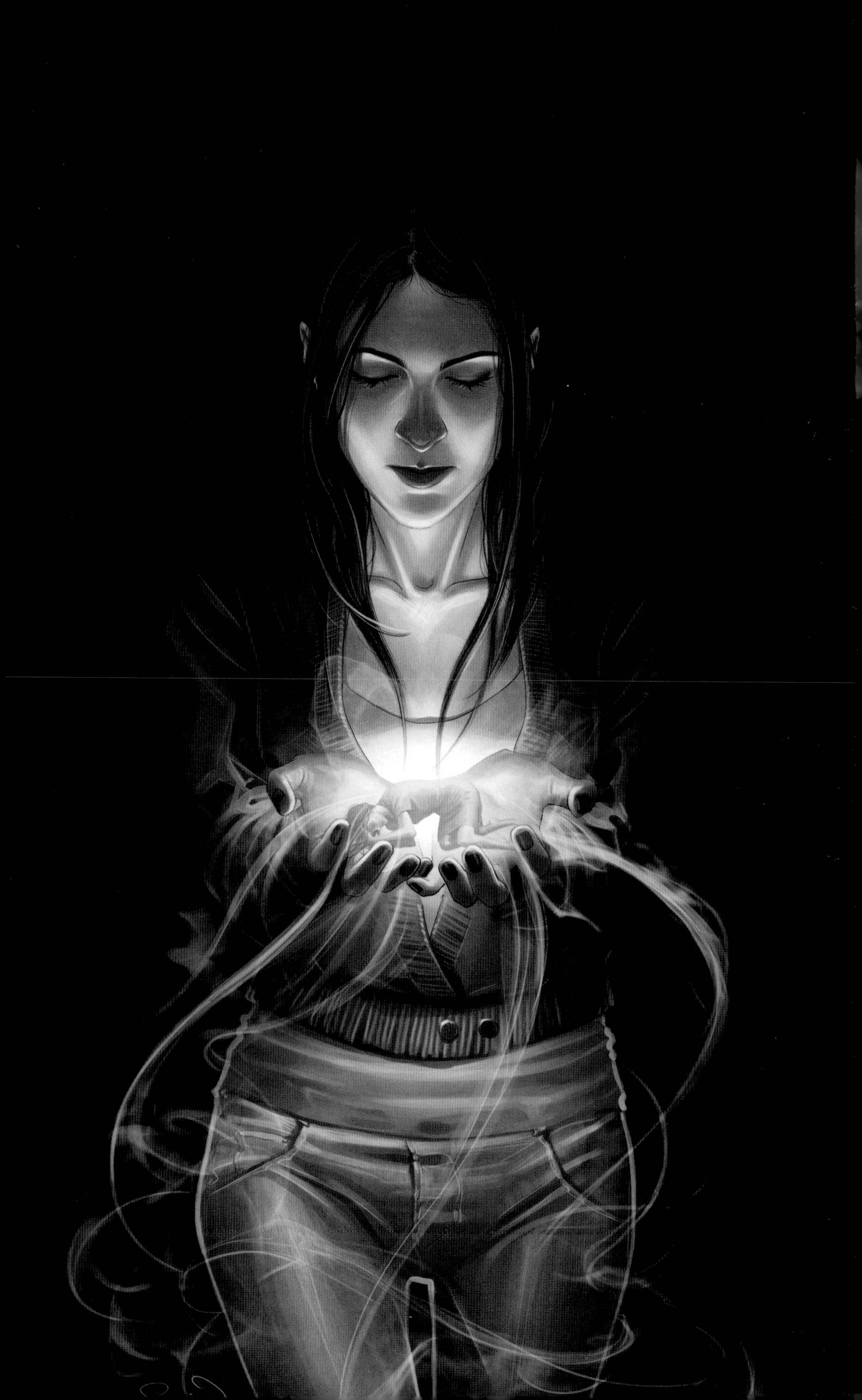

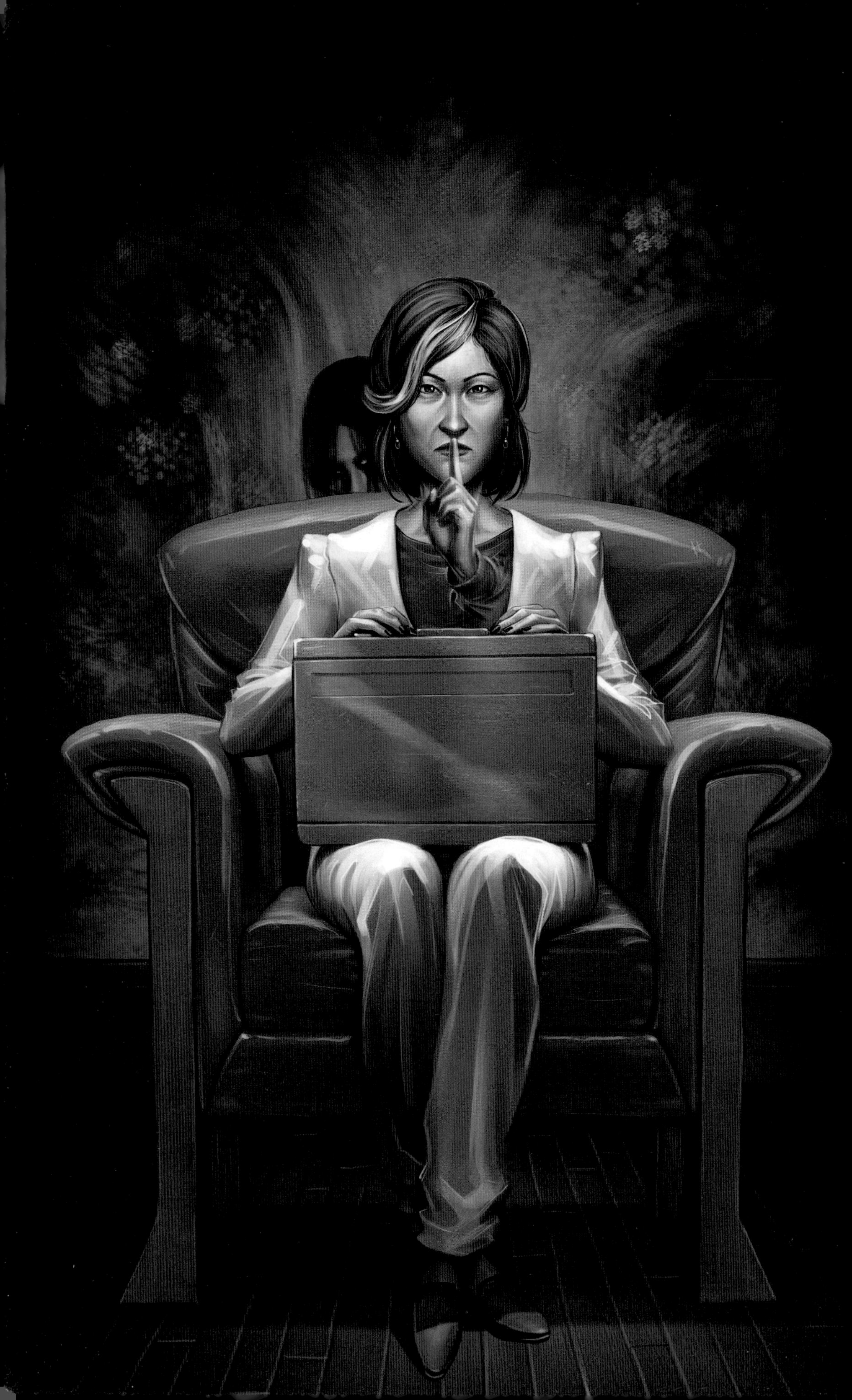

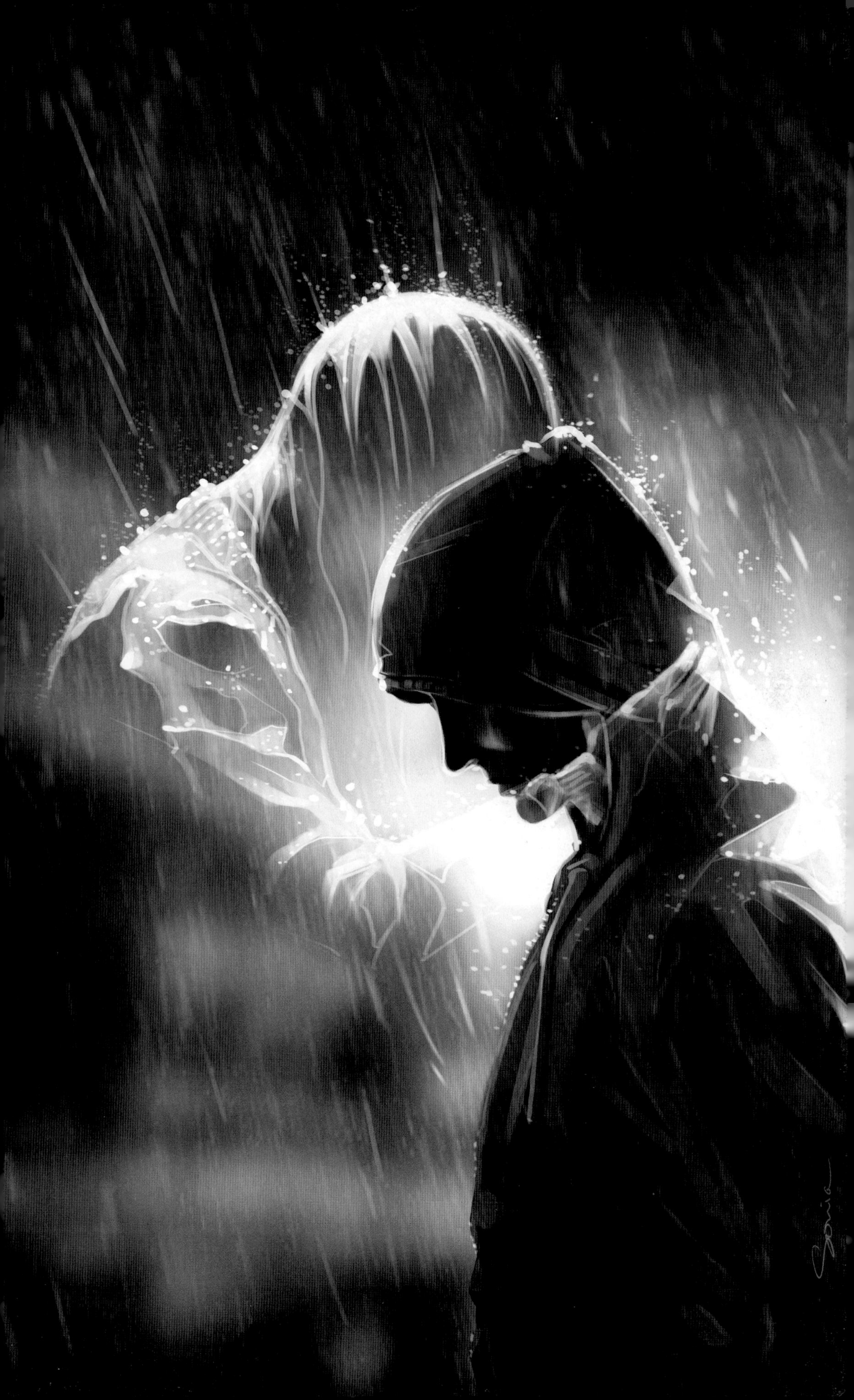
Sonia

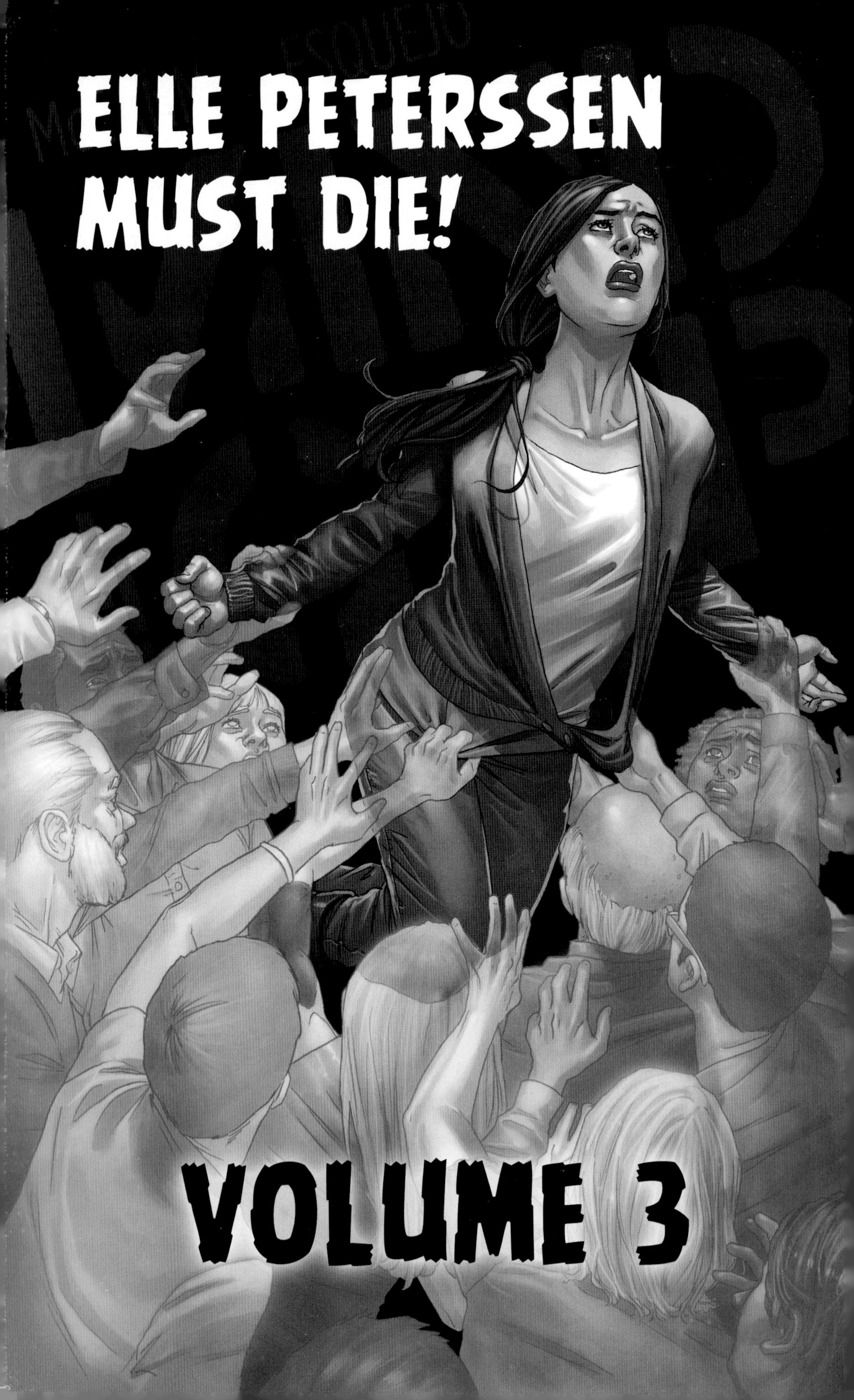
ELLE PETERSSEN
MUST DIE!
VOLUME 3

ERYONE IS A SUSPECT.

NO ONE IS INNOCENT.

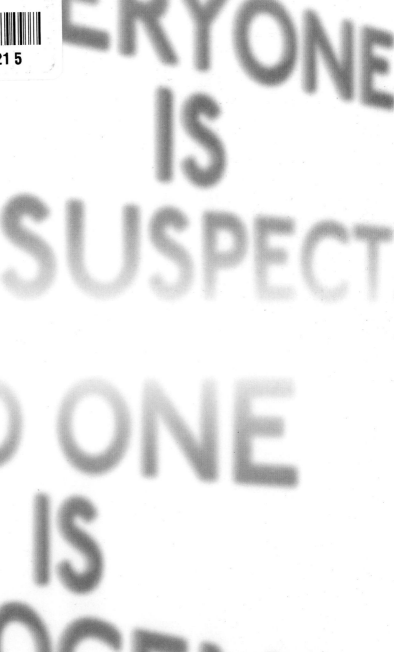

"I can honestly say I have no idea what Jim McCann is cooking up but I can't wait to see what happens next. 5/5 stars." - ComicVine.com

"This is a book that mixes spirituality, relationships, and family into a thriller that makes it hard to put down." - Examiner.com

"A paranormal thriller/mystery graphic novel that non-comic book readers will enjoy." - BoingBoing.net

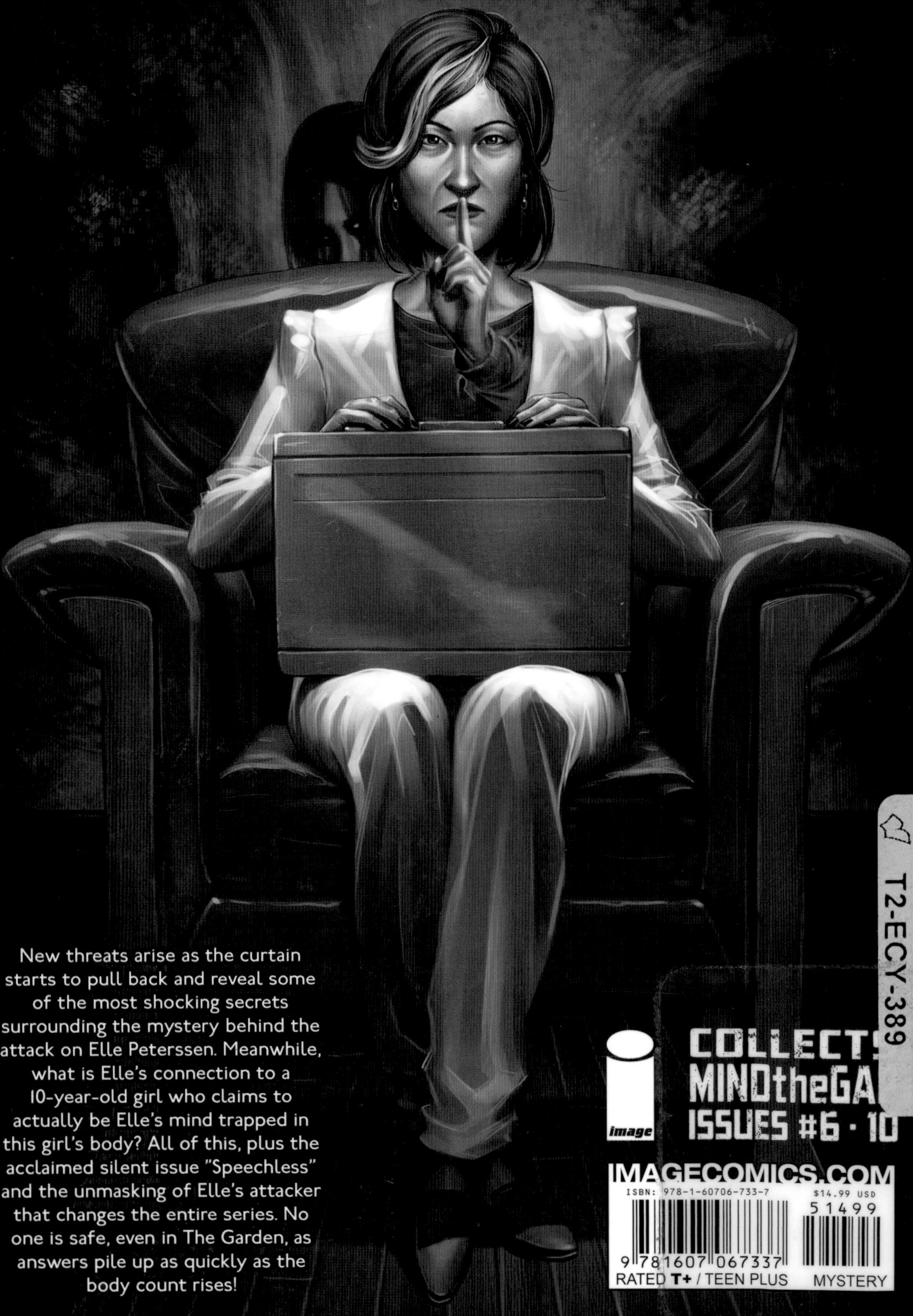

New threats arise as the curtain starts to pull back and reveal some of the most shocking secrets surrounding the mystery behind the attack on Elle Peterssen. Meanwhile, what is Elle's connection to a 10-year-old girl who claims to actually be Elle's mind trapped in this girl's body? All of this, plus the acclaimed silent issue "Speechless" and the unmasking of Elle's attacker that changes the entire series. No one is safe, even in The Garden, as answers pile up as quickly as the body count rises!

COLLECTS MINDtheGA[P]
ISSUES #6 - 10

image

IMAGECOMICS.COM

ISBN: 978-1-60706-733-7
$14.99 USD
9 781607 067337 51499

RATED T+ / TEEN PLUS
MYSTERY